Left Parties in National Governments

Also by D. Hough; M. Koß; J. Olsen

THE LEFT PARTY IN CONTEMPORARY GERMAN POLITICS

Left Parties in National Governments

Edited by

Jonathan Olsen
*Associate Professor of Political Science,
University of Wisconsin-Parkside, USA*

Michael Koß
Lecturer in Politics, University of Potsdam, Germany

and

Dan Hough
Reader in Politics, University of Sussex, UK

© Editorial matter, selection, and conclusion © Jonathan Olsen, Michael Koß and Dan Hough 2010
All remaining chapters © respective authors 2010

All rights reserved. No reproduction, copy or transmission of this publication may be made without written permission.

No portion of this publication may be reproduced, copied or transmitted save with written permission or in accordance with the provisions of the Copyright, Designs and Patents Act 1988, or under the terms of any licence permitting limited copying issued by the Copyright Licensing Agency, Saffron House, 6-10 Kirby Street, London EC1N 8TS.

Any person who does any unauthorized act in relation to this publication may be liable to criminal prosecution and civil claims for damages.

The authors have asserted their rights to be identified as the authors of this work in accordance with the Copyright, Designs and Patents Act 1988.

First published 2010 by
PALGRAVE MACMILLAN

Palgrave Macmillan in the UK is an imprint of Macmillan Publishers Limited, registered in England, company number 785998, of Houndmills, Basingstoke, Hampshire RG21 6XS.

Palgrave Macmillan in the US is a division of St Martin's Press LLC, 175 Fifth Avenue, New York, NY 10010.

Palgrave Macmillan is the global academic imprint of the above companies and has companies and representatives throughout the world.

Palgrave® and Macmillan® are registered trademarks in the United States, the United Kingdom, Europe and other countries.

ISBN: 978–0–230–23650–9 hardback

This book is printed on paper suitable for recycling and made from fully managed and sustained forest sources. Logging, pulping and manufacturing processes are expected to conform to the environmental regulations of the country of origin.

A catalogue record for this book is available from the British Library.

A catalog record for this book is available from the Library of Congress.

10 9 8 7 6 5 4 3 2 1
19 18 17 16 15 14 13 12 11 10

Printed and bound in Great Britain by
CPI Antony Rowe, Chippenham and Eastbourne

Contents

List of Tables	vii
List of Abbreviations	viii
List of Contributors	xi

1. From Pariahs to Players? Left Parties in National Governments
   Jonathan Olsen, Dan Hough and Michael Koß — 1

2. The Norwegian Socialist Left Party: Office-seekers in the Service of Policy?
   Jonathan Olsen — 16

3. The French Extreme Left and Its Suspicion of Power
   David Bell — 33

4. Between a Rock and a Hard Place: The Governing Dilemmas of Rifondazione Comunista
   James Newell — 52

5. A Poisoned Chalice? Finland's Left Alliance and the Perils of Government
   Richard Dunphy — 69

6. The Spanish United Left – The Belated and Troublesome Transition from Policy- to Office-seeking
   Tània Verge — 87

7. Close to, but Still Out of, Government: The Swedish Vänsterpartiet
   Michael Koß — 105

8. The Danish Socialist People's Party: Still Waiting After all These Years
   Dag Arne Christensen — 121

9. From Pariah to Prospective Partner? The German Left Party's Winding Path towards Government
   Dan Hough — 138

10. Ready to Get Their Hands Dirty: The Socialist Party and GroenLinks in the Netherlands 155
    Dan Keith

11. Conclusion: Left Parties in National Governments 173
    Jonathan Olsen, Dan Hough and Michael Koß

Bibliography 186

Index 203

Tables

1.1	Left parties' participation in statewide governments in western Europe since 1990 (selected countries)	4
2.1	Election results in Norway, 1997–2009	17
4.1	Percentage of the vote obtained by RC and the PDS in the local elections of 1991	57
4.2	Voting support and membership of RC, 1992–2006	60
5.1	Recent general election results in Finland	71
5.2	Outcome of the 2009 European Parliament election in Finland	84
6.1	The PCE's and IU's electoral results in legislative and regional elections	88
6.2	Ideological placement of the IU and the Spanish electorate	93
7.1	Electoral results of the Left Party in national elections, 1982–2006	116
8.1	The Danish SF's electoral support, 1960–2007	126
8.2	Governments in Denmark since 1973	127
8.3	Socialist parties' performances in Denmark	128
8.4	SF's formal constraints on coalition bargaining, 1973–95	131
9.1	The PDS's electoral performance in eastern parliaments, 1990–2005	142
11.1	Ideological distances between left parties and social democratic parties, 1990–2003	176
11.2	The relative electoral strength of left parties and their coalition partners, 1990–2009	178
11.3	Segmentation and block dynamics, 1990–2009	180
11.4	Election results of left parties, 1990–2009	183

Abbreviations

AG	Working group within the German Left Party
ATTAC	Association for the Taxation of Financial Transactions for the Aid of Citizens
BWK	Association of West German Communists
C	Conservatives (Denmark)
CD	Centre Democrats (Denmark)
CDA	Christian Democratic Appeal (Netherlands)
CDU	Christian Democratic Union (Germany)
CFSP	Common Foreign and Security Policy of the EU
CiU	Convergence and Union (Spain)
CMP	Comparative Manifesto Project
CPN	Communist Party of the Netherlands
CPP	Christian People's Party (Denmark)
CSU	Christian Social Union (Germany)
CU	Christian Union Party (Netherlands)
D66	Liberal Party (Netherlands)
DC	Christian Democratic Party (Italy)
DKP	Communist Party of Denmark
DKP	German Communist Party
DNA	Labour Party (Norway)
DP	Proletarian Democracy (Italy)
EEA	European Economic Area
EFTA	European Free Trade Area
ELP	European Left Party
ENPP	Effective number of parliamentary parties
FDP	Free Democratic Party (Germany)
FP	People's Party (Sweden)
GDR	German Democratic Republic
GL	GroenLinks (Netherlands)
GUE/NGL	European United Left/Nordic Green Left
ICV	Initiative of Catalonian Greens (Spain)
IG	Interest group within the German Left Party
IMF	International Monetary Fund
IU	United Left (Spain)
KD	Christian Democrats (Finland)
KD	Christian Democratic Party (Sweden)

KESK	Centre Party (Finland)
KOK	National Coalition Party (Finland)
L	Liberals (Denmark)
LP	Left Party (Germany)
M	Moderates (Sweden)
MP	Green Party (Sweden)
MWP	Mecklenburg Western Pomerania
NKP	Norwegian Communist Party
PASOC	Party of Socialist Action (Greece)
PCE	Communist Party of Spain
PCF	Communist Party of France
PCI	Communist Party of Italy
PD	Democratic Party (Italy)
PdCI	Party of Italian Communists
PDS	Democratic Party of the Left (Italy)
PDS	Party of Democratic Socialism (Germany)
PP	Popular Party (Spain)
PPR	Party of Radicals (Netherlands)
PS	True Finnish Party
PSI	Socialist Party of Italy
PSOE	Social Democratic Party of Spain
PSP	Pacifist Socialist Party (Netherlands)
PvDA	Social Democratic Party (Netherlands)
RC	Communist Refoundation (Italy)
RI	Italian Renewal Party
RKP	Swedish People's Party (Finland)
RV	Radical Liberal Party (Denmark)
SA	Rainbow Left (Italy)
SAK	Central Organisation of Finnish Trade Unions
SAP	Social Democratic Workers Party (Sweden)
SD	Democratic Left (Italy)
SD	Social Democratic Party (Denmark)
SDP	Social Democratic Party (Finland)
SEA	Single European Act
SED	Socialist Unity Party (Germany)
SF	Socialist People's Party (Denmark)
SF	Socialist People's Party (Norway)
SKDL	People's Democratic League of Finland
SKP	Finnish Communist Party
SKP	Swedish Communist Party
SP	Centre Party (Norway)

SP	Socialist Party (Netherlands)
SPD	Social Democratic Party (Germany)
SV	Socialist Left Party (Norway)
UL	Unity List (Denmark)
Ulivo	Olive Tree Coalition (Italy)
V	Left Party (Sweden)
VAS	Left Alliance of Finland
VIHR	Green Party (Finland)
VPK	Left Party Communists (Sweden)
VS	Left Socialist Party (Denmark)
VVD	Liberal Party (Netherlands)
WASG	Electoral Alliance for Labour and Social Justice (Germany)
WEU	Western European Union
WTO	World Trade Organisation

Contributors

David Bell is a Professor of Politics at the University of Leeds. He has co-written monographs on the French Socialist Party and on the French Communist Party and a textbook on 'French Politics' (Manchester University Press, 2007). He has published widely in various professional journals and is an editor of a number of books on French politics. He is currently working on a book on the French left due to be published in 2011.

Dag Arne Christensen is a researcher at the Stein Rokkan Centre for Social Studies at the University of Bergen. His doctoral thesis, published in 1999, analyses the EU policies of the left-socialist parties in Scandinavia. He has published in journals such as *Party Politics*, *Scandinavian Political Studies*, *West European Politics* and *Local Government Studies* (forthcoming). He has also been an Editor of *Scandinavian Political Studies*.

Richard Dunphy is Senior Lecturer in Politics at the University of Dundee. His books include: *The Making of Fianna Fáil Power in Ireland, 1923–48* (Oxford University Press, 1995), *Sexual Politics* (Edinburgh University Press, 2000), *Contesting Capitalism? Left Parties and European Integration* (Manchester University Press, 2004), (with John Barry and Brian Baxter, eds) *Europe, Globalization and Sustainable Development* (Routledge, 2004) and (with David Gowland and Charlotte Lythe, eds) *The European Mosaic*, third edition (Palgrave Macmillan, 2006). He is currently working on a study of the European Left Party (for Manchester University Press). He is associate editor of the journal *Perspectives on European Politics and Society*.

Dan Hough is a Reader in Politics at the University of Sussex. He has recently co-written a monograph on Germany's Left Party (Palgrave, 2007) and a textbook on *The Politics of the New Germany* (Routledge, 2007). He has published widely in journals such as *Party Politics*, *Journal of European Public Policy*, *German Politics* and *Regional and Federal Studies*. As well as being an Editor of *German Politics*, he is also Secretary of the International Association for the Study of German Politics (IASGP).

Dan Keith is completing his doctorate on 'Programmatic and Ideological Change in Western European (Post-) Communist Parties' at the University of Sussex. He is a co-author of 'Towards an analytical framework for party mergers – operationalising the cases of the German Left Party and the Dutch GroenLinks' (forthcoming in *West European Politics*).

Michael Koß is a Lecturer in Politics at the University of Potsdam. His recent books include *The Politics of Party Funding: State Funding to Political Parties and Party Competition in Western Europe* (OUP, 2010) and *The Left Party in Contemporary German Politics* (with Dan Hough and Jonathan Olsen) (Palgrave, 2007). He has published in journals such as *Regional and Federal Studies, Elections, Public Opinion* and *Party Politics* as well as *German Politics*. He is a member of the executive of the International Association for the Study of German Politics (IASGP).

James Newell is Professor of Politics, University of Salford. Recent books include *Parties and Democracy in Italy* (2000), *The Italian General Election of 2001* (ed., 2002), *Italian Politics: Quo Vadis?* (ed. with Carlo Guarnieri, 2005), *Italian Politics; Adjustment Under Duress* (with M. Bull, 2005), and *The Italian General Election of 2006* (ed. 2008). He is co-editor of the *Bulletin of Italian Politics*, and a member of the Executive Committee of the UK Political Studies Association. His new book, *The Politics of Italy: Governance in a Normal Country*, is due to be published by Cambridge University Press in January 2010.

Jonathan Olsen is Associate Professor of Political Science at the University of Wisconsin-Parkside. He is author of *Nature and Nationalism: Right-Wing Ecology and the Politics of Identity in Contemporary Germany* (St Martin's/Palgrave, 1999) and co-author (with Dan Hough and Michael Koß) of *The Left Party in Contemporary German Politics* (Palgrave, 2007). He has published widely on political parties and political extremism in various professional journals and is on the executive board of the International Association for the Study of German Politics (IASGP).

Tània Verge is a Lecturer in Political and Social Sciences at the Universitat Pompeu Fabra (Barcelona, Spain). Her research interests include party politics and gender and politics. Her work has been published in *Regional and Federal Studies, Representation – The Journal of Representative Democracy, South European Society and Politics*, and *The Journal of Women, Politics and Policy* (forthcoming). She is the author of several book chapters and two books on Spanish political parties and on gender representation in Spanish political institutions.

1
From Pariahs to Players? Left Parties in National Governments

Jonathan Olsen, Dan Hough and Michael Koß

Over the last two decades western European party politics has undergone a number of far-reaching changes. One of these changes has been the rise in the number of new parties and also an increase in the political relevance of longer-lived, but hitherto largely marginalised, older ones. Broadly speaking, these parties fall into one of three distinct camps – Green parties, parties of the far right, and parties of the far left. One of the most interesting common features of these three types of party is their initial – and in some cases, still existing – disdainful attitude to striking bargains and entering government alongside other actors. The first of these three party types, Green parties, were initially considered non-coalitionable by their opponents, and for many years they themselves also deliberately rejected participating in national governments, making a virtue out of the necessity of their 'anti-partyness' (Frankland and Schoonmaker, 1992; Poguntke, 1993; Tiefenbach, 1998; Shull, 1999; Burchell, 2002). This changed slowly at first, but by the late 1990s most green parties had become 'coalitionable', even if many have not yet actually been part of a national government (Lees, 2000; Poguntke, 2002; Hough, Koß and Olsen, 2007: chapter 4).

Far right parties, in their different guises, have also traditionally been considered beyond the coalitionable pale (Betz and Immerfall, 1998; Norris, 2005; Mudde, 2007). However, in the last decade some of these parties – such as the Austrian Free Democrats and the Italian National Alliance – have begun to move into government. Their institutionalisation, to be sure, has been more uneven than that of Green parties. Although parties of the far right have also enjoyed a relatively long (if somewhat spotty) parliamentary presence at the statewide and sub-state level, their participation in coalitions has had varying results, with some governments enjoying a degree of stability while others have been characterised by extreme instability and, indeed in a few cases, the effective death or slow decay of the far right parties involved (Minkenberg, 2001; Heinisch, 2003; Luther, 2003).

Finally, far left parties – or more simply 'left' parties, distinct from their social democratic, 'centre-left' cousins (more on the nature of this distinction below) – have also begun the transition from outsider to insider party. Surprisingly, however, the entrance of several of these actors into statewide governing coalitions, their increasing participation in sub-state governments, and, in general, their position as possible coalition partners across most of western Europe have received relatively little scholarly attention. This is particularly so when compared with that which Green parties or parties of the radical right have achieved (see Bale and Dunphy, 2006 for an analysis of the notable exceptions). To be sure, path-breaking studies on the European left after the fall of the Berlin Wall, such as that by Martin Bull and Paul Heywood (1994), remain in many ways the core texts from which analysis of left parties still begins; yet such studies are now inevitably out of date in addressing the new challenges and strategic choices that these parties face. A significant amount of often highly illuminating work has, perhaps unsurprisingly, been done on the rejuvenation of (former) communist parties in central and eastern Europe (see, for example, Waller, 1995; Ziblatt, 1998; Ishiyama, 1999; Bozóki and Ishiyama, 2002; Grzymała-Busse, 2002; Hough et al., 2006), but this has little direct relevance when analysing the hard choices that left parties are faced with (in terms of coalition politics at least) in western Europe. This is in spite of the fact that some of the newest and most innovative research has indeed looked to adapt these findings to the western European context (Keith, 2010). Some of the more recent studies of left parties in 'old Europe' have curiously sidestepped these questions, and they have tended to be either richly informative descriptions of left parties in particular countries (see, for example, Bosco, 2001; Botella and Ramiro, 2003; and, for a particularly good summary of all European left parties, see March, 2008), analyses of left party attitudes towards particular international institutions (Dunphy, 2004) or detailed analyses of intra-party conflicts and power tussles (see, for example, Hudson, 2000). While undoubtedly broadening our knowledge of how these actors have developed politically, organisationally and ideologically, this body of research still tends to more or less completely neglect issues of when and under what conditions contemporary left parties cross the Rubicon and become parties of government. In short, the vast majority of previous research on left parties after 1989 tells us precious little about why and how left parties enter government, what they actually do when they get there, and what happens to them (and the party systems where they are active) subsequently.

The apparent dearth of comparative literature on left parties is all the more surprising when one considers that since 1990 left parties in eight European democracies (as well as, if one looks farther afield, New Zealand) have, at one time or other, either entered national governments as coalition partners or acted as support parties. They are therefore arguably as significant to executive government in the last decade as their Green brethren (see Table 1.1).

Of course, left parties *have not* seen masses of voters stream to support their cause. Many poll regularly vote shares between 5 and 10 per cent and very few indeed regularly compete eye-to-eye with the largest social democratic party. They have nonetheless found themselves in politically more opportune settings, as social democrats in particular have increasingly sought to bring left actors into the coalition equation. In some cases left parties are already enjoying ever greater opportunities to influence national policy from inside governing coalitions (see Table 1.1 above). Whether in government or out of it, however, it may be that for left parties their time in the spotlight has arrived: recent worldwide economic problems have shifted more attention to parties of the left, which, in many cases, offer substantial policy alternatives to the pro-market economic consensus that has dominated mainstream economic policy in advanced industrial democracies in recent times. Subsequently, those left parties not yet in government are finding themselves forced to consider the basic question of whether they should give up a traditional oppositional role with a view to actually shaping policy outcomes.

It is this basic question which we put under the analytical microscope in this book. Our intent here is to scrutinise the choices left parties make for entering or not entering coalition government (be it as formal coalition partners or as support parties) and the conditions that shape, affect and frame these strategic choices. As our various case studies demonstrate, although the precise nature of the debates within left parties differs across time and space, the basic question of whether to participate in government – and the factors that shape this choice – is pertinent in all countries where left parties exist. Once left parties join coalition government, moreover, further questions arise. Do these parties perform as well in government as they talk in opposition? Are parties of the left ready to practise politics as the 'art of the possible' and adjust their policies to the hard business of governing, despite inevitable

Table 1.1 Left parties' participation in statewide governments in western Europe since 1990 (selected countries)

Country	Party	Most recent national election result (per cent)	Period in government	Previous government experience before 1990?
Cyprus	Progressive Party of Working People	31.1 (2006)	2003–Present (Presidential system)	No
Denmark	Socialist People's Party	13 (2007)	1993–2001 (support party)	Yes (support party, 1966–8)
Finland	Left Alliance	8.8 (2007)	1995–2003 (coalition partner)	Yes (predecessor a coalition partner 1944–8, 1966–71, 1975–6 and 1977–82)
France	French Communist Party	4.29* (2007)	1997–2002 (semi-presidential system; coalition partner)	Yes (coalition partner 1981–4)
Germany	Left Party	11.9 (2009)	No	No
Italy	The Left – Rainbow (Communist Refoundation; Party of Italian Communists; the Democratic Left; and the Federation of the Greens)	3.1 (2008)	1996–1998**; 2006–2008 (coalition partner)	No
Netherlands	Socialist Party	16.6 (2006)	No	No
Norway	Socialist Left Party	6.2 (2009)	2005–present (coalition partner)	No
Sweden	Left Party	5.9 (2006)	1998–2006 (support party)	No
Spain	United Left	3.8 (2008)	2004–8 (support party)	No

* In first round of voting, legislative elections.
** Communist Refoundation only.

claims of ideological betrayal by some of their members (and, indeed, voters)? Or, on the contrary, do they promise much and deliver frustratingly little when actually given the opportunity to take part in national governments? It is these kinds of questions that this book also aims to analyse.

Defining and classifying left parties

The first place to begin, of course, is with an understanding of just what 'left' parties are – their ideological and programmatic distinctiveness from other party families – and to trace something of their family origins. This is not quite as straightforward as it might appear. In contrast to some other party families (with the possible exception of the far right), it is more challenging to classify left parties in their present guise as a clearly defined party family. Such classification was easier to do in the early post-war years, as (at least some of) these actors were Communist parties – with their classic themes of revolution and the eventual rule of the working class – which had split from social democracy sometime after 1917. However, things became much more complicated as the Cold War wore on. Some of the more traditional Communist parties – initially in places such as Denmark and Sweden, but soon in other parts of the continent – were beginning to move away from Moscow's dogmatic line towards more flexible, less doctrinaire ideological stances. Left-libertarian parties were also arising out of the new social movements of the 1960s in parts of Northern Europe. The 'Eurocommunist experiment' of the PCI in Italy and the PCF in France also further blurred the traditional line between communist and socialist/social democratic parties. Classification of these parties became even more difficult after 1989 when various parties on the left split, merged with other parties and groups, renamed themselves, and otherwise redefined their overarching political values and policy goals.

One illuminating approach to making sense of this rich mosaic is to classify left parties on the basis of their attitude to the prevailing economic and political system. This involves a basic split between those that want significant and deep-rooted change to the structures that underpin liberal democratic institutions as well as the market-based economic system ('radical left parties') and those that simply denounce capitalism and view liberal democracy as a sham, rejecting all forms of compromise and accommodation with actors in the prevailing system ('extreme left parties'). Whereas the 'extreme left' stresses its revolutionary identity and the importance of the extra-parliamentary struggle

(March, 2008: p. 3), the 'radical left' supports the notion of democracy (in theory at least), but rejects the global neoliberal consensus and the marketisation and liberalisation that have, thus far, inevitably appeared to come with it. The 'extreme left' sees the market as anathema to any notion of social justice and human equality, and views bourgeois democracy as nothing more than a tool that capitalists use to cement their own positions in society. The 'radical left', on the other hand, accepts that the market may have a small, limited and highly restricted role to play in wealth generation, but very much within the context of an economy that is driven, and organised, around issues of social justice and economic equality. The 'extreme left' is now much more marginal than the 'radical left', but such parties do still exist – albeit on the fringes – of party politics in places such as Portugal and Greece. What unites these parties, as Luke March observes, is an 'identification of economic inequity as the basis of existing political and social arrangements' and a common belief that achieving 'collective economic and social rights' is their key goal (March, 2008: p. 3).

March's framework cannot, and indeed does not, neglect the real-world diversity of these parties. However, in reality *all* party families possess shades of grey and areas of ideological inconsistency, and we subsequently feel justified in taking a 'big tent' approach to understanding what constitutes the left party family, and therefore which parties should be put under the analytical lens in this book. Left parties may be reformed communist parties such as Sweden's *Vänsterpartiet*, Denmark's *Socialistisk Folkeparti*, and, with a number of caveats, the Finnish *Vasemmistoliitto*. They can also be much more orthodox or traditionalist Communist parties such as the *Parti Communiste Français* or the *Partito della Rifondazione Comunista* in Italy. Left-libertarian parties and parties with a distinct heritage in the tumultuous politics of the 1960s and 1970s (as the post-war social democratic left began to fragment) also exist, such as the Norwegian *Sosialistisk Venstreparti* and the Dutch *Socialistische Partij*. Finally, there are also parties that oscillate somewhere within this left ideological territory, such as Spain's *Izquierda Unida*, as well as parties that have emerged from a combination of origins, such as Germany's *Linke*, whose roots indeed lie in the old East German Communist Party but which has nevertheless evolved – especially after its merger with disaffected social democratic groups from western Germany – into something else entirely.

To recount these diverse origins and distinctive histories, however, is not to say that these parties do not have a clear and distinguishable ideological and programmatic core. They all reject the alleged neoliberal consensus and they reject the processes of marketisation and globalisation that it has brought with it. They have major reservations about the EU project, because of both its democratic deficit and its alleged facilitator role in supporting capitalism in Europe. They still seek to achieve full employment as well as much more redistributive tax regimes. They largely reject market mechanisms as a fair way of allocating resources. They are all keen to stress their solidarity with oppressed peoples across the globe and they are vehement in their rejection of US-inspired 'imperialism'. Finally, most left parties incorporate Green perspectives (especially in those countries without strong Green parties and/or a high degree of environmental consciousness) and feminist themes (even if these many of these parties themselves are still largely male-dominated). Left parties – as defined here – subsequently have enough in common to be compared and contrasted with one another. What is particularly interesting and timely (if not unique) about these parties, however, is the way in which they are being increasingly confronted with some very basic choices concerning their respective roles in their party systems – choices which can fundamentally affect their identity as parties.

Understanding left parties' strategic choices: An analytical framework

To understand the choices and dilemmas facing left parties as they try to accommodate themselves to the business of governing, we can use a conceptual model of party behaviour given its fullest articulation by Kaare Strøm (1990a; Müller and Strøm, 1999), a model we fruitfully employed in our previous study of the German Left Party (Hough et al., 2007) and which Tim Bale and Richard Dunphy have highlighted elsewhere (Bale and Dunphy, 2006). This model's trichotomy of party goals as centring on 'policy, office, or votes' can certainly encompass left parties in addition to more mainstream parties.[1] Indeed, for our purposes here, we can think of the 'policy, office, or votes' framework as providing a helpful perspective on the question of how and under what conditions left parties enter national government.

Coalition theory has long posited that coalitions come into being because of both policy and office considerations on the part of parties. Put very simply, most scholars have come to the conclusion that parties seek to maximise their office gains and minimise their policy distances with coalition partners by seeking 'minimal connected winning' coalitions. Although this is generally true in explaining coalition behaviour in the aggregate, in looking at how particular coalitions emerge in any one country at any one point in time, context and constraints of the political system play crucial roles. In terms of context, for example, the distances between parties in a multiparty system generally reflect differences across a variety of policy dimensions. Whether a party chooses to enter coalition government, in short, will depend upon which issues become salient for that party (and its coalition partners) at that point in time, and which issues do not (Narud, 1996). The policy salience question is difficult to capture with formal models. Furthermore, within any political system there are varying constraints on coalition formation that also affect actors' choices, among them institutional, cultural and historical, and situational constraints (see the discussion below). These constraints limit what is possible at any one time in any one national setting. If we want to understand exactly what conditions a party's choice to enter government in any country at any particular time, we therefore have to peer inside the 'black box' of party decision-making (Müller, 1997).

Overall, Strøm's heuristic provides us with a framework that can help us interpret what we find when we look inside this black box. At its most basic level, this framework suggests that all parties move within a triangle defined by three strategic choices: a 'policy' goal in which a party seeks to maximise its impact on public policy, implementing its policy agenda in the purest, most consistent way (pure and consistent, that is, with the party's identity and ultimate aims); an 'office-seeking' goal whereby parties attempt to attain political power and maximise the benefits of office by gaining significant ministerial portfolios or other governmental positions for their supporters; and a 'votes' goal whereby parties attempt to maximise their share of the vote in electoral competition with other parties, regardless of whether or not such vote maximisation leads to office. The strategic goals are quite obviously 'ideal types', inasmuch as no party can be completely described as seeking 'office' (or policy or votes) only. However, parties do appear to prioritise one party goal – to have a 'primary party goal' – over the other party goals at any one point in time (Harmel and Janda, 1993).

Thus, a party might prioritise an 'office' goal for a period of time, then later (in the event, say, of electoral loss) recalibrate its strategy to give more weight to policy implementation or vote maximisation. What is important here is that parties face inevitable opportunity costs when manoeuvring within these parameters: prioritising a 'policy' goal can (and often does) impact the ability of a party to maximise its share of the vote or to serve as coalition partner, since being uncompromising in a policy area is unlikely to attract coalition partners or (in many cases) voters. In the perfect world of parties, of course, a party's policy commitments would be perfectly in line with its other goals, such that it could pursue its (purest) policy objectives while simultaneously gaining both votes and office. However, parties themselves are quite aware that achieving all three objectives in their maximum form is not possible. Cognisant of these conflicts between party goals, parties have to make 'hard choices' – de-emphasising one party goal or another so as to accommodate other party goals. This is clearly illustrated when parties move to reform or dilute their policy commitments so as to become electable (vote-seeking) or coalitionable (office-seeking).

So what kinds of things affect parties' choices? The literature on parties indicates that there are at least four clusters of factors that seem to be important in shaping parties' decisions within the parameters of policy, office, and votes:

1. *Institutional factors.* Institutions shape incentives. More specifically, they help parties frame choices when they do their own goal-setting. Such factors include the electoral system, institutional governing traditions, or parliamentary rules and procedures. Countries in which 'strong parliaments' or committee systems exist and subsequently grant the political opposition a significant policy impact may heighten the priority given to policy-seeking goals while dampening office-seeking ones. Similarly, institutional governing traditions that make minority government an accepted 'normal' condition may also dampen office-seeking goals. For left parties in countries with a tradition of minority government and/or strong parliament, for example, office-seeking goals may have traditionally been given a much lower priority than elsewhere. So recognition of the impact of the institutional framework is subsequently vital in understanding why left parties enter government, and what they are able to achieve (or not achieve) when they get there.

2. *The party system and the nature of electoral competition.* Parties' decisions to enter or not enter government will depend on the kind and degree of competitiveness in the party system. This could include the socio-political cleavages in society and the number of spatial dimensions of competition, the history of relationships between parties, and the kinds of issues that gain saliency. A country with a more fragmented party system will – all other things being equal – tend to produce parties that give more weight to office-seeking goals than countries with less fragmented party systems (Müller and Strøm, 1999). The history of relationships between parties can also obviously condition the 'policy,

office, votes' dynamic, since a strained relationship can effectively blackball theoretically attractive coalition options. For example, some left parties have (or have had) very difficult relationships with their social democratic brethren. This can make entering government an extremely difficult decision, regardless of electoral outcomes.

3. *Organisation and the internal dynamics of parties.* A change in leadership has long been seen as a crucial factor in explaining the evolution of parties' primary goals (Harmel and Janda, 1993; Harmel et al., 1995). However, the impact of organisation and the internal dynamics of parties goes beyond leadership issues and includes changes in the balance of power within a party (i.e. the ascendancy of one faction over another), the relationship between the leadership and the party rank and file, and the organisational rules of the party that might severely limit the manoeuvrability of the leadership. To take a very straightforward example, factions within a party opposed to the office-seeking strategy of the leadership can, given sufficient organisational strength, frustrate leaders' ability to carry out this strategy and/or stage a coup to install a different leadership. This fight between factions can be seen in various left parties over the last two decades, and it has significantly impacted their decision on whether or not to enter government.

4. *Situational factors, including 'external shocks'.* Situational factors include a wide variety of specific events, both exogenous and endogenous, that impact parties' hard choices. Situational factors could include things such as the personalities of leaders at the time of coalition discussion (where leaders do not get on well, deals are harder to seal); the state of the economy at the time of coalition discussions (leading some parties to reject the 'poison pill' of coalition government); or specific, often spectacular, events (for example political scandals) that trigger sudden elections or new coalition discussions. Undoubtedly the most significant of these situational factors, however, are 'external shocks' to a party. And the most recognisable of external shocks are electoral shocks. An unexpected electoral loss often prompts a party to re-evaluate its primary goal and replace it with another one as the party goes through much soul-searching about both party strategy and policy. Research on Green parties, for example, has shown that electoral losses while still in opposition are a key factor in moving these parties into government at the next election (Dumont and Bäck, 2006). However, external electoral shocks can also come from unexpected electoral success: this confronts a party with the prospect of entering coalition government that it previously did not have. Such 'electoral

success shocks' seem to be especially pertinent to parties that have traditionally been opposition parties, such as left parties.

Left parties' hard choices

The framework of policy, office, votes is one that can be used to analyse all political parties (Bale and Dunphy, 2006). Thus it should go without saying that left parties are basically no different from other parties in the hard choices and trade-offs they face. However, there are a number of things that make these trade-offs especially difficult for left parties. First of all, parties on the left have historically wrestled with the question of how to 'deal with' parliamentary democracy more than other types of parties. For most of their history, left-wing parties have pondered over whether to question or reject parliamentary democracy *per se*, in good Leninist style, as a capitalist charade that in reality represses the working class; or whether instead they should seek to change the system from within, fundamentally reshaping capitalist structures and democratic institutions. Although most of the contemporary left parties considered here have long since moved closer to the latter position, some of their members are nevertheless policy purists, giving priority to policy objectives and sacrificing office (and often votes too) on the altar of ideological purity. This is completely consistent with a core piece of these parties' identity: many of their followers are attracted to this type of party precisely because they perceive it to be a party that 'stands apart' from the other parties; that is, a party that pursues overarching, systemic change and is willing to articulate clear, radical and uncompromising policy prescriptions.

However, all parties in parliamentary democracies – at least once they decide they want to decisively influence political life rather than sit grumpily on the sidelines – must eventually give some priority to office-seeking goals as part of working 'within the system'. Expanding a party's goals to include office-seeking also leads to some emphasis on vote maximisation, since without a good electoral performance a party cannot hope to enter government (or, in the case of multiparty parliamentary systems, to enter into executive coalitions). Vote maximisation and office-seeking goals in turn lead almost invariably to the de-emphasising of policy objectives, at least in their ideologically purest form. Thus left parties tend to become more de-radicalised over time. Still, shifting the weight it gives to each goal or replacing one primary goal with another remains a very difficult choice for any party, most especially when it comes to giving office-seeking goals more priority.

The intersection of left parties' more purist ideological identity with new political opportunity structures and changing party system dynamics, which have thrust them into the role of possible coalition partner, is therefore bringing these parties' hard choices into sharp relief. Their challenge is to continue to articulate a distinguishable political vision and a set of clear policy principles; at the same time, they must be able to compromise them so as to get into a position where they actually have the power to implement their policies. Left parties are quite aware of this dilemma.

Second, left parties' hard choices are especially acute given that most of them (as Table 1.1 indicates) have had little experience of coalition government in comparison to more 'mainstream' parties. Entering coalition governments constitutes a fundamentally new phase or stage in their 'lifespan', a metaphor Pedersen (1982) uses to convey the evolution of political parties from their very beginning to their maturity (and, in some cases, death). Pedersen outlines four stages of a party's life – declaration (announcing the intent to become a party), authorisation (meeting the requirements necessary to be recognised as a party), representation (winning seats in parliament) and relevance. Deschouwer (2008) has taken Pedersen's model one step further in exploring the distinctive characteristics of 'newly governing parties'. Drawing on Giovanni Sartori's (1976) definition of a party's 'relevance' within a political system as consisting of either its 'blackmail potential' (a party's ability, via its electoral power, to impact other parties' coalition strategies) or its 'governing potential' (coalitionability, in other words), Deschouwer argues that 'governing' has to be added as a crucial, and qualitatively new, phase in a party's lifespan. Governing presents benefits to a party, undoubtedly, but also has severe impacts: it almost certainly results in the dilution of policy commitments (as the discussion above notes) and (very frequently) punishment at the next election.

Deciding to enter government is an especially hard choice for parties new to it because of at least four factors. First, as discussed above, being a coalition partner risks sacrificing an important part of a party's core identity, such as that of left parties which have conceived themselves as standing apart from or above the 'establishment'. Being a part of government thus involves a deep existential transformation for left parties. Second, in contrast to more mainstream (governing) parties, being new to government means that political 'normality' has been previously defined by party members and voters as *not* being in government. This 'abnormal' situation is thus likely to generate much more scrutiny and soul-searching on the part of activists and voters than happens in established parties; it also inevitably provokes more media attention simply because it is unusual (Deschouwer, 2008). Third, being new in government also means operating without an established pattern or model for governing, as parties new to government often grope for answers to questions which they have never before faced. Along with this, being new in government means (most probably) negotiating with a more experienced coalition partner, where the risk is run of being taken advantage of. Together, this means that the experience of coalition government is likely to be a rockier one than is the case for more established parties. Yet, as Buelens and Hino (2008) have shown, being new in government is almost certain to bring electoral loss at the next election, especially if the party is less centrist and more ideologically extreme. Left parties, especially ones without any experience, thus face a difficult decision over whether to enter government in the first place and, as a direct result of crossing the Rubicon, they will also run significant electoral and political risks at a later date.

Plan of the book

All the contributors to this volume are subsequently seeking to identify common patterns in both the nature of the hard choices that left parties are faced with and also the outcomes that tend to be spawned. The frameworks introduced above shape these discussions accordingly. We proceed inductively, examining a number of the most prominent cases in advanced industrial democracies. Chapters 2–5 analyse cases where left parties have actually entered coalitions. We purposely ignore the somewhat anomalous case of Cyprus (for more on this case see Dunphy and Bale, 2007), choosing to look instead at Norway (Jonathan Olsen), France (David Bell), Italy (James Newell) and Finland (Richard Dunphy). The common experience of being in government has not translated into identical outcomes for parties in these countries. We seek to understand why that has been the case and which conditions were at work in bringing these parties into government in the first place. Chapters 6–8 analyse cases where left parties have not taken the 'final step' into a genuine coalition but have instead acted as support parties. Being a support party is something of a 'halfway house', and, although it has certain advantages, it also clearly has its limitations. The cases put under the microscope here are Spain (Tània Verge), Sweden (Michael Koß) and Denmark (Dag Arne Christensen). Finally, Chapters 9 and 10 look at cases where strong left parties exist, but they have not – as yet – entered national governments; namely Germany (Dan

Hough) and the Netherlands (Dan Keith). In the last statewide election in both Germany and the Netherlands, the left parties scored impressive electoral gains and were seen as among the clearest 'winners' of these elections. Nevertheless, left parties in both countries were shut out (or shut themselves out) of coalition government. Why? What factors conditioned these parties' choices? What factors will be at play in the future?

Throughout each case study, authors have employed a unified framework to understand why decisions were taken, as well as to understand the ramifications these choices have for the future. Along with this, authors have attempted to construct a narrative of each party's development that will help the reader understand the contextual field within which each moves, as well as the constraints (external and internal) under which each operates. Accordingly, each chapter considers four sets of questions.

First, each author gives a little background and explains the most important contextual factors that shape the strategic decisions that left parties have to make. More specifically, this will entail a discussion of the historical origins of the party and how (if at all) these origins impact on the party's attitudes/decisions towards entering government. Institutional and party systemic factors such as electoral rules, traditions of government and the nature of party competition will also be analysed in so far as they impinge on the party's (in)ability or (un)willingness to enter government. The initial section of each chapter will also briefly introduce any relevant situational factors – electoral shocks, prominent personalities and so forth – as well as party organisational features of note.

The second set of questions discusses ideological and programmatic issues. More specifically, the extent of the impact of government participation – or the prospect of it – on ideological and programmatic orientation will be put under the analytical microscope. If change has occurred, when did it do so (i.e. pre-, post- or during government) and what were the causes and consequences of both entering government and aiming (if indeed it was the aim) to become more coalitionable? Finally, what policy accomplishments can the party lay claim to, and how does this match up with original aims?

Third, each author will analyse the core policy stances of his or her respective left party. This will enable the editors to analyse in the concluding chapter what the core of the anti-capitalist agenda within left parties actually is, before assessing the limits, constraints and opportunities that exist in attempting to implement this policy package. Areas such as the party's attitude to the European integration project will be analysed, as will attitudes towards the much maligned process of economic globalisation. Links to various non-parliamentary bodies (particularly in the context of anti-globalisation strategies) will also be touched upon. Authors will also analyse what this set of policy preferences means for relationships with the centre-left and with other left or Green parties in their own countries.

The respective case study chapters will conclude by looking at future electoral and political prospects. Authors will attempt to shed light on how the party has been impacted electorally by government participation or support. Given that we would expect some sort of de-radicalisation during a period in government, each chapter will say something on what happened after the party left government. Do we see a party maintaining the more moderate positions that it found itself taking in government, or does it return to the more radical positions of yesteryear? Do we see evidence of a comprehensive linear move towards the political centre or are the party's policy positions something much more ad hoc?

These case studies will be followed by a final substantive chapter (Olsen, Hough and Koß) which draws the key strands from these case studies together. We try, in other words, to make sense of what we have learned from each of the case studies. Are there common patterns of decision-making on policy, office and votes that can be seen among left parties, or are such decisions completely context-dependent? Do left parties differ significantly not only from more mainstream parties but from other, more radical parties in the way in which they ultimately make their hard choices? Does the extent to which a left party de-radicalises depend on whether or not the party has participated in government; and, if so, does it depend upon it having been a full coalition partner rather than a support party? Do left parties radicalise once again in the opposition or is there 'no turning back' after participation in government? Although we may not be able to definitively answer these questions, we will be able to approach answers to them with some degree of confidence gained from our empirical data.

Note

1. Sometimes the literature on parties' strategic goals includes a fourth goal, that of 'internal party unity.' See Sjøblom (1968); Harmel and Janda (1993).

2
The Norwegian Socialist Left Party: Office-seekers in the Service of Policy?

Jonathan Olsen

The Socialist Left Party (*Sosialistisk Venstreparti*, SV) originated as a splinter party of the dominant centre-left Labour Party (DNA) in 1961, as Norway's membership in NATO and that organisation's nuclear policy sparked a walkout of the far-left faction within the DNA. Known initially as the Socialist People's Party (SF), the party was, at most, a minor electoral irritant to Labour throughout the 1960s, and by the end of the decade it was near total collapse. Yet it rebounded as a result of mobilisation against Norway's possible EEC membership in 1972: leading the 'No' camp, SF, the anti-EEC opposition within the (otherwise pro-EEC) DNA, and representatives of the Communist Party (NKP) joined forces in a 'Socialist Electoral Alliance', which after a period of consolidation into one party (with most of the Communist Party representatives returning to an independent NKP) renamed itself the Socialist Left Party in 1975.

Despite its early 1960s heritage, in reality SV was really a product of the New Left of the early 1970s and represented a break with the traditional, 'materialist' politics of an older left, giving priority to issues – such as anti-militarism, grassroots democracy, solidarity with the third world, and green politics – beyond the traditional class cleavage (Christensen, 1996). The party's origins, policy positions, political orientation and commitment to democracy all mark it as a party of the radical left, rather than of the extreme left (as discussed in Chapter 1 of this book). Since the late 1970s, SV has enjoyed a permanent parliamentary presence, hovering between 5 and 12 per cent of the vote. Although the party lent its support to Labour minority governments on specific policy issues from time to time, it had until recently never been asked to participate as a full coalition partner (or even as a formalised support party) in government.

Rebuffed by Labour, SV basked in its outsider status, seeing itself as a left-wing corrective to its larger brother on the centre-left. Indeed, entering into a formal centre-left coalition government in the 1960s, 1970s, 1980s or even the early 1990s was just as unthinkable for SV as for Labour. Office-seeking goals were entirely off the table, and the SV pursued policy goals and, to a much lesser extent, vote maximisation.

In 2004, however, the DNA, SV and Centre Party (SP, the former Agrarian party) agreed to a form a pre-electoral coalition pact committing all parties to form a coalition if they jointly obtained a majority in parliament. The 2005 national election brought this centre-left coalition to power with a six-seat majority, despite a substantial electoral loss of a quarter of its previous vote by the SV (see Table 2.1). This was a quite remarkable development, and one that broke with all previous tradition. Although common from 1900 to 1940, multiparty cabinets were the exception rather than the rule in Norway after 1945: since that time there have been only nine cabinets that included more than one political party, none of which had, prior to 2005, included DNA (Narud and Valen, 2007). Moreover, roughly two-thirds of all Norwegian cabinets since 1945 have been minority cabinets (whether single- or multiparty), and DNA had never before participated in a majority government with other parties.

This chapter will examine how the SV came into government for the first time in its history, discuss SV's performance in government and speculate on the impact (electoral and otherwise) government participation has had on the party. In analysing how SV came to give substantially more weight to office-seeking goals, the chapter will highlight several factors. The most prominent of these are the changing nature of party competition in Norway over the last decade; evolving features of

Table 2.1 Election results in Norway, 1997–2009 (figures in percentages)

Party	1997	2001	2005	2009
DNA	35.0	24.3	32.7	35.4
SV	6.0	12.5	8.8	6.2
Red Alliance	1.7	1.2	1.2	1.3
Centre Party	7.9	5.6	6.5	6.2
Christian People's Party	13.7	12.4	6.8	5.5
Left Liberals	4.5	3.9	5.9	3.9
Conservatives	14.3	21.2	14.1	17.2
Progress Party	15.3	14.6	22.1	22.9
Others	1.6	4.3	3.1	1.3

parliamentary government in Norway that have provided institutional incentives to DNA and SV to enter into coalition government; 'electoral shocks' to DNA and SV that affected the strategic choices of each party; and new leadership in SV that guided an often fractious party toward more accommodation with Labour. Beyond these factors, two 'situational' issues that have come to dominate Norwegian politics over the last decade – Norway's oil wealth and the issue of European Union membership – also created a new context for coalition possibilities and set the parameters for the factors discussed above. The first issue, Norway's oil wealth, has made all governing parties in Norway 'vulnerable to charges that the "richest country in the world" can surely afford better public services...' (Sitter, 2006: p. 574). After 2001, this issue helped bring an electorally chastened DNA – which for the previous few years had been pursuing a more neoliberal, fiscally conservative economic policy – closer to the positions of the SV and Centre Party. Meanwhile, the bracketing of EU membership as a live issue removed a powerful obstacle to formal co-operation between the three parties. SV's origins lie in its opposition to the EU and its scepticism regarding NATO;[1] these constitute the party's policy 'heartland'.[2] While the saliency of NATO as an issue has declined considerably since 1989, the question of EU membership continues to be very important in Norwegian politics.[3] Taking EU membership off the table after 2001 thus made co-operation between SV, Labour and the equally EU-hostile SP a real possibility.

The changing situation of the Labour Party in Norwegian electoral politics

Bringing SV into government depended heavily on making the DNA much more amenable to a coalition with SV than they were previously. An important precondition for making the Labour Party ready, in turn, to ask the SV to join a coalition government was DNA's fall from a hegemonic position in the Norwegian political system. Labour's dominance of post-war Norwegian politics is deeply rooted in the social compromise between labour and capital, and between agrarian and urban interests, negotiated before the World War II (Mjøset et al., 1994). Still, by the late 1960s changing socio-economic structures, a significant rise in the level of education, and increased urbanisation and geographic mobility led to the erosion of the salience of traditional cleavages in Norwegian society – with significant demographic and electoral consequences for DNA, the shrinking of its traditional working class being the most obvious one (Strøm and Svåsand, 1997).

At the same time, the Keynesian economic policies of the DNA started to produce macroeconomic failures in the 1970s that gave Labour the image of being unable to effectively manage the economy. As with other social democratic parties in western European democracies, DNA – in order to remain competitive electorally – had to find new ways of combining its goals of social justice and economic prosperity. Much like other social democratic parties in western Europe (albeit later, and not nearly as deeply), DNA thus set out on a 'third way', that is, an attempt to achieve its traditional goal of social justice through new economic means (Green-Pedersen and van Kersbergen, 2002). In electoral terms, changes in the social structure and the move away from Keynesianism prompted social democratic parties such as DNA to increase their attempt to try and win over voters in the middle of the political spectrum, with fiscal disciplinary measures being the most obvious way these parties could demonstrate to the electorate that they could govern responsibly.

This new strategy was not without its risks, however. The DNA's dilemma – familiar to all modern social democratic parties – was the need to guard its left flank while simultaneously governing enough from the centre to guarantee votes from the middle of the political spectrum. By the late 1990s, this balancing act had become increasingly precarious for Labour. From a one-time high of 48.3 per cent in 1957, DNA fell into the low forties by the mid-1960s, culminating in the disastrous 1973 election where it scored a mere 35.3 per cent. Even though the party rebounded in the next several elections, by the late 1980s and early 1990s it looked as if Labour would never again recover its historic highs.

Besides the declining electoral strength of the Labour Party and the outsider status of SV, the Norwegian party system since the 1960s has also been characterised by a bloc of non-socialist parties, which in various combinations have provided the main governmental alternative to minority Labour governments, with only a limited 'crossing' of the blocs. There were two basic permutations of this non-socialist coalition: a centre-right coalition, which since the 1960s has been the main coalition alternative; and a 'centrist' coalition option, which included the Liberals, the Centre Party and the Christian People's Party (but not the Conservatives). The role of the Centre Party in these two coalition variations has been critical. SP's break with the Conservatives in 1993 (discussed below) and its failure in the late 1990s to forge a strong majority for a centrist coalition have meant that Labour still finds itself in a very strong position in the Norwegian party system. In addition, Labour and (especially) the SV have benefited electorally from the lack of a viable green party in electoral competition, as is the case in Finland and Sweden. Still, the difficulties of the non-socialist opposition in forming strong, stable governments also meant that Labour's claim on government office for much of the 1990s rested 'as much on anything on the inability of the non-socialist parties to provide a coherent alternative' (Madeley, 1998: p. 188) as on its own political popularity.

In 2000, Labour once again took office after the centrist government was brought down by an alliance of both left and right parties. DNA's new leader, Jens Stoltenberg, fashioned himself into a social democratic reformer in the mould of Tony Blair. Under Stoltenberg, a former minister for oil and energy as well as finance minister, DNA pressed for the partial privatisation of the state energy and state railway sectors, restrictive use of moneys generated by the state Petroleum Fund, a reduction in the number of government civil servants, initiation of fiscal reforms in health care, and the introduction of private schools alongside state schools. Not surprisingly, Labour depended on support from the centre-right to push through these measures. However, Labour's popularity in office sank, both among its traditional voter groups (such as the unions) and also among newly courted centre-right voters. Consequently 'the fiscal restraints which he [Stoltenberg] displayed failed to endear him any longer to voters of the centre and right, many of whom called for a looser regime which would use the country's oil wealth to fund both increased expenditure on public services, transport and pensions *and* cuts in taxation' (Madeley, 2002: p. 214).

By the 2001 election, an increasing number of voters were frustrated with the two viable governing alternatives with which they were faced – either a Labour minority government or a coalition of the centre-right (Aardal and Valen, 1997). The election subsequently proved to be a watershed for Labour. It appeared that, for at least some DNA voters, the Stoltenberg government was seen to have shifted too much towards the right. Meanwhile, SV saw its vote total in 2001 go up dramatically, from 6.0 per cent in 1997 to 12.5 per cent in 2001. SV's gains at the 2001 election appeared to be a perfect illustration of the 'vacuum thesis', the theory that, once a party moves away from one segment of its electorate (such as unions), rival parties have the opportunity to win votes among those whose policy preferences are no longer articulated by their former party (Patton, 2006; Neugebauer and Stöss, 1999). Of course, the SV has always soaked up voters to the left of DNA, as it has occupied the farther-left end of the political spectrum since 1961. Still, in the 2001 campaign, SV scored one of its best electoral results ever by sounding positively Labour-like, advocating an expansive welfare state and society's responsibility towards society's least well-off groups. Concretely, SV's platform included the need to improve public services (funded by using more of the Petroleum Fund than was advocated by Labour); full provision of Kindergarten places for all (and at reduced rates); a return to higher 2004 levels of taxation; and opposition to a greater role for private schools and private hospitals. SV combined this message with one attacking the 'neoliberal' policies of the DNA, while stressing SV's own green and feminist credentials, its opposition to unfettered globalisation, and its support for an equitable and peaceful world order (Socialist Left Party, 2005). Not surprisingly, then, much of SV's increase in the 2001 election could be traced to disillusioned Labour voters, especially among Labour's traditional trade union clientele. In the following election in 2005, these disillusioned DNA voters would return to Labour's fold, accounting in part for SV's electoral losses.

It gradually became clear after the 2001 election to the majority of those in DNA that Labour would have difficulty ever regaining its historic electoral highs. Moreover, it became clear to many within Labour that the minority model of government it had preferred was under serious strain, with Stoltenberg's predecessor as DNA leader, Thorbjørn Jagland, already suggesting in the late 1990s that more formalised co-operation with other parties might be needed (Allern and Aylott, 2007). Indeed, Norwegian minority governments in the late 1990s experienced an increasing number of unexpected parliamentary defeats, demonstrating that the traditional minority government model with ad hoc support on particular issues was coming under some strain (Rommetvedt, 2003; Strom, Narud and Valen, 2005). At Labour's national council meeting in 2004, Stoltenberg argued that Labour no longer had the electoral strength to govern effectively as a minority government in this way (Heidar, 2005). He also floated the idea, however, that some kind of negotiated majority in parliament short of a full coalition with SV and SP might suffice, a suggestion the other two parties flatly ruled out (Heidar, 2005). DNA was thus faced with several strategic alternatives: it could move farther towards the centre-right and try to win over voters from the bourgeois parties and/or cut a deal with the centre-right parties (for example, by tempting the Christian People's Party into supporting a minority Labour government). This was anathema to the left wing of DNA, far from a guaranteed vote-winning strategy, and not necessarily certain to be supported by the centre-right (Sitter, 2006). The other choice was to try to forge a formal centre-left coalition with the SV and, if possible, the Centre party. In the event, DNA's national party convention in 2004 endorsed a pre-electoral coalition of the three parties and empowered Stoltenberg to negotiate with the SP and SV after the election (Allern and Aylott, 2007).

The role of the Centre Party

In addition to the changes involving DNA, the role of the Centre Party (SP) in bringing SV into government was crucial. Despite a 'crisis agreement' (*Kriseforliket*) in 1935, the Centre Party was, unlike its counterpart in Sweden, unwilling to enter a lasting electoral pact with Labour (a so-called 'red–green' alliance) after this time, and preferred coalitions with the non-socialist bloc (Allern and Aylott, 2007). Indeed, while the SP's youth organisation in the 1960s favoured an alliance with the DNA, it found little support in the party as a whole (Christensen, 2001). Since that time, SP's preference for a centre-right or centrist coalition has been based on its traditionalist, rural concerns – concerns that until recently were largely at odds with Labour's modernising agenda.

In 1989 the Centre Party entered a coalition government with the Conservatives and Christian Democrats that had a weak parliamentary basis (only 62 out of 165 seats). Although its voters shared more cultural values with the Conservatives, the SP was more sceptical towards the tax-cutting and privatisation policies of its coalition partners. It was also emphatically opposed to EU membership, and even opposed the European Economic Area agreement (EEA), a document governing non-EU states' relationship with the EU. This put it at odds with the Conservatives, long-time champions of Norway's EU membership. As the EU membership issue became more politically salient, the coalition broke apart and a Labour minority government again assumed power. Given its traditional distance from Labour, and the added fact that DNA was also in favour of EU membership, SP after 1993 therefore pursued an office-seeking strategy involving the centrist coalition option, which it portrayed as a '3rd centre of gravity' to the two main options of centre-left and centre-right government (Christensen, 2001). This strategy came to fruition after the 1997 election with the first Bondevik cabinet. However, as discussed above, this government had an extremely weak parliamentary basis (42 out of 165 seats) and fell in 2000 over, amongst other things, the issue of the EEA, with Labour once again assuming power.

At this point, the Centre Party began to rethink its electoral and parliamentary strategy once again. Although traditionally the ideological distance between Labour and the Centre Party on the one hand, and

SV and Centre Party on the other, was significant, this ideological distance had begun to narrow greatly during the 1990s. As measured by Knutsen's longitudinal study of ideological placement of parties by experts (1998), the Centre Party by 1993 had clearly undergone significant ideological change since the 1980s: the Liberals and Centre Party had exchanged places, with the Liberal Party moving to the right and the SP to the left. Furthermore, SV and Centre were no longer separated by a vast ideological distance, with SV moving towards the political centre. Similarly, Narud's (1996) analysis of voters and parliamentarians in Norway demonstrated that voters and parliamentarians alike placed the Centre Party significantly more to the left during the 1990s than they had previously. Moreover, this same study found that the Centre Party's parliamentarians had become much more hostile to the Conservatives and, while preferring a coalition with the Christian People's Party, were much more open to a coalition that would include not only Labour but also the SV. For its part, SV preferred the Centre Party and DNA as possible coalition partners. Thus, even though SV and SP were separated by some policy differences, the two parties had considerable sympathy for each other as coalition partners (Narud, 1996). This was attributable, in part, to their common anti-EU position. As this issue became more politically salient after 1993, SV and SP had the policy potential for a firm basis of co-operation. Yet the narrowing of the ideological distance between the two parties appears to go beyond this. As Christensen (2001) has noted, the EU issue 'fuelled a massive Centre Party critique of modern capitalism' that shows striking affinities with SV's own economic position. Moreover, SP's core policies today – more subsidies for agriculture, better financing of local government, current levels of public ownership, the use of the Petroleum Fund as a source of government spending – are just as compatible with a broad centre-left coalition as with a centre-right one. After the 2001 election, SP began to explore seriously a centre-left coalition option with talks between SP and SV on specific areas of policy.

SV's changing attitudes towards government participation

Beyond the question of specific policies of a Labour–SP–SV coalition government, SV's unwillingness to abandon its traditional 'outsider' role and to seriously consider being bound by a formal coalition arrangement was the last, and certainly the most important, obstacle that had to be surmounted. This shift away from a strong emphasis on policy-seeking (and, to a lesser extent, vote-seeking) to a strategy that now included office-seeking goals was hastened by several factors. First, although the 'policy influence differential' – the difference between the ability of formal coalition partners and parties not in the executive to influence policymaking – has not been as great in Norway as in other liberal democracies, it is nevertheless still very real.[4] Just as importantly, in liberal democracies parties that find themselves in the role of supporting minority governments (either in a formalised arrangement or in an ad hoc fashion) are quite aware of the difference in power available to those parties in government and those outside it. By 2001 the thinking within SV was that, in order to be able to have the kind of influence on government policy that SV desired, entering a coalition would have to be seriously considered. More specifically, unless Labour – having experimented with a more centrist, 'neoliberal' politics – was bound by a coalition agreement and forced to constantly negotiate with coalition partners it would pursue policies directly opposed to the interests of the SV (Elvik, 2007; Lysbakken, 2007; Seierstad, 2007). SV leaders eventually came to believe that the main policy goals of the SV were being frustrated outside government and therefore could be best achieved through an alliance with Labour and SP – much more so than could be achieved in the opposition or acting as a support party (Lysbakken, 2007; Seierstad, 2007).

In truth, the barrier to entering a formal coalition with Labour and the Centre Party was not nearly as high for SV in 2005 as it had been during the 1960s, 1970s, and 1980s, when the relationship between Labour and SV was not particularly good. As early as the 1970s some within SV had argued that a coalition with the DNA should at least be considered, including the former party leader Fin Gustavson (Christensen, 2001; Seierstad, 2006). SV party congresses had consistently ruled this out – a position reiterated strongly in 1997 in the form of a specific resolution rejecting this option. Yet, despite this resolution, relations between the two parties had begun to grow warmer by the early 1990s. Indeed, the rhetoric and hostility that had characterised the relationship between DNA and SV during the 1960s and 70s had diminished considerably while atoperated on important pieces of legislation.

Seen in this way, the sometimes turbulent relationship between the two parties from 1993 to 1997 can be seen as something of a detour in the road of SV's slow evolution to acceptable coalition partner. This detour appears to have been spurred on by the rank and file's frustration with the unresponsiveness of the party leadership as well as a fear of a loss of SV's political profile should the party continue to advocate too close co-operation with Labour. The immediate cause of the worsening relationship between the two parties was a statement by then SV leader Erik Solheim after SV's 1993 party congress that appeared in the major media. Solheim was quoted as saying that the SV wanted actively to work towards a coalition with Labour, despite the 1993 congress's explicit attachment of strict conditions – most importantly, the inclusion of the Centre Party and Norway's withdrawal from the EEA – to such a coalition (Christensen, 1998). The explicit attachment of conditions for a coalition government was in itself an indication of SV rank and file's unwillingness to take final, realistic steps towards co-operation (given the fact that Labour would view these conditions as unacceptable). Be that as it may, the party's rapid decline in opinion polls shortly thereafter, and a deeply disappointing election result of 7.9 per cent in the 1993 election, mobilised the youth wing of the party to actively contest SV's movement towards Labour, and in 1997 an SV party congress explicitly rejected any coalition – in fact, any significant co-operation – with Labour (Aardal and Valen, 1997; Madeley, 1998; Seierstad, 2006).

Significantly, however, the same party congress elected a new party leader, Kristin Halvorsen, who had a greater ear for the style and sentiments of the party base and thus signalled a less divisive, more unifying leadership style than that of Solheim. Indeed, the reason for the change of leadership was not so much a question of Halvorsen being more or less open to coalitions with Labour *per se* than Solheim but of her greater sensitivity to the inner-party democratic style of SV – and thus to the attitudes within the party base. Party leadership change thus resulted in subtle changes in personnel, and strategic and tactical reorientation. In the wake of the party's explicit rejection of any co-operation with Labour, SV suffered a drop in opinion polls and another disappointing (for many in SV) result at the 1997 election. By this time, it appears, SV voters, as well as party members, were frustrated both with too eager an embrace of a coalition with Labour and with an overly frosty relationship (Seierstad, 2007). Consequently, while the following party congress in 1999 reprimanded the SV parliamentary group for supporting Labour's position to support NATO actions in Kosovo, at the same time it supported a motion to try to establish some form of binding co-operation with Labour and the Centre Party (Seierstad, 2006, 2007).

By 2001 SV's relationship with Labour had improved to the point that SV made a momentous shift in direction, declaring at its spring 2001 annual conference that its goal after the parliamentary election the following autumn would be a government coalition of the three parties, provided policy differences could be narrowed. Although SV's offer was not yet reciprocated by DNA, the 2001 election had several important spin-off effects for SV that would impact its strategic considerations going into the 2005 election and its ultimate decision to enter a coalition with Labour and SP. First and foremost, the 2001 election seemed to change the power relationship between DNA and SV, with SV within 12 percentage points of its larger partner. For many within the party, this made the possibility of having a relatively large impact in influencing government policy much more probable, thus ensuring that the policy-seeking goals of the party might come some way towards being satisfied (Holmås, 2007; Jensen, 2007; Lysbakken, 2007; Seierstad, 2007). Moreover, the increasing support of the trade unions made it possible to exert stronger pressure on DNA, increasing the perception within the SV that the party would be able to negotiate with its still-larger partner from a position of strength (Elvik, 2007; Holmås, 2007; Lysbakken, 2007; Seierstad, 2007).

Second, there was a perception in SV that refusing to leave its oppositional role after the 2001 election would have severely disappointed those new voters who had voted for the party. Indeed, to refuse to consider being in coalition government when the party was finally asked to do so would have been to consign SV to the permanent role of a protest party. Seen from this perspective, the 2001 election acted as something of an 'electoral shock' for SV: it presented, for the first time, the real potential of entering government, thus confronting the party with the possibility of power. The disappointing election result in 2005, in turn, further underscored the desirability of an office-seeking strategy: given that one possible reason to stay in opposition is the fear of vote loss at the next election, electoral losses while still in the opposition can convince parties that coalition government is worth the risk. The third spin-off of the 2001 election was the coming to power of a centre-right government that often depended on votes of the far-right Progress Party to achieve some of its policy goals. Moreover, it soon became clear that the centre-right government would continue, if not extend, the neo-liberal policies and attacks on the welfare state of the previous Labour minority government (Lysbakken, 2007). Better to be in government and attempt to push public policies back to the left – to hold Labour's feet to the fire – than to stand by and see a new centre-right government in power, further dismantling the welfare state.[5]

Fourth, as a result of its poor election result in 2001, DNA was driven into opposition. As discussed above, it seemed DNA did begin to tilt back toward the left, with a resulting narrowing of policy distance between SV and Labour. Fifth, the personal relationship between the leaders of the SV, Kristen Halvorsen, and Labour's Jens Stoltenberg helped pave the way for SV's eventual entry into a coalition government. These two party leaders had long served together in parliament and got on quite well. Such good relationships had not always been the case: during the 1960s and 1970s the two parties and their leaders clearly despised each other, and while the relationship had improved over the course of the last two decades there was still clearly some animus between the party leaderships. Halvorsen was able to bring different factions together in the party and work towards an understanding within the party on its relationship with the Labour Party (Jensen, 2007; Langeland, 2007).

SV at the bargaining table and in office

In April 2005 SV's party congress unanimously endorsed the decision to work for a coalition government of DNA, SV and SP, and a government came to fruition after that autumn's election. In the formal coalition agreement, the three parties supported (among other things) continued public ownership of hydro power and oil resources; keeping the level of overall taxation at the same level as in 2004; reversing a reduction in unemployment benefits in place from the previous government; and educational reform. The most important aspects of the coalition agreement, however, were the compromises each party committed itself to in regard to some core foreign policy concerns. These concerns were negotiated in September 2005 and presented as a declaration of the planks of a common platform (named the 'Soria Moria' declaration after the Oslo hotel where the parties had undertaken the negotiations). While Labour agreed not to seek EU membership for the duration of the coalition (satisfying SP and SV), SV agreed not to put Norway's membership in NATO into question (a point of conflict with both DNA and the Centre Party). Meanwhile, the Centre Party agreed to support the government in regard to current membership in the EEA (requiring that Norway accept all relevant new EU legislation) as a trade-off for the agreement not to seek EU membership. In addition, all three parties committed themselves to helping to reduce the debt of developing countries and working to reform international institutions and agreements such as the World Bank, IMF and the WTO. Furthermore, they supported the idea of having a clear UN mandate as a precondition for Norwegian participation in international military operations and pledged themselves to increase the level of foreign/developmental aid given by the government to poorer countries around the world (Office of the Prime Minister, 2005).

Putting the broad outlines of the coalition agreement into practice has, however, been considerably more difficult for the three coalition partners. SV in particular has been challenged to defend its policies against Labour as well as vis-à-vis SP.[6] SV has had to compromise on environmental issues with the Centre Party, as the latter represents the interests of Norway's rural districts, where development is often favoured over environmental protection. For example, SV and SP fought over particular statements by Agricultural Minister Lars Peder Brekk (SP) that ranchers should be allowed to kill wolves when they threatened livestock (Berglund, 2008a). More importantly, although SV (with the support in this case of SP) is against offshore oil exploration activities near Lofoten (in Norway's north), Stoltenberg and DNA would ideally like to go ahead with this, but in any case have sought to delay a decision until more information can be gathered about the consequences. This has clearly angered some supporters of SV (Berglund, 2008b). SV also suffered a major policy defeat when Labour refused to force the oil and gas industry to further restrict its CO_2 emissions. SV has also clashed with Labour on a proposed tightening of the law governing political asylum (a fight SV lost) and on sending additional troops to Afghanistan (another loss, with SV against and SP and Labour for). Furthermore, a threatened veto in 2008 against Labour's decision to purchase new fighter planes from the US (and used by NATO) rather than from Sweden (SV's choice) failed to materialise (Goll, 2008). SV's policy defeats have produced the expected grumbling among SV supporters (and some within the parliamentary group) that SV has been too ready to compromise on its core issues of environmental protection and a non-militaristic and independent foreign policy.

Moreover, the policy achievements of SV in government have not always been easy to identify. SV has resisted full implementation of the services directive, has pushed DNA to set tough environmental standards for Norway's state-owned energy company, *StatoilHydro*, and has induced the government to adopt certain ethical guidelines to govern investments from the Petroleum fund (Berglund, 2007a). Finally, SV was also able to push through an aggressive expansion of state Kindergartens (now at some 98 per cent of coverage for citizens seeking a spot) and put a stop to (further) privatisation of schools. Still, like other small parties in coalition government, SV has had some difficulty in being able to trumpet its policy successes, especially those achievements which can be seen as largely defensive and 'negative' (i.e. preventing 'worse' policies – from the perspective of the party – from being adopted).

Nationwide local elections in September 2007 brought home the depth of dissatisfaction with SV among some of its core voters. While nearly all the other parties (including Labour and SP) gained votes, SV lost about a quarter of its previous seats in local councils. Political observers traced the electoral loss to unease among SV's core voters about compromises the party had made, as well as to the perceived failings of SV environmental minister Helen Bjørnøy (who was seen as largely ineffective and who was replaced after the election by Erik Solheim) and SV Education Minister Øystein Djupedal, with teachers (traditionally strong supporters of SV) complaining that the new government had not substantially improved schools since coming to power (Tisdall, 2007).

Despite its organisational difficulties and problems in being able to point to significant policy achievements, however, SV appeared to rebound in the polls in the two months preceding the election. This bounce in the polls was ultimately misleading, however. As this book was going to press national elections (see Table 2.1) returned the three-party coalition to power by a whisker. The continuance of this centre-left coalition occurred despite SV's loss of nearly a quarter of its 2005 support, as it sank to 6.2 per cent of the vote. The glass can certainly be seen as half-empty for SV, for its vote losses undoubtedly reflect the disappointment some of its supporters felt about SV's compromises over environmental and foreign policy issues during the party's first term in office. However, vote losses also probably reflect the fact that some SV voters from 2001 and 2005 were only 'on loan', so to speak, from DNA; these centre-left voters returned to the DNA in this election, with Labour increasing its share of the vote some 2.7 per cent over its 2005 figure. The glass can be seen as half-full: SV preserved most of its 'core' vote despite the expected incumbency losses, and there was never any doubt that, despite some grumblings, the base of the party was behind continuing the coalition government with DNA and SP. Indeed, the party tried to make a convincing case that, in combination with its coalition partners, it was able to reverse the 'neoliberal' course of Norwegian politics over the last half-decade, has moved forward significantly on several environmental areas, and has managed to keep the economy on track and maintain the welfare state during an extremely challenging global economic downturn.

That SV was able to contain its vote losses – as well as preventing a significant opposition within the party to continued government participation from materialising (with a party congress in the Spring of 2009 voting unanimously to continue the three-party coalition) – owes something to its principled opposition to oil exploration in Lofoten as well as to skilful party management on the part of Halvorsen. It also owes something to deputy party leader Audun Lysbakken, a rising star in SV. Though only 30 years old, he headed the party organisation from 2006 to 2008, became an MP later that year, and now heads the party electoral list going into upcoming elections. He has extensive experience at the local level, is extremely sensitive to the party base, and is quite popular within the party – very possibly because of his connection to the rank and file. He is also considered to be farther to the left than Halvorsen. Nevertheless, he is entirely loyal. Thus Lysbakken brings a significantly amount of ('street' or 'party base') credibility to the party in office, even while it has had difficulty in claiming policy successes.

Conclusion

In explaining how SV came into government for the first time in its history, this chapter identified several important factors. The most important factors here lie in the party system and the changing nature of party competition in Norway over the last decade. This has created different opportunity structures for SV and its coalition partners. Institutional factors have also played a role, as Norway has witnessed changing dynamics in the nature of its parliamentary government, which have provided more incentives to DNA and SV to enter into coalition government. There have also been 'electoral shocks' to both the DNA and SV that have affected the strategic choices of each party. Finally, the new leadership of SV guided an often fractious party towards more accommodation with Labour, one that guided the party towards a historic accommodation with its larger cousin on the left.

This chapter also illustrated how SV's opportunity structures have been conditioned by the two issue areas that have dominated Norwegian politics over the last decade – Norway's oil wealth and the issue of European Union membership. SV's trajectory for the last 15 years or so could be characterised as a kind of 'two-steps forward, one-step back' movement towards coalitionability. The consensus that gradually emerged in SV throughout the 1990s – aided by the aftermath of the 2001 election – was that the traditional weight given to vote-seeking in the party's strategic calculations and SV's self-positioning in a purely opposition role were leading the party to something of a dead end. Policy goals, in other words, could no longer be best achieved by remaining in opposition. When the SV was asked to join government, therefore, it readily accepted. Yet SV's experience in government has been somewhat rocky. In particular, the SP has suffered some environmental and foreign policy losses in debates with its coalition partners. Moreover, participation in coalition government resulted in electoral losses for SV in 2007 and more recently in the 2009 national election. Despite this fact, it would be hard to imagine that SV will ever be content to be merely a party of principled opposition, sitting on the sidelines of power, rather than a possible coalition partner.

Notes

In writing this chapter I was able to draw on discussions with many Norwegian political experts and key political players. My thanks especially to all those members of SV's parliamentary delegation and Central Party office who agreed to sit down for interviews with me. Thanks also to several anonymous reviewers for *Scandinavian Political Studies* and to Dag Arne Christensen for their critical comments that helped to make this chapter much better. Finally, my deepest thanks to Thomas Spence, formerly of the *Aftenposten* and now Vice-President of the Norwegian Journalist Union, for speaking to me on several occasions, sharing his deep knowledge of the Norwegian political scene. These conversations were of incalculable value in the researching of this chapter.

1. The rejection of EU membership is, of course, given rational arguments. In SV's 2005 election manifesto, the party lists five reasons it rejects EU membership, among them the purported lack of democracy and transparency in the EU, a rejection of the EU's economic policies that 'complicates the struggle against unemployment and for leveling out social conditions', and the claim that membership would deprive Norway of control over its natural resources. *Different people. Equal opportunities. Election Manifesto of the Socialist Left Party of Norway (SV), 2005–2009*, at www.sv.no (accessed 5 June 2009).
2. As Narud (1995) has argued, certain issues are fundamentally intertwined with a party's identity; they constitute a 'heartland' upon which parties seek to build public support. A party will change from a co-operative to a competitive strategy if 'heartland' issues become salient. Conversely, a party can change its strategy from competitive to co-operative if such issues do not become salient or are otherwise taken off the table.
3. SV's identity as an anti-EU party is not just historical legacy: in a 2007 poll for Norway's leading daily, *Aftenposten,* 73 per cent of SV voters were against EU membership. 'Labour voters Say No', *Aftenposten* 5 November 2007, at www.aftenposten.no/english (accessed 5 June 2009).
4. 'The emerging picture of the Storting is that of a pragmatic, decentralized, consensus-building institution, where the opposition has ample opportunity to influence policies' (Strøm, 1990b: p. 210). Strøm suggests Norway has a strong parliament owing to several factors: a parliamentary Board of Presidents with significant opposition representation; conferences between parliamentary leaders of various parties; and permanent legislative committees with fixed areas of specialisation where real legislative work is done, proportionately distributed among all the parties.

5. 'In the 2005 Parliamentary elections we find ourselves at a crossroads, facing a choice between values. The right wing is dismantling the welfare state, it is awarding tax breaks to the richest, and it is tying Norway even closer to the US foreign policy. We want to go in another direction' (*Socialist Left Party* 2005: p. 3).
6. Much of this section draws on conversations with Thomas Spence of the *Aftenposten* (see the unnumbered note above).

3
The French Extreme Left and Its Suspicion of Power
David Bell

Introduction

One of the curiosities of the last 20 years has been the disappearance of the revolutionary left from Europe, but its persistence in France. This Marxist left has been a feature of French politics since the Third Republic and is therefore not novel. Current movements on the left are not, in this context, a surprise, nor are they attributable to particular contemporary factors. They are not, in other words, a mere reaction to the more recent crisis in politics, although the parties have nonetheless tried to adapt their appeal to the challenges of the contemporary world (Perrineau, 2003; Perrineau and Ysmal, 2003). This left remains, as has always been the case, uncomfortable with exercising power, and has laboured in what Bergounioux and Manin have termed self-reproach (*'remords du pouvoir'*) (Bergounioux and Manin, 2005). In part the French left's difficulty with issues of government participation has its roots in the founding of the socialist movement in the Republic. The assumption has been that unless everything changes then nothing changes: the revolutionary position is consequently that a new form of non-capitalist socialist society is necessary for real change to occur. Any ameliorations are a diversion from the revolutionary task that falls to the workers' movement. A diversion from this revolutionary vocation is therefore nothing short of betrayal.

On the left, and in the twenty-first century, left-radical movements everywhere consequently face a 'social democratic dilemma': what is the route to power in a western society? This is expressed in the tension between revolution and parliamentary reform. Socialists took, after some hesitation, Bernstein's view that democracy is both the means and the end, both the means of the struggle and a constituent part of socialism (Gay, 1962). This view never took root on the extreme left in France, and the Communist and Trotskyite ideologies paid little attention to social organisation. Hence a divide that has run through left-wing politics in France almost more than anywhere else in the western world was born.

A distinction, widely used on the left, also has to be made between the use of 'bourgeois' institutions and the participation in government. For the early Marxists, the National Assembly, and elections at all levels, were a means of advancing their cause and of promoting the socialist message. Trotskyites and Communists, taking their cue from Lenin's (1997) condemnations in *Left-wing Communism*, ran candidates in elections and used the platforms available to them (not for them the anarchists' dismissive claim that elections are a trap for the stupid). However, governing was another matter, as this was at odds with the strategy of consciousness-raising and of showing how the capitalist system could not deliver on workers' demands. To fall into the embrace of Assembly or Senate politics was, to use Marx's term, 'parliamentary cretinism' and thus, for the extreme left, to be avoided (Marx, 1852: chapter 5). Despite this affected disdain for the electoral arena, Communists were clearly proud of their electoral performance both pre- and post-World War II, and it validated their position as an anti-system party both in France and in the broader global movement. Trotskyites have also found that the chase for votes has the same allure, giving them greater legitimacy and a pre-eminence (in their own eyes) on the far left. However, for the Marxist left, the main theatre must remain the class struggle in all its aspects but particularly in industry, services and the trade unions. Contemporary Trotskyism has kept this precept, although the division runs through the Communist Party, dividing the 'revolutionary' from the parliamentary left.

Origins of the non-socialist left in France

In the late nineteenth century the Republicans, and later the loosely grouped 'Radicals', promoted the parliamentary Great Revolution as their own. At that time two forces were set in opposition: a monarchist opposition and a Republican movement. The Republicans claimed the inheritance of the Great Revolution, the Monarchists the authority of the Monarchy whilst condemning the 'decadence' of parliamentary government (Gildea, 1992). When the socialist movement began to emerge in the last years of the nineteenth century, it found it difficult to carve out a space in the party system. Much of the nascent French

Socialist movement disseminated the Marxist message that the next 'revolution' would be the proletarian revolution, and that therefore the institutions of the Republic were not 'theirs', not legitimate, and that the management of 'bourgeois affairs' was not their vocation (Bergounioux and Manin, 2005). Like many socialists, they expected the revolution immanently and thought that this would resolve the problems of participation in government and of parliamentary reform. Socialist revolution would install the regime of the proletariat, thus dissolving the dilemma of participation that confronted the parliamentary left.

Socialist Party (Section française de l'international ouvrière – SFIO) suspicion of participation in government continued despite an effective contribution to fighting in World War I. In response to the rise of the Communist Party (Parti Communiste Français), leaders argued that their party was really 'revolutionary' and that this vocation was not negated by the PCF's rise. Leaders such as Léon Blum contested methods adopted by the Communists, but not the aim of the 'revolutionary' transformation of society: the elements of the strategic impasse for French socialists were in place. On the one hand the party needed centrist support to make up a majority in the Assembly, but on the other it was undermined from the left by a powerful party that accused it of 'sell-out' when it 'collaborated' with 'class enemies' (Robrieux, 1980). This was a persistent problem through the 1920s and was exemplified by the left-wing coalition of the 'Cartel des gauches' attacking the SFIO from the left for class collaboration. Thus French social democracy remained weak, while the Communist political machine propagated the ideology of the Communist movement in impressive unity of purpose (Lazar, 1997). French Communism ran newspapers, publishers, study circles, film clubs and popular events such as fêtes and socials that were well organised, elaborate and highly efficient at propagating the Marxist message. It is not surprising, in view of the subsequent generations who were socialised into politics through the PCF (either as activists or as objects of propaganda), that the ideas of revolutionary socialism have had a long shelf life. SFIO leader Blum asserted that the revolutionary transformation of society was for the long haul (not the overnight coup) and made the distinction between the 'conquest of power' at some distant point in time (and that would therefore be 'revolutionary') and the exercise of power as a majority coalition in parliament (Moreau, 1998; Berstein, 2006: chapter 7). It was possible to see, Blum said, French society being won over by the exercise of power. That would lead to the eventual conquest in unproblematic circumstances (Lacouture, 1974).

French Communism pursued a different path. Government participation was not a major issue for the PCF during its years of subordination to Moscow. French communism's policies on elections and on government participation were decided in the CPSU for Soviet foreign policy reasons, and hence there followed a series of abrupt changes of position and reversals in policy. In 1934 Stalin decided that Hitler's seizure of power was a greater threat than that posed by the 'bourgeois' capitalists. Thus the PCF leadership, with exemplary discipline, repudiated its past actions and allied with Socialist and 'bourgeois' parties in what became the Popular Front. After the Popular Front victory in the election of 1936, the question of participation was secondary for the PCF and it could have taken portfolios in the government. The alliance of the SFIO, Radicals and Communists that won the election had left open the question of the participation of the PCF in government – and the distribution of Cabinet posts – and the Communists chose not to take up portfolios. Furthermore, at liberation the PCF entered government and held several ministries but the Communist line – consistent in its inconsistency – changed to non-co-operation with the onset of the Cold War, and then to co-operation again in 1956 after Khrushchev's secret speech. This phase was abruptly terminated at the end of the 1970s when the Communist Party's policy swung once more in a decidedly pro-Soviet direction, supporting the Soviet invasion of Afghanistan.

A policy-seeker without policy preferences?

The final PCF participation in government while the world Communist movement still existed took place in particularly unpropitious circumstances. In 1981 the presidential elections proved to be the next test. Communist leaders ran an election campaign that was almost as much anti-Socialist as against the outgoing centrist President Giscard. Despite this hostility, François Mitterrand became French President and the Socialists swept to an absolute majority at the ensuing general election. The Communists had dropped their outright hostility to the Socialists and sought to save their Assembly seats with the prospect of government posts not an issue. Communist support was not at that point necessary, but the PCF nevertheless decided that it wanted to be a part of the 'historic' victory of the left and bargained for four ministerial posts. These four posts were minor, but the PCF's broader supporter base – in such places as the CGT trade union – made their disagreements with the president increasingly clear from the beginning. In 1984 the PCF quit the government, declaring that the experiment had been a failure (although Communist activists and voters seem to have regarded it as positive) and the bad experience – as the leadership saw it – became part of the party's folklore (Courtois and Lazar, 1995).

There followed, after 1984, an unremitting slide in Communist electoral fortunes. Communists tried to make the best of their increasingly marginal status, exploiting the government's difficulties but – when pushed – supporting the left. With the collapse of the world Communist movement in 1989–91, the raison d'être for the party also disappeared. Hence in 1994, under the new leadership of Robert Hue, the CPF embarked on a series of changes. However, in this the PCF was a victim of the 'de Tocqueville syndrome' in which the institution loses its grip at the moment it liberalises: party discipline, once a feature of Communism, diminished, the party sundered into an archipelago of baronies and the cell system was abandoned. In this context of the ideological turmoil of the 1990s and Communist Party weakness, participation in a socialist government became again a possibility, one which (perhaps) might give the party a new purpose.

This was the position when the 'plural left' of Communists, Socialists, Radicals, Greens and independents unexpectedly won the snap general election in 1997. For the first time since 1978 the PCF increased its representation in the Assembly (to 34 deputies) although it was at the same time that the Italian Communist Refoundation leader (Bertinotti) rejected the idea of joining a Socialist-led government there. A referendum of party members approved participation by 80 per cent and the move seems to have been strongly supported by Communist sympathisers (90 per cent approved). Maxime Gremetz, the orthodox hardliner, was the only Communist deputy not to support Premier Jospin's investiture (*Nouvel observateur*, 20 November 1997).

Party leader Robert Hue, under investigation for illicit party funding, did not join the government, but other leading figures, Jean-Claude Gayssot and Marie-George Buffet (who later became party leader), did indeed take portfolios. Once again the Communist ministers behaved with 'bourgeois' propriety and gained a reputation as solid administrators. One of the first actions of Gayssot was to privatise Air France, and the Communists remained in a government that went on to engage in more privatisation than any of its predecessors. There was no evidence of Communist objections to this, and no original contributions to budget issues or tax policies. In 1998, the 150th anniversary of Marx's Communist Manifesto, only one PCF budget amendment was proposed – lowering VAT on chocolate – and that was dismissed. Governmental tenure proved to be a strategic impasse as it was hard to discern any PCF influence on government. Its leadership played the role of loyal collaborator in the left's administration but it was not able to show what it had gained as a result. If participation meant simply endorsing the Socialist agenda then what use was it? If the PCF had an alternative then what was that? Neither question was, or has yet been, satisfactorily answered by the party leadership.

A new(ly buttressed) contender: The PCF under siege from the left

'Comrade 4 per cent' Robert Hue could have made the PCF a force on the left (in the way that the Left Party is in Sweden), but the party also had to bury many of the Communists' old ideas and in particular turn towards the problems of internal reform (when, where and what for?), something that the 'revolutionary perspective' had enabled them largely to avoid until then. Hue faced the difficulty of demarking the PCF from the Socialists, against aggressive minor parties and also unrestrained Trotskyites, all of whom were using imaginative tactics in exploiting the problems of the marginalised ('sans') and the popular distrust of European integration. In 2002 the election result was a further humiliation for the PCF, although it was not brought low enough to accept the invitation to merge into a unified party of the left that would replace the Socialists and the Communists. Again this result was attributed to the party's participation in government and its solid support for the Socialist Party. Following its poor election result in 2002, the PCF convened a national conference that ended up being nothing short of a shambles, with Hue being 'promoted' to party President (an honorific position) in a clumsy attempt to disguise his defenestration and apparatchik Marie-George Buffet replacing him. Despite a new National Secretary, the Party still struggled to find a role. It was able to exploit anti-system movements and in particular opposition to the Lisbon Treaty, yet it was still neither capable of uniting the far left nor able to be the leader of the left of the left. Germany's *Die Linke* has been admired as an example of the sort of formation – somewhere in between the Socialists and the Trotskyite left – that the PCF should be trying to promote, although at other times the ambition of the leadership has been to create a cartel of non-capitalist parties. Trotskyite ambitions, now appearing ever more realistic, have been to replace the PCF as the party of the working class and the dominant formation on the left of the left. Communism's strategic position, and its stance on government participation, therefore remain studiously ambiguous. It is half on the anti-socialist left and half a part of the extreme 'alternative left' that sees itself as distinct from other left-wing groupings.

In 2007 the party's presidential candidate, Marie-George Buffet, was able to garner only 707,327 votes (1.93 per cent), a result that was a further humiliation even though the PCF did manage to win 1,115,790 votes (4.29 per cent) at the subsequent general election. This share of the vote was only slightly below the PCF's 2002 total, and it managed to get 18 deputies elected – enough to form a group in the Assembly. It was once again buoyed by its local activism and at the 2008 local elections suffered only a relatively slight decline. The Socialist Party competed fiercely against it in some cities, but the PCF lost a number of important bastions (including Calais), although it remained in a rough equilibrium with its previous position. Its local strength is impressive and it boasts 10,000 local councillors in 500 towns, much more than its nearest rivals on the left. Thus French Communism, diminished as it is, is still the third party in local government. It remains the biggest formation on the far left, with 78,779 paid-up members (although, in the tradition of the reporting of membership figures, it claimed an exaggerated 134,000 members).

Of PCF members, 15 per cent are workers and 18 are white collar, although this is a decline from the 46.5 per cent workers it claimed to have in its ranks in 1997 (Platone and Ranger, 2000). This waning of political force and the diminution of its presence in the working class is of significance because the party's remaining tenuous foothold on political relevance is maintained only through alliances with the Socialist Party. It talks of a 'break' with capitalism even while it is trying to safeguard its position in the system and use its resources. It is therefore caught between an effective submission to the Socialists and a Marxist radicalism. Its principal gain from the alliance strategy of the 1960s and 1970s was local (and regional) government, but this ties it into the mainstream left and makes it impossible to fully break with the Socialists. Inside the party the factions opposed to the links with the Socialists (mainly older hard-liners but also some seeking an 'alternative left') are a manageable minority. However, the feeling persists in the Party leadership that the 1981–4 and the 1997–2002 participations in government were a prelude to disaster for the party. This situation of 'co-dependence' between the Socialists and Communists is often disguised by talk of the 'unity of the left' that is assumed to lie near to the surface. In fact, however, the differences between the two parties of the left, PS and PCF, have been historically persistent and very deep.

Socialists, on the other hand, have possible alternatives to a Communist alliance and these factors limit the PCF's autonomy vis-à-vis a future government of the left. Since 2002 the Communists have avoided the central question of government participation, largely as it has not been a pressing one in recent years. Instead the PCF has sought to rebuild a position on the left through the mobilisation of anti-European sentiment. This has not been successful; although able to structure the balance of power – through its superior resources and organisation – on the left, it has been repudiated as the leader of that movement. French Communism, having lost its role in the Communist world system, has yet to find a new vocation. Unlike the post-Communist parties elsewhere in Europe, the niche issues of ecology, human rights, anti-war and anti-European integration have been taken by more nimble minor parties. Communists have tried to associate themselves with these issues but have not been able to make them their own. Overall a sense of purpose is therefore lacking in a once confident party. Communist candidates appeal to an older electorate – one that remembers the struggles of the once mass party – and has failed to make headway with younger voters. Moreover, amongst the young there is vigorous competition from the far left – and amongst these the various Trotskyite formations.

A growing political force: The non-socialist, non-communist left in France

French Communism's search for a new position on the left was complemented by an alliance of anti-European factions that split from the Parti Socialiste. Thus a new group (moving to party status) was located on the left and sought a more 'socialist' platform possibly in association or alliance with the Communist Party. These new left-wing groups inside and outside the Socialist Party have all sought to extend bridges to the extreme left Trotskyite, anti-globalisation, and anti-free market movements. At the PS's Reims Congress in November 2008 the left faction in the Socialist Party polled a meagre 18.52 per cent and drew the conclusion that there was no place for their members in a party where they felt that they had been marginalised. This minority withdrew to form the 'Parti de Gauche' (Party of the Left) in February 2009, just before Besancenot's proposed new party could get under way, and its leader or 'president' was the former PS senator Jean-Luc Mélenchon, assisted in the Party's National Bureau by the PS Federation of the North's Marc Dolez. This Parti de Gauche, conscious of its nascent weakness, sought alliances in a Front de Gauche – left–wing alliance. One of the points of reference for the quickly assembled Front de Gauche with the PCF was the German Left – *Die Linke* – which brought together the left of the Social Democrats under its former leader Oskar Lafontaine, and the ex-Communist PDS (based mainly in the East). Unlike *Die Linke* in Germany, the Front de Gauche lacks the leadership as well as the opening on the left that enabled the *Linke* to poll 11.9 per cent in the federal election of 2009, and, of course, it has rivals on the extreme Trotskyite left that the German party has not. The Front de Gauche is a formation that defines itself as 'marxist' but, as is the general rule, claims that the 'revolution' will come through the ballot box. In the election to the EP in 2009 it allied with the PCF to form the joint 'Front de Gauche list' and managed to get five MEPs elected: two communists, two Parti de Gauche (including Mélenchon in the south-west) and one Communist from the overseas department of Réunion.

Activity by the Trotskyite left is not a marginal phenomenon in France. As a force on the left of the Socialists, the extreme movements pull the party away from the centre and from the route familiar to other western social democratic parties – the strategy once dismissed by the left as *'Blairisme à la française'*. In policy terms the Trotskyite platforms that compete with the Front de Gauche and with the PCF are not particularly strong or persuasive, but Trotskyite parties excel at presenting the case for the prosecution (of capitalism) rather than at finding remedies. Trotskyite parties have maintained their revolutionary purity by standing clear of government commitments in institutions that they believe can only promote 'bourgeois' interests in a capitalist society. In fact the electoral process serves a different purpose – although it is useful for other functions, such as 'consciousness raising' and for recruitment, and in showing how the 'bourgeois' state is incapable of delivering on workers' interests. Hence the Trotskyite platforms have been deliberately unrealistic, demanding impossible concessions from 'capital' that will be rejected but will 'raise the awareness' of the working class. The extreme left perceives elections as a part of the revolutionary process. However, energies and hopes should not be placed on elections, since these are not the site of political transformation. The 'revolution' is the only means of working-class emancipation. Any detraction from that is a sell-out to the bourgeoisie. All the Trotskyite parties claim to be internationalist and they all have links with small parties in other countries both in Europe and beyond, but these 'internationals' have no real presence on the international stage.

Arlette Laguiller, who stood for the fourth time as the Lutte Ouvrière candidate (LO) for the presidency, polled 5.3 per cent (1.6 million votes) in 1995, and this was the electoral breakthrough for Trotskyites. It came, ironically, from an organisation that set no store by elections and electoral success. In the 2002 presidential election four candidates claimed the Communist heritage of anti-imperialism, anti-globalisation, anti-neoliberalism (or capitalism), anti-fascism and anti-racism (a 'product of capitalism'). None of them saw their vocation as being to support the parliamentary left. At these elections one shock was that the Trotskyite extreme left polled over 10 per cent of the votes and the Communist Party was displaced as the main Marxist party, with the Ligue communiste révolutionnaire's (LCR) candidate Olivier Besancenot emerging for the first time into public notice and consolidating a position as the most attractive figure in the new constellation. Besancenot gave the LCR, a more libertarian and adventurous formation prominent in campaigns and in student life, a prominence that had hitherto eluded it. For many years the Communist Party vote had been sliding, and the Trotskyite left had been rising, but the PCF's decision to support its ministers undoubtedly left a space on the left open to the more opportunist elements of the extreme left.

It is possible that the PCF's loss of monopoly on the 'Marxist trademark' has allowed these Trotskyites to claim a legitimacy that was previously denied to them, but the discrediting of the Soviet experiment has not embarrassed the Trotskyites, who, in one way or another, were always critical of the USSR. Extreme left parties evoke issues that were once Communist – a distrust of the market economy, hostility to the USA and the EU, anti-Israel, scepticism concerning political reform, and an emphasis on equality, as well as simple solutions, permanent protest and the centrality of conflict and radicalism in politics. Laguiller's language even recalled the cliché-laden discourse of previous Communist leaders, with talk of the 'proletariat against bourgeoisie' and the poor against the rich, although Besancenot was more nuanced. The LCR, for example, has always called on its supporters to 'defeat the right' by voting for the left in elections, although the LO has been more circumspect, even calling on Laguiller's supporters to spoil their votes rather than to vote for Chirac in 2002 to keep Le Pen out. The LO was widely criticised for this and, although hardly a resounding endorsement, its view changed in 2007 when Laguiller called for LO supporters to vote for the Socialist on the second ballot. Many of these themes have very old origins and recall the nationalism, anti-capitalism, anti-liberal and anti-parliamentary Jacobin and Catholic movements of the Great Revolution.

There are three main Trotskyite forces on the extreme left (the PCF apart) and they each have their position in the unions – a point that should not be overlooked. By consolidating their extra-system strengths they have exercised an influence on the party system itself and pulled the system leftwards. These parties are involved in a competition for the dominant position on the extreme left, a competition that is at the expense of the parliamentary left in what is an attempt to outbid their rivals in repudiation of 'reformist' politics. Before the rise of the Trotskyite challenge in the 1990s, the PCF was by far the dominant force on the left of the Socialists and treated the Trotskyites, when it condescended to notice them, with disdain. But the situation has changed and the PCF, once sovereign, now has to face challenges in its strongholds and in its fiefdoms (such as the unions) and even has to negotiate with the Trotskyites, taking, sometimes, a secondary position in campaigns.

Trotskyites exert their pull on the PCF, and that also influences the Socialists through the need to retain the left of the left's support. This Trotskyite triptych is composed of the Lutte Ouvrière, the Ligue Communist Révolutionnaire (which in late 2008 became the Nouveau parti anti-capitaliste – NPA) and the PdT (Parti des travailleurs). Lazar remarks that in all probability they recruit from the unions, the young and intellectuals (Lazar, 2003). These parties all put up candidates at presidential elections (the first Trotskyite candidate was Alain Krivine in 1969) but more in the expectation of attracting recruits and funds than of influencing policy or making bargains. At local, regional and European levels the LCR and the LO have sometimes formed alliances and have won seats (as they did in 1977, 1979, 1983, 1999 and 2004), but the collaboration has been very difficult, and has usually broken up in acrimony. Each of the parties believes that it alone has a route map to the revolution, each has a sense of identity and hegemonic ambition that surfaces when alliances are proposed, and they have all lost support as a result of sectarian squabbles.

Of these Trotskyite groups, Lutte Ouvrière is the most traditional, believing other parties to be lackeys of the bourgeoisie, and thus hostile to mainstream politics and (usually) to alliances. It refuses to reform and compromise, and maintains a programme of world revolution. It is 'workerist' to a self-destructive degree, rarely looking beyond the bounds of the old working class. In keeping with this outlook it places heavy, almost exclusive, emphasis on the workplace and union struggle and the need to preserve or protect jobs from outside 'capitalist' threats (in their various forms). It is therefore indifferent (or hostile) to parliamentary parties. Given this outlook, it has striven to outflank parliamentary parties: it has set up cells and publications in workplaces and in this has had some success; but Lutte Ouvrière concentrates on the workers' struggle and it is quite rigid to the extent that it neglects, or dismisses, other social issues. It is anti-EU, but has regarded its opposition to integration as well as other issues such as globalisation, ecology and human rights as detractions from the main revolutionary task: increasing the power of the workers (Laguiller, 2002: p. 172). In the 2008 local elections LO sought out alliances with the PCF and PS and managed to get 79 councillors elected (14 on LO lists and 69 on combined lists of the left). The LO has permitted some differences of opinion and one of LO's internal opposition factions, L'Etincelle, opposed these alliances and was accused of flirting with Besencenot's new party – a party that many of those accused later joined.

Pierre Lambert's Courant 'communiste internationaliste' is devoted to infiltrating mainstream organisations like the unions – something that makes its exact influence unfathomable. Unsurprisingly, this is the least well known of the Trotskyite parties. In 1991 Lambert formed the 'Parti des travailleurs' and the Trotskyite faction is – ostensibly – one component of the party. This party claims to be heterogeneous, and does not proclaim its Trotskyite affiliations, although the Trotskyites are dominant and provide the leadership. In June 2008 it became the Parti ouvrière indépendant (POI), led by four National Secretaries, including Daniel Gluckstein (who had been PdT's presidential candidate in 2002) and Gérard Schivardi. It was formed under the banner 'For Socialism, Republic and Democracy', although it does not proclaim to call for a revolution. It expects rather to determine policy through other organisations. It is strongly anti-European and defends local government as well as the French secular traditions, and to that extent eschews the grandiloquent ambitions of the other parties. However, its new platform includes the commitment to end exploitation and to socialise the means of production. Repeating a staple of the LO, this party also includes demands for all job losses to be subject to legal control (or administrative refusal).

Gérard Schivardi, PdT's presidential candidate of 2007, was presented as the 'candidate of mayors' and PdT has consistently presented itself as the champion of local autonomy. According to its programme, the capitalist world is in its last stage of self-destruction and imperialism (through the USA and EU, in particular) is in its most aggressive phase (Lazar, 2003). This analysis enables it to defend the social rights of the workers and lead the fight against outside 'imperialisms' on behalf of – in effect – the nation and its local communities. Local government aside, PdT's infiltration into secular associations and into the unions has given it considerable influence (Bourseiller, 1997). In José Bovè's agricultural union – *Confédération paysanne* – it is strong, and it is also very active in the non-communist Force ouvrière union confederation. In the leading instances of FO, once the principal reformist union confederation, memberships often overlap and PdT has prioritised action in the unions. However, in a curious reversal of 'revolutionary priorities', it is willing to work in local government but dismisses the national arena – and portfolios – as part of the capitalist system.

The LCR was less addicted to secrecy than the other formations and had a more open culture, in keeping with its mission to create a workers' party with a very wide supporter base (at times it even implied that the revolutionary vocation might have fallen into other hands than those of the working class). Over a long period the LCR permitted divergences in opinion and factions, and was relatively diverse, to the extent of recruiting other small minorities and Trotskyite groups. It had a membership largely consisting of public service and educational members but, possibly, a new 'workers and intellectuals party' was in the first stages of formation here. The LCR had had some substantial intellectual backing and sought to mobilise the social movements in France over the last three decades, resulting in a dispersion of its activities across a broad front of left-wing, human rights and economic (job protection, working rights etc) causes. Its activists were in numerous pressure groups on the left (such as ATTAC, SOS-Racisme, Porto Alegre and against the Iraq War) and it dispersed its energies in these causes – not always with success (for example, the attempt to promote Pierre Juquin as a new formation to the left of the PCF at the end of the 1980s). It probably gained the most from the anti-Lisbon Treaty 'no' campaign with a left-wing emphasis that swept aside the mainstream left (Communists excepted), although it was not the main force within it.

A neo-Trotskyite movement: The New Anti-Capitalist Party

In 2002 the LCR's Olivier Besancenot was a product of the party's internal organisation, but – unlike an apparatchik – he presented a youthful, humorous and fluid outlook in a mediatised political world in which he was, more than most candidates, quite at home. Besancenot represents the Trotskyite search to replace the Communist Party on the left, as well as a determination to reject reformist politics and, by that token, government participation. There was a rejuvenation of the LCR after Besancenot's presidential campaign, and this continued into 2007: a quarter of activists were under 30 and half were under 40 (quite unlike the PS, which has a conspicuously ageing profile). This support comes from a group wanting rapid change (not necessarily revolution), which rejects the mainstream Socialists. This ascension took place in three stages after the first breakthrough in 2002: in the opposition to the Lisbon Treaty in the referendum of 2005, in the anti-CPE demonstrations of spring 2006 and then in the 2007 presidential election. These stages were a rejection of 'reformist' politics and were outside the mainstream political left; they were to a large extent based on the rejection of the established parties of the left.

Besancenot, and the new party created as his vehicle, will, if they achieve their objective, unite the left and create a dynamic force contesting the PCF's position in the party system. This will present major difficulties in the creation of a governing coalition of the left and will, at least initially, be an obstacle to participation in government or to the support of the parties on the left with a governmental vocation. Besancenot presents a non-sectarian face to the voters, but the 'Révolution' faction from which he emerged was a hard-line group demanding a break with the orthodox left by supporting spoiling tactics at general and local elections (not standing down for others on the left). Besancenot's book (*Révolution*) deals less with Trotsky than with the 'crimes' of capitalism, France and 'state terrorism', but it is not clear that it renounces violence even while it places great hopes in the 'soviet' model – in this book renamed 'councils' or collectives'. In its last major campaign, the local elections of 2006, the LCR performed well. It polled 5 per cent where it stood and half its lists were alliances with others on the radical left.

Besancenot's presidential campaign of 2007 was not a triumph, but the other Trotskyite candidates performed worse and – with 4.08 per cent and 287,019 more votes than in 2002 – the LCR emerged as the major far left force pushing aside Laguiller's LO, the Greens ('Verts') and the Communist Party. LCR's platform at this election was similar to Laguiller's in its representation of the communist prescriptions of nationalisation of the means of production, planning 'autogestion' as well as the recycled demands for a shorter working week and the abolition of world economic organisations, but also with a denunciation of globalisation and human rights restrictions. But Besancenot, unlike Laguiller, had managed to combine the opposition to free market liberalisation with postmodern, ecological and 'multicultural' values emphasising personal liberty and rights. Unsurprisingly, Besancenot began to be described as 'ministerial material'; moreover, Besancenot was more popular than the LCR, and in polls is regularly approved of by the public. Much rides on Besancenot's future ambitions and on whether he is content to stay as a tribune calling down anathema on the system on the margins of mainstream politics (as Le Pen appears to have been from the right).

Besancenot's most adventurous move was the dissolution of the LCR and the creation of the Nouveau Parti Anticapitaliste (NPA) with a peculiar megaphone logo. This makeover had been planned in advance, but Besancenot was able to use his momentum after the presidential election of 2007 and the internal quarrels of the mainstream left, as well as his own media presence as 'the best opponent of the President'. This party is based on the old LCR but reaches out beyond that Trotskyite formation in the hope of federating the 'anti-capitalist left'. Some of the new members wanted to drop the 'revolutionary' aspect of the programme, but Besancenot's preference for the term prevailed even though it defined itself as against the free-market neoliberalism they regarded as prevalent. Besancenot's party promoted an inclusive amalgam of LCR and other leftists but emphasised their independence of the Socialists as well as repudiating alliances with other groups for the European elections (some internal groups were more inclined to alliances than others, but they were minorities). One of its founding principles was on the one hand to repudiate all governing posts with the PS, at national and local level, but to maintain 'social action' in the movements of 'sans' in French society. NPA's new organisation was partly electoral and partly workplace, reflecting this ambiguity, and the NPA would continue to ride the two horses that the LCR had ridden: of electoral participation and activity in, or leadership of, the social movements.

It was hoped to develop the NPA as a party of about 10,000 members (probably three times those of the LCR it replaced, although it claimed 9,123 members when it was founded). This creation of the new party was not without collateral damage: a minority in the LCR, led by Christian Picquet, was evicted in a Leninist 'purge' and internal opposition reduced. However, the new party permitted internal factions to organise and express points of view, and there were three motions before the founding Congress. Besancenot's supporters were in a huge 83 per cent majority and the principal figures were former LCR (including all the leaders of lists for the European elections) members.

Despite the setback of the 2009 European election, at which the new party (with 4.88 per cent of the vote) failed to win a seat, it still made political headlines. This was in large part a result of Besancenot's ability to promote himself and the inability of the other parties to find a riposte to the new President Sarkozy. Polls testify to the public's appreciation of the frank and outspoken newcomer and of his fight with the conservative right. Besancenot thus emerged as one of the principal personalities of the left and a political figure of growing stature. Contrary to the line of the new NPA, the majority of Besancenot's voters wanted to see Besancenot in government. What the NPA lacks – and this has bedevilled other groups on the extremes of French politics – is the network of local supporters (mainly in local government) that would enable it to build up effective support ready for a parliamentary or regional breakthrough. It could, like the Front National, continue to make a political splash at presidential elections (where no power is distributed) and impede the progress of the mainstream left, but its refusal of alliances and rejection of deal-making makes it an unforeseeable partner. The NPA's commitment to opposition reinforces the difficulty of the mainstream left in forming governing coalitions. In the past the Socialists (and Communists) have been quick to adopt new movements, giving (for example) the greens' portfolios more attention, but the NPA is not amenable to such blandishments. Thus the pluralism on the left includes an anti-system party that will not co-operate, and that in itself marks it out as exceptional.

The institutional opportunity structure of the extreme left in France: The unions as a breeding ground of non-socialist movements on the left

One distinctive aspect of the French system is the status of the trade unions. They, although with only 9 per cent of the workforce in them (5 per cent of the private sector), are weak in comparative terms, but are well represented in the public sector and capable of bringing the country to a standstill. Unions are important on the left as sources of support, of funds and of activists. They rarely feature in party system theory, but in France they are the dark matter that affects the rest of the party system, pulling it leftward and creating obstacles as well as possibilities. Unions are politically marked, and political union confederations have long been in place; each confederation having a different political outlook (Communist, Socialist, Christian Democrat, leftist etc).

Marxist parties have been adept at infiltrating organisations and the unions all have their Marxist currents even when not controlled by the Marxist parties. Furthermore, the revolutionary aspect is strongly present. Communists have long controlled the CGT but the current state of the Communist Party, wrought by internal squabbles, means that the CGT has acquired the autonomy from the Party's directives that they once claimed, but did not in fact have. In the last few years the CGT leadership has used its autonomy to move in a reformist direction and to develop its own position independent of the Communist Party. It is, by many measures, the biggest of the union federations, and it has been an object of infiltration, particularly by the LO – though for the CGT the extreme left has been an irritant rather than a threat.

Unlike the PdT (which objects to the religious aspect of the unions), the LCR has been active in the reformist CFDT (The union confederation the Confédération française démocratique du travail) where its 'revolutionary' message has had some uptake; this was at the origin of the split that led to the formation of Solidaire, Unitaire Démocratique in 1981 (SUD – officially Union syndicale Groupe des Dix-Solidaires). SUD was based at that time on the postal unions but subsequently became an important new force. Serious upheavals in the public sector, in opposition to government measures, gave the far left impetus through the 1990s. These unions have not restricted themselves to workers' rights issues but have been involved in political anti-globalisation, unemployment and other movements and are supporters of the left of the left's Fondation Copernic (its principal think tank).

There is a continuing lip service to the autonomy of the unions from politics, but the practice of political and union activists on the far left being interchangeable has continued. By 2008 several unions had joined the confederation and claimed 80,000 members in 36 branches. After a split from the teachers' union, the FSU (Fédération syndicale unitaire) was formed in 1993 from the amalgamation of Trotskyite and pro-Communist factions, and it became the principal education union. Activists of the former teachers' union are the main force in a small confederation of extreme left unions – the Union National des Syndicats Autonomes. Both UNSA and USS are small in absolute terms, but are bigger in the public services, where they are active forces and contribute to the leftward pressure on the left's parties. In 2008 the USS took 3.8 per cent of the vote for the personnel of the labour tribunals ('Prud'homals), an increase of 2.31 per cent, but still remained the junior partner. For the extreme Trotskyite left (and to a lesser extent the Communists), the strike movements and the workplace activism are their recruiting ground, and their energy is devoted to that rather than to electoral politics. From the Trotskyite point of view the reform activities of the mainstream parties are peripheral and their calculation is not electoral.

Policy-seeking without policies and policy-seeking against office-holders: The strategic peculiarities of the non-socialist left in France

It is tempting to fall back on the notion of French political culture to explain the persistence of the extreme left in its Communist and Trotskyite forms into the twenty-first century. This could be another facet of the weakness of French social democracy as compared with other European countries. There is an organised extreme left and it can draw on the resources of a long and deeply held political culture of radicalism, but it is prepared to make use of opportunities on the left as they arise. As a result, the Parti Socialiste is torn by sectarian disputes and is deprived of its 'natural' audience on the left and in the popular classes but still dependent on a centre (Christian democrat and neo-Gaullist) vote to bring it a winning margin. Pressures from the extreme left widen the divisions over policy issues (such as Europe) and mobilise activists in ways very difficult for the mainstream left to manage. Unlike the Communist Party, a party that is still amenable to coalition with the mainstream left, the Trotskyite left is free from the taint of the totalitarian regimes of the Communist bloc and able to distance itself from them while re-emphasising the utopian themes and humanitarian issues of the Marxist left.

President Sarkozy reputedly said to the Socialist leader, François Hollande, that 'the right has taken twenty years to deal with the extreme right, today it's your turn.' However, the extreme right appealed to an audience that went beyond the traditional confines of the right, whereas the audience for the extreme left is restricted in the main (though not completely) to the groups that think of themselves as being on the left. For the analogy to be complete the evidence of an ability by the Trotskyite parties to expand the audience of the left would have to be stronger (Pingaud, 2000). In addition, there is no evidence that a loyal core vote has developed. Thus Trotskyite parties may prove not to be permanent fixtures of the party system (union and movement activity is another matter). On the extreme left the general outlook of the parties is negative – anti-capitalist – and their positive proposals are flimsy or non-existent. This extreme left, for governmental purposes, plays a destructive role: it prevents the left from making appeals to the centre and floating voter. Strategies that are common to other socialist parties are thus not possible or are inhibited by the vigour of the extreme Trotskyite left. Yet, given the location of its voters on the left, there is a gap between the leadership (hostile to participation) and the supporters, who are willing to see it as a support force of the mainstream left and welcome its main personalities in government posts.

4
Between a Rock and a Hard Place: The Governing Dilemmas of Rifondazione Comunista

James Newell

Introduction

Italy is an unusual case in that, until very recently, outsider parties of the left (and right) were significant, taken-for-granted and seemingly permanent features of the political landscape. After World War II, the second largest party was the Italian Communist Party (Partito Comunista Italiano, PCI). Its outstanding electoral performances (as compared with communist parties in other western democracies) meant that it was always 'system relevant' in Sartorian (1976) terms, while its permanent exclusion from office was one of the cornerstones of what was most distinctive about the Italian party and political systems. That is, the Cold War dread of communism, and thus the absence of any feasible governing coalitions not built around the large centre-placed Christian Democrats (Democrazia Cristiana, DC), reduced electoral pressures on the governing parties to enact coherent legislative programmes – by rendering alternation in government impossible. Parties relatively free of pressures to enact coherent legislative programmes were, consequently, unable to construct coalitions with any real cohesion and therefore power vis-à-vis the legislature. Hence governments were highly unstable – there were 50 between the election of the Constituent Assembly in 1946 and the general election of 1994, easily a European record – and their party components had to rely on clientelism and patronage as the only alternative to policy as a basis for competition between them, a feature also giving the Italian system notoriety on the European stage.

But if, cross-nationally, it was unusual for the main party of opposition to have outsider status in this way, it was not at all unusual from the perspective of Italian history. In all three of the regimes – liberal, Fascist and republican – that succeeded each other after Italian unification in 1861, the forces of opposition were considered inherently illegitimate by those in government, with the result that, prior to the 1990s, peaceful alternation in power, of the kind exemplified by the 'Westminster system of government', was never possible. And, since the forces of government in each case saw their mission as being less to 'govern' than to defend the state against the forces of opposition seen as 'usurpers', they spent much of their time seeking to co-opt, in various ways, those whose support might otherwise go to reinforce the power of the opposition.

It is no accident, then, that *'trasformismo'* is an Italian word, for it was in liberal Italy that the tradition of 'turning (potential) enemies into allies' became an established art of government. In a parliament weakly structured by party, governments sustained themselves in office on the basis of constantly shifting majorities through the offer and distribution of rewards to potential supporters. By bringing about the inclusion of deputies of conflicting opinions within single governing coalitions, *trasformismo* ensured that the centre of gravity of governments would always lie in the middle of the political spectrum; and by bringing together 'moderates', opposed to radical republicans and reactionary Catholics alike, it served to defend the unified state and its constitution.

Later examples of the practice included the Lateran Pacts of 1929 by which Mussolini bought implicit Church support for his regime; the invitation to the Socialist Party (Partito Socialista Italiano, PSI) to join the government in 1963, definitively detaching it from the orbit of the PCI and strengthening the DC's hold on office; and the practice of *'consociativismo'* involving the PCI itself. This term entered the political lexicon from the 1970s to refer to the way in which – in exchange for assistance in the passage of legislation in a parliament of weakly cohesive governing parties – the PCI was given both policy concessions and access to certain key positions within Parliament (notably, the chairs of a number of permanent committees). By thus allowing the PCI to be involved in the legislative process without being formally involved in government, Italy's political elites were able to resolve the dilemma of the impossibility of admitting the PCI to government and the obvious dangers to regime stability, given its popular support, involved in the opposition's *total* exclusion.

In the case of each of the three regimes the ultimate failure of efforts to contain the forces of opposition by co-optation led to a crisis of the regime itself (Salvadori, 1994). Hence it was only after regime collapse that the opposition was able to gain full access to government as a legitimate political actor. The latest of these regime crises – the one that began in the wake of the collapse of the Berlin Wall in 1989 – illustrates this rather strikingly. Brought on in part by the PCI's own transformation, involving the renunciation of communism and the adoption of a new name, the crisis brought the disintegration of the DC and its governing allies, unable any longer to make capital out of *anti*-communism. To be sure, this was not a collapse of the regime in the sense of any kind of *constitutional* overthrow, but it did bring a transformation of the *party* system and consequent change elsewhere in the political system radical enough to support the argument that Italian democracy itself had changed its nature (Fabbrini, 2009; Morlino, 2009). There is no real anomaly, then, in widespread use of the terms 'First' and 'Second Republic' to refer, respectively, to the periods between promulgation of the 1948 Constitution and the early 1990s, and from the early 1990s to the present. Nor is there much that is unusual in the fact that the transition between the two regimes has coincided with the now former Communists' entry to government. As with the demise first of liberal and then of Fascist Italy, so here, too, a formerly excluded opposition party gained office thanks only to a regime change for which it had been wholly or partly responsible.

From this perspective, the journey towards government that Communist Refoundation (Rifondazione Comunista, RC) undertook after the start of the new millennium was wholly in keeping with Italian political traditions. When it joined the government in 2006 it was in a sense merely repeating a course of action that the remainder of the former PCI had already undertaken 10 years earlier when the Democratic Party of the Left (Partito Democratico della Sinistra, PDS[1]), encompassing most of the former Communists, joined the government led by Romano Prodi. And, as we shall see, there were significant parallels between the forces propelling it towards government, the dilemmas it had to grapple with once there and the consequences of its government experience, and the forces, dilemmas and consequences that its predecessors on the Italian left had experienced when they too had made this journey.

With this in mind, the remainder of this chapter is structured as follows. We begin with an account of the origins of RC in order to fix its status as a member of the category of parties with which this volume is concerned, and to establish a baseline from which its subsequent trajectory may be understood. We then describe the processes by which the decision to enter government came about, showing that it was very much a coerced choice, the forces driving it being incomparably more powerful than the party itself, let alone any one component within it. We then discuss its experience in government, and the consequences, before showing, in conclusion, what similarities there were with the case of the PSI 40 years earlier. Doing this helps throw light on the extent to which RC's experience has something to tell us about the causes and consequences of radical left parties' participation in government generally.

Origins

The politico-organisational traditions of those giving birth to RC were three in number. First there was the 'pro-Soviet' wing of the PCI surrounding Armando Cossutta. As with the second tradition – the anti-capitalist left of the party – its emergence as an organised force had been very much bound up with the PCI's decline following the demise, in 1979, of the second of the two 'national solidarity' governments.[2] On the one hand, efforts to recover the numerous additional, but weakly attached, voters acquired in the years immediately preceding 1979 required change, implying a dilution of the party's communist identity. On the other hand, maintenance of the commitment of activists required that identity to be sustained. One of the consequences of this conflict was a relaxation of democratic centralism, providing greater space for contrasting ideological tendencies to compete for the support of activists. Relaxation also meant that when party leader, Achille Ochetto, proposed that the PCI be transformed into a non-communist party with a new name, the prospect that a breakaway could lead to a new party of more-than-marginal significance was a real one: democratic centralism had given the leaders considerable authority by enabling them to pose as embodiments of the unity and continuity of the entire organisation (Bertolino, 2004: p. 39). Now openly divided over Ochetto's proposal, they were revealed to be mere faction leaders – in disagreement, moreover, over the party's very identity. Thus, the prospect that the innovators would be able to take the activists compactly with them was much reduced. If this enhanced the prospects for the 'Movement for Communist Re-foundation' now spearheaded by the Cossuttiani, then in order to avoid the new organisation being hopelessly handicapped by their conservative and backward-looking image they were obliged to share power in the Movement with the ex-PCI left. The third tradition was the one represented by Proletarian Democracy (Democrazia Proletaria, DP), the small party that had sought to keep alive the traditions of the new left and which now merged with the

Movement, aware that the latter's emergence effectively reduced its own political space to almost nothing.

So, in terms of the distinction made in Chapter 1 of this volume, the new party was not of the 'extreme left'. While parties in this category share the anti-capitalism of the 'radical left', what arguably distinguishes them is an unqualified commitment to revolutionising the institutions of the state. They therefore repudiate as a matter of principle any governing vocation, and adhere rigidly to democratic centralism. RC has never been a democratic centralist organisation: emerging through the confluence of a variety of political leaders, each with his or her own political resources and geographical power base, it has experienced persistent factional competition and has thus been denied strong leadership capable of imposing decisions on the party.

Factional competition places RC in the 'radical-left' category, defined, in this volume's first chapter, in residual terms, as including parties that are not of the 'extreme left', but that do not clearly belong to the traditional communist or socialist/social democratic families either. Thus, although RC has had within it Trotskyist factions whose outlooks would fit the 'extreme-left' category, they have never been dominant. Although RC has the term 'Communist' in its title, the other term, 'Re-foundation', has facilitated the coexistence within it of those wanting the traditions of the old PCI to be revived in the new organisation and those convinced by the alternative implication of the term 'Re-foundation', namely, that the communist tradition needed to be rethought. The party is not a social democratic organisation. 'Social democracy' usually designates a commitment to removing the injustices of capitalism through legislation designed to *regulate* it, and therefore implies a strong governing vocation. Most in the party wanted the *supersession* of capitalism. And, though not opposed to governing on principle (unlike the 'extreme left'), they felt strongly that any governing prospect was strictly subordinate to programmatic questions; for they looked at least as much to civil society as to the institutions as the preferred terrain of political contest. These features also confirmed RC's status as an outsider party.

A party has to fulfil two criteria in order to be an outsider party worth examining. It has to have 'blackmail potential', and to be without 'coalition potential' (Sartori, 1976). The outsider parties that have emerged in Europe in recent years have distinguished themselves as such by 'disturbing' (Deschower, 2004) the electoral competition and the quest for power of the older established parties. But they cannot do this without being able to affect competition among the remaining parties (i.e. without blackmail potential), and without it they are of little significance for the political system as a whole. By remaining without coalition potential – that is, by remaining, through choice or circumstances, unavailable for government formation – a party underscores its outsider status by confirming that it is unwilling or unable to compete for public office on the same terms as its rivals.

RC fulfilled both criteria from the start. The local elections of May and June 1991 – the first after its emergence – showed that it was able to monopolise the space it sought to occupy; that the geographical distribution of its vote closely mirrored that of the old PCI; and that it was occasionally able to outrun the PCI's main successor (Table 4.1). Its ability to affect the outcome of competition between the remaining actors in the system was shown by Roberto D'Alimonte and Stefano Bartolini (1997), who calculated, for each of the single-member Chamber constituencies for the 1994 and 1996 general elections, the difference in the votes obtained by coalitions' candidates, and the sum of proportional votes obtained by the parties fielding the candidates. These calculations suggested that, at both elections, significant numbers of voters supporting centre-left parties with their proportional votes were, however, unwilling to support, with their single-member constituency votes, the coalition's candidates when these candidates were drawn from RC – an effect that was much smaller, or else ran in the opposite direction, when the candidates were drawn from other parties.

Concerning coalition potential, it is important to understand that the post-1989 regime crisis, and the 1993 electoral law reform,[3] brought the emergence of a transformed – bipolar rather than tripolar – party system, and made the construction of potential governing coalitions, prior to the vote, essential. The post-1993 period thus saw the

Table 4.1 Percentage of the vote obtained by RC and the PDS in the local elections of 1991

	RC		PDS	
	% votes	Seats	% votes	Seats
Municipal elections 12 May	5.9	14	14.3	40
Municipal elections 30 June	12.8	7	13.6	11
Municipal elections 24 November	5.6	11	10.1	22
Sicilian regional election	3.2	1	11.4	12

Source: Bertolino, 2004: p. 67, table 1.2

emergence of two large (if shifting) electoral coalitions – of centre-left and centre-right – competing for overall majorities in Parliament. From then on RC was in a position 'to determine... at least one of the possible governmental majorities' (Sartori, 1976: p. 122).

However, its coalition potential remained at most partial, and highly incomplete. From the beginning there had been two perspectives competing for ascendancy within the party (Bertolino, 2004: p. 103). One saw the 1991 split as the opening up, within the Italian left, of a division that ought one day to be closed by using the party's communist electoral following as a bargaining counter within a framework of broadly social democratic assumptions. The other saw the 1991 split as definitive, seeing the Italian left as increasingly divided between 'two lefts' – one with a governing, the other with an oppositional, vocation – from which it inferred a need continuously to mark the differences between RC and the more moderate PDS. Hence, the party was never able to make itself available for the construction of majorities in support of a government or potential government without the risk or the actuality of a split. Thus, after the centre-right Berlusconi government elected in March 1994 fell, and the party found its votes indispensable to the support of an alternative government, its parliamentary contingent was divided in the votes of confidence giving birth to the interim Dini government (January 1995 – May 1996), some leaving shortly thereafter to form the Comunisti Unitari. And, while its parliamentary contingent gave critical support to the centre-left 'Olive-tree' (Ulivo) government that took office following the general election of 1996, by the autumn of 1998 it was no longer able to do so in a united fashion, leading to the breakaway of the Party of Italian Communists (Partito dei Comunisti Italiani, PdCI). This event confirmed RC's outsider status by bringing about the departure of those most ready to bow to the pressures of bipolar electoral competition, to give priority to an alliance with the remainder of the centre-left and to look to the institutions of Parliament and government as the preferred terrain of political contest.

Other parties also placed limits on RC's coalition potential. Thus, the centre-left Ulivo coalition that made its electoral debut in 1996 excluded RC in part on the insistence of some of the actors located near the centre of the political spectrum – with the result that the coalition (Ulivo + RC) that defeated Berlusconi and the centre-right that year was not a coalition for government at all but a mere electoral alliance: an expedient arising from the nature of the electoral system, allowing RC to keep high in the campaign the profile of its separate identity.

The journey towards government

At its fifth congress in April 2002 (with the centre-right back in office following Berlusconi's 2001 election victory) RC's position was still that the remaining centre-left parties could be distinguished from 'Berlusconism' in terms that were quantitative, not qualitative, and that no long-term alliance with them could be contemplated in advance of agreement on the programmatic content of such an alliance. By contrast, at the sixth congress in March 2005, the majority resolution set 'the objective of a coalition of forces to give life to an alternative programme for a government in which RC and the forces of the alternative left are present as members', thus ratifying the decision now to search for an alliance in *advance* of programmatic discussions. Space restrictions preclude discussing the evidence in detail, but that the shift in position was a matter not of choice, but of necessity, can be seen from the degree of *ideological* overlap between the fifth congress theses and the majority resolution approved at the sixth congress despite the difference in the *pragmatic* outcomes of the two meetings.

Given the nature of the electoral system at the time of the 2005 congress and the increasingly entrenched bipolar character of the Italian party system, some kind of alliance with the remainder of the centre-left was essential if the party was to avoid electoral meltdown.

- Where two coalitions compete for an overall majority of seats, rational voters will support an unaligned third party only if it is among the two best placed in their constituency. The results of the 2001 election, when RC fielded its own independent candidates in the single-member constituencies for the Senate contest, confirmed that not even in the central 'red-belt' regions was there a Senate constituency where the party came anywhere near to fulfilling this criterion.
- Post-war social changes, including increasing urbanisation along with rising levels of education and of geographical and social mobility, had increased the likelihood of rational voting by weakening voters' long-term commitments to parties: in 2001, among those whose vote in the Chamber's proportional arena went to RC and who were old enough also to vote for the Senate (where the vote is acquired at 25), 30.9 per cent cast their Senate vote for the Ulivo (Italian National Election Study Data, 2001), rather than sticking with a party whose votes risked bringing defeat for the Ulivo to the advantage of the centre-right.
- Social changes had in turn left the party unable to do much itself to inculcate long-term commitments among its followers and thus to

protect itself from the electoral consequences of strategic shifts: its capacities came nowhere near those of the PCI, which had been able, in some parts of the country, to sustain loyalty by acting as the pillar of an entire political subculture. One indicator of RC's weakness was the ratio of its membership (itself in a state of long-term decline) to its voters. While the PCI had about 20 members for every 100 voters, RC struggled to manage five (Table 4.2).
- By 2005, it was clear that centre-left voters were more strongly attached to the coalition than to any of its constituent parties and united more by opposition to Berlusconi than by anything more positive. RC thus risked massive hostility if it took an independent stance, as this would have weakened the forces opposed to the entrepreneur.

Bearing in mind that even party leader Fausto Bertinotti felt that non-institutional forms took precedence over institutional forms of political struggle, RC might have been unwilling to bend to the requirements of immediate-term performance in a parliamentary election had the party's organisational survival not been so closely tied to such performance. While the human and material resources it could count on through its branches were modest – in 2001, only 20 per cent of the *circoli* had over 100 members – the central party organisation had, in compensation, been playing an increasingly significant role. Once it had become clear that RC's place in the national party system would be central and not marginal, the party's leaders had decided to increase the resources invested in the central bureaucracy (Bertolino, 2004: pp. 277–8). However, its efficacy was heavily dependent on the party's professionalisation, which in turn depended on its success in getting candidates elected to public office. Moreover, approximately two-thirds

Table 4.2 Voting support and membership of RC, 1992–2006

	1992	1994	1996	2001	2006
Chamber elections: no. of votes	2,202,574	2,334,029	3,215,960	1,868,113	2,229,604
No. of members	117,463	113,580	127,073	92,020	92,752*
Members as % of voters	5.3	4.9	4.0	4.9	4.2

* Figure is for 2005

Sources: http://www.ecn.org/reds/prc/VIcongresso/prc0502VIdestini.html
http://it.wikipedia.org/wiki/Rifondazione_Comunista

of the party's income came from the state, thanks to the system of public funding of parties, with the amounts accruing to them being perfectly correlated with their vote totals (Newell, 2000: p. 77).

A mere electoral coalition of the kind RC had agreed to in 1996, the last time the centre-left had won an election, was not possible. Such an arrangement, provided it involved no programmatic compromise or prior commitment as to the party's stance in the aftermath of the election, would have satisfied even those in the party most critical of party secretary Bertinotti's search for alliance. But the remainder of the centre-left would have refused any arrangement that did not involve a prior commitment to assume governing responsibilities and thus a programmatic agreement: the last time the centre-left had conceded a mere electoral coalition it had subsequently fallen from office, thanks to the refusal of 21 of RC's 34 deputies to support it in a confidence vote on the Finance Bill in the autumn of 1998.

Finally, in December 2005, the centre-right rushed a new electoral law through Parliament apparently designed to reduce the likelihood of its defeat in the forthcoming election or, if it lost, to make life difficult for the incoming centre-left government. The new system was one of proportional representation, with lower exclusion thresholds for aligned than for non-aligned parties and a majority premium for the party or coalition with most votes. It thus removed the problem of the summability of votes, which previous elections had shown worked to the disadvantage of the centre-right.[4] By enabling the formation of electoral coalitions without the need for parties to agree on joint candidates, thus allowing voters to support a coalition without having to cast a vote for a candidate drawn from a party other than their most preferred party, it held out the prospect of a dramatic increase in seats for RC, which in fact saw its tally go up from 15 between deputies and senators to 68 at the 2006 election. The problem for both it and the centre-left as a whole was that, given the expectations of each party concerning the likely behaviour of the others, the majority premium and exclusion thresholds of the new electoral system placed them under pressure to construct the broadest coalitions possible. For RC this increased still further the pressures on it to fall into line; for it meant that third forces outside either of the two main coalitions would be very few and thus almost entirely ignored by the media in the campaign. For the centre-left as a whole, which was highly fragmented as it was, this meant that it would find it very difficult to govern if it won the election. It did win, and RC found itself taking office along with eight other parties in a government whose survival depended upon the support of every one of its individual components.

Experience in office

The experience of government was unhappy in the extreme. Constantly berated for behaving 'irresponsibly' by anyone whose support for it was less than fervent, RC found itself caught in the classic dilemma: if it sought to exploit its indispensability as a means of advancing the causes of most concern to its core supporters, then, by appearing to put the survival of the government in jeopardy, it risked losing the support of more recently acquired but less strongly attached supporters.[5] On the other hand, if it bowed to the resulting pressures, it was exposed to the criticism of core supporters who would immediately accuse it of having sold out. The dilemmas and resulting pressures were made the more acute by the sheer fragility of the government's hold on office. Its nine parties reflected the entire ideological span that ran between clericalism on the one hand and Trotskyism on the other. The slimness of its Senate majority, together with its fragmentation, meant that its survival depended on the success of daily efforts to cajole not just single parties, but every individual parliamentarian located near its margins. The electoral system by which it had come to office gave no incentives to any of its party components to behave cohesively, but quite the opposite.

RC's response was to manage the dilemma as best it could by attempting to keep one foot in and one foot out of government. Thus, at the end of 2006, it supported the Finance Law (which, it said, was 'not the flower in the government's buttonhole' (Mauro, 2007a)), while also publicly supporting a national teachers' strike, called for 16 April 2007, against some of the effects of that law (Calculli, 2007). When, in January 2007, the Government announced its decision to accede to US requests for expansion of its military installations in Vicenza, RC participated in demonstrations against a decision that touched directly on one of its 'flagship' themes (peace and anti-militarism), while RC ministers were notable for the 'softly, softly' approach they took to the unrest.[6]

RC was terrified of bringing down the Government because of what it would have meant in terms of reminders of the autumn of 1998. Then, the split with the Cosuttiani, which had been the direct consequence of that episode, had led to the loss of 21 of 34 deputies, eight of 11 senators, 36 of 62 regional councillors, 22 of 117 provincial secretaries and four of 20 regional secretaries. Between 1998 and the following year, membership had dropped by 20,995, the number of branches by 371. The split brought the departure, in disproportionate numbers, of the most professionalised of its cadres; it meant that the party now had a direct competitor (the PdCI) in an area of the political spectrum it had once monopolised; and it saw its share of the vote decline from 8.6 per cent in 1996 to 4.3 per cent in the 1999 European elections (Bertolino, 2004: pp. 125–7).

In fact, RC's electoral support had arguably begun to decline *before*, not *after*, its 1998 decision and may thus have been a *cause* rather than a *consequence* of it. It therefore exemplified the other horn of the party's dilemma, one well illustrated by the comments of disillusioned leftists that rapidly began to appear on the Internet in the period following 21 February 2007.[7] This was the day on which Prime Minister Romano Prodi resigned after losing a vote on an important foreign policy motion as a result of the decision of two of the Government's nominal supporters – Fernando Rossi (recently departed from the PdCI) and Franco Turigliatto of RC – to abstain. Prodi was sent back by President Napolitano to Parliament, where he won a confidence vote a week later. But the event led to Turigliatto's swift expulsion from RC and party Secretary Franco Giordano's acid denunciations of the senator's abstention as an action not against the Government (which had survived) but against RC (Mauro, 2007b).

It was not surprising, then – and was certainly not because of some strange and unaccountable sympathy for parliamentarians of the centre-right – that, in July 2006, Bertinotti (by then President of the Chamber of Deputies) could be found proposing that a way be sought to broaden the base of the Government's majority – while echoing, in early March 2007, ex-Socialist Giuliano Amato's suggestion that the Government might rely on 'variable' majorities in Parliament (Passarini, 2007). Such a solution would have *strengthened* RC's position, *not* weakened it, for it would have restored to the party some autonomy by relieving it of the burden of responsibility for the Government's survival.

Nor was it surprising that the period following the 2006 election saw various splits in the party. Although none led to the departure of any parliamentarians, each was symptomatic of the tensions created by a range of issues – from Afghanistan to the Finance Law, pensions reform and the Government's proposals concerning civil partnerships – on which RC had been obliged to support measures it was unhappy with or which fell far short of what it would have liked.

The consequences

At the general election following the fall of the Prodi government in January 2008, RC's candidates competed as part of a single list, the Rainbow Left (la Sinistra l'Arcobaleno, SA), fielded jointly with the PdCI, the Greens and the Democratic Left (Sinistra Democratica, SD), a small group that had broken from the DS. In 2007, the DS had merged with former Christian Democrats with the ambition of creating a party – the Democratic Party (Partito Democratico, PD) – capable of dominating, if not monopolizing, the political ground to the left of the centre in the way Silvio Berlusconi was able to dominate the ground to the right. For Walter Veltroni, who led the PD, the experience of the Prodi government had shown that attempting to beat the centre-right by constructing the broadest coalitions possible was ultimately a losing strategy as they were subsequently incapable of providing stable government. He therefore now proposed to 'revolutionise' the party system by fielding his own party (almost) without allies and by insisting that remaining centre-left parties would have to sacrifice their separate identities by fielding their candidates as part of the PD's own lists. Thereby, even if he lost the election, his action would most likely result in a radical simplification of the party system: remaining centre-left parties would have to choose between bowing to his conditions or facing probable exclusion from Parliament altogether through failure to surmount the 4 per cent exclusion threshold; supporters of these parties would be forced to choose between voting for them or the party (his own) with the best chances of stopping Berlusconi. RC was content with the 'consensual divorce' from Veltroni represented by its involvement in the separate SA: like Veltroni, it too needed to distance itself from memories of the litigious and unpopular Prodi government and from any kind of coalition that might seem as if it were offering a rerun of that experience. And just as Veltroni was seeking to hegemonise the centre left, in exactly the same way the SA seemed to offer RC, as the only component capable, on its own, of surmounting the exclusion threshold, the opportunity to hegemonise the radical left.

The election outcome was an unmitigated disaster for RC and the SA, which took just 3.1 per cent of the vote and therefore failed to elect anyone. For the first time in the history of the Italian Republic, Parliament was without a single member claiming to represent the socialist or communist traditions. The causes of this outcome were essentially twofold: the unpopularity of the outgoing government generally, and the reactions of the SA parties' former supporters to the dilemma of government involvement. Flow-of-the-vote figures produced after the election showed that the largest outflow consisted of those who had apparently heeded Veltroni's call to cast a 'useful vote' (*un voto utile*) by supporting his party, followed by those who abstained or voted for one of the minor parties of the extreme left (Buzzanca, 2008; Corbetta et al., 2008; Mannheimer, 2009).

But, even more than an electoral disaster, the outcome was a financial and organisational disaster. By tying the available funds closely to the proportion of the vote a party receives, the system of public party funding meant that, in total, the SA parties would receive €13 million, as compared to the €51 million they had received in 2006 (Lopapa, 2008). It was true that, though they had been expelled from Parliament, they had not ceased to exist as social forces and that those who had deserted them at the election might be persuaded to return to the fold (Ricolfi, 2008). The problem was that without parliamentary representation they risked being more or less ignored by the media; and, having suffered such a large cut in the financial resources available to them, their capacity to overcome this handicap was severely weakened.

At the inevitable post-mortem following the election, two positions emerged. One was that of Nichi Vendola, president of the Puglia region, who felt that the SA had been unsuccessful because it had been a discordant federation. What was needed was a constituent process uniting all those parties willing to rethink fundamentally what being on the left now meant. By overcoming division, such a pluralistic organisation would, by virtue of its size, enable profitable engagement with the other large parties in the Italian political system, and find an interested audience among pressure-group activists, in the trade unions and among the new social movements. However, at the party's congress at the end of July, Vendola's position was beaten by that of ex-Social Welfare minister, Paolo Ferrero. His view was that inherent in Vendola's position was a danger of liquidation of the party – whose organisational reinforcement was, on the contrary, necessary if one were to avoid the twin dangers of left unity being deprived of specific horizons, and the risk of conflict among the potential constituent parties over what the nature of the new organisation was to be.

The Vendola–Ferrero division refused to die down after the July congress, continuing to simmer during the subsequent months before boiling over in December in a public row between Ferrero and Piero Sansonetti, editor of the party's paper *Liberazione* – guilty, in Ferrero's view, of sponsoring moves by Vendola to promote the formation of a united left party that would compete with RC (Newell, 2009). The inevitable recriminations eventually brought a party split. Presenting itself divided at the June 2009 European elections and facing a 4 per cent threshold introduced by the Government and opposition in February,

RC added to its loss of the seats it had had in the Chamber and Senate the five it had had in the European parliament as well.

Discussion and conclusion

RC's experience of government has been one that it was essentially obliged to undertake as the means of avoiding the enormous electoral and organisational risks it would have faced in turning its back on the 'opportunity'. Second, the experience was one which, by burdening the party with responsibility for the government's survival, created intractable dilemmas for it. Third, as a consequence of these dilemmas, the experience has left the party much weaker than it was before it entered government. In all three respects, the similarities with the experience of the PSI, 40 years earlier, are striking:

- Then, the PSI too was subject to pressures to join the executive it was not in a position to resist. Caught between a large competitor to its left (the PCI) and a large competitor to its right (the DC), and having been obliged to distance itself from the PCI after the events of 1956, it was, ineluctably, brought closer to the DC and to government: with the centre party unable to construct stable governing majorities without the support of the Socialists, there would have seemed little point in voting for a PSI which, having turned its back on the opposition, then refused to join the government either.
- Once in government, the PSI, like RC after it, was subject to ferocious pressures to moderate its objectives – pressures which, in its case, included awareness that President Antonio Segni (who took the highly unusual decision, in July 1964, to summon General Giovanni De Lorenzo, head of the Carabinieri, as part of the consultations leading to the formation of a new government) was contemplating the appointment of a government of technocrats if the parties were unable to agree on the basis for a government involving the PSI. It subsequently came to light that, at the beginning of 1964, De Lorenzo had developed the 'Solo' counter-insurgency plan involving the arrest and detention of those deemed to pose a threat to 'public security'.
- Finally, like RC, the PSI too was much weakened by its participation in government, suffering a major party split as a consequence and gradually losing its ideals as it became ever more closely associated with the practices of clientelism and patronage which the governing parties generally relied on to maintain themselves in power.

All this suggests to us that, far from being the unique consequence of specific circumstances, RC's experience exemplifies more general patterns and tendencies. These do not invite optimism on the part of supporters of the radical left, and they suggest the following conclusions. Radical-left parties seek to use the formal equality of liberal democracy to reduce substantive inequalities in the distribution of power. But, precisely because power *is* distributed so unequally, these parties face massive obstacles in the way of building electoral majorities behind their programmes. As minorities, then, they are either excluded from government or else invited to join when their participation is made necessary by the need to build governing majorities. However, their minority status, and the underlying power imbalance this status reflects, mean that the parties are unable to participate on their own terms and that once in government they are unable to achieve most of their goals even when – or perhaps *especially* when – they are numerically indispensable. Their inability to achieve much of what they stand for gravely weakens them. Electoral participation is not, therefore, promising terrain for radical-left parties. Unfortunately for those with a commitment to radical-left agendas, it is not at all clear in the early years of the twenty-first century what alternative avenues are available to be explored.

Notes

1. Later called the Left Democrats (Democratici di Sinistra, DS).
2. Holding office between July 1976 and March 1979 these were minority governments, staffed by the DC alone, which remained in power thanks to the external support or at least abstention of the PCI. Taking office at a time of considerable tensions caused by economic difficulties, and by violence from the extra-parliamentary right and left, they represented the apogee of *consociativismo*, a prelude, PCI leaders hoped, to their eventual admission to government. Their hopes proved unfounded.
3. From 1993, three-quarters of the seats in both chambers of Parliament were distributed according to the single-member, simple plurality method (encouraging the formation of electoral coalitions of left and right involving stand-down agreements among allied parties) and one-quarter proportionally (which parties could therefore compete for independently). For the Chamber of Deputies, voters cast two ballots: one for their preferred candidate in their single-member constituency, the other for their preferred party in the proportional arena.
4. The previous law placed parties under pressure to field joint candidates in single-member constituencies while also forcing them to consider whether the addition of an extra partner to the coalition would increase or decrease the coalition's vote total. If there were parties intensely disliked by the

supporters of other parties in the coalition, then it was reasonable to suppose that those supporters might refuse to support a joint candidate drawn from the disliked party.
5. The potential losses were not insignificant: in 2006 its vote in the Chamber of Deputies election amounted to 2,229,464: 20 per cent more than the 1,868,659 votes it had won in 2001.
6. When asked in a *Repubblica* interview whether he would participate in the 17 February demonstration, RC's minister of Social Affairs, Paolo Ferrero, replied simply that he hadn't decided. This was after stating that, when he attended the funerals of two Italian soldiers killed in Iraq, he had taken off the pacifist badge he always wore because he didn't want it 'to seem somehow offensive' (Lopapa, 2007).
7. See, for illustrations, the blog posts that appeared on the PartigianaMente web site: http://partigianamente.splinder.com/post/11297256

5
A Poisoned Chalice? Finland's Left Alliance and the Perils of Government
Richard Dunphy

Introduction

This chapter considers the very mixed experience of coalition government participation of the Left Alliance of Finland (Vasemmistoliitto – VAS). The party participated in government in Finland from 1995 to 2003, yet without any clear gains in policy terms and certainly without success in halting a slow electoral decline. Indeed, that decline has somewhat accelerated since the experience of government. Despite that, many VAS leaders remain convinced that government participation was the only option open to the party and that a strategy of 'oppositionism' would have merely hastened the party's isolation and decline. The party now faces major strategic questions about how to conduct itself in opposition – and how best to facilitate a return to government office, if possible in 2011 when elections are due.

VAS was created in April 1990. Its founding programme made only a passing reference to 'socialism' as one of the influences upon the party – along with feminism and ecology, for example. The emphasis was upon the need for a new party, dedicated to forging a type of 'red–green' left politics. In reality, however, ideological renewal was less profound than it seemed and many of the problems and internal divisions of the 'old' were carried over into the 'new'.

VAS had its origins in the People's Democratic League of Finland (SKDL), formed with Soviet support in November 1944 and dominated by the Finnish Communist Party (SKP).[1] The SKDL was a major force in Finnish politics, polling 23.5 per cent in the national election in March 1945 and remaining around or above the 20 per cent mark until the 1970s. Support dropped to between 15 and 20 per cent during the 1970s and to between 10 and 15 per cent in the 1980s. Although the SKP and the SKDL elected new and more reform-minded leaders in the mid-1960s, who tended to identify with Italian-style 'Eurocommunism' and with Dubček's Prague Spring reforms, both organisations were plagued by divisions between reformers and so-called Stalinists for the next 20 years. The SKDP participated in coalition governments with the Social Democrats and Agrarians (or Centrists) in 1944–8, 1966–71, 1975–6 and 1977–82. Government participation, especially in the 1970s, further exacerbated internal party divisions. These divisions were not straightforward; one cannot, for example, speak in tidy schematic terms of reformers being in favour of government participation and neo-Stalinists being opposed. On the contrary, both factions were divided in their estimation of participation, so that at one point one might identify up to four separate and competing groups.

In a sense, VAS's participation in coalition government in the period 1995–2003 might be interpreted as nothing new – given that its predecessor had a long history of government involvement. The surface appearance of continuity, however, masks two important differences between the earlier and later periods of government participation. Finland's unusual and somewhat ambiguous position during the decades of the Cold War – a neutral capitalist democracy intent on maintaining good relations with its Soviet neighbour – helps explain why the convention to exclude Communists from government from the late 1940s until the end of the 1980s never applied in quite the same way as it did in, for example, France and Italy (although the SKDL's omission from government in the 1948–66 period did reflect some elements of ideological polarisation (see Lindén, 2005). Secondly, the SKDL had participated in government in the earlier period as a party of some considerable political weight, whose presence within the ambit of government helped to consolidate Finnish democracy on the basis of consensus politics. When VAS participated in government from 1995, the world around it had changed fundamentally. The USSR had collapsed. When the Finnish economy (which traded heavily with the USSR) and Finnish politics (accustomed to the 'Finlandisation' model) recovered from the shock, a new consensus steered the country in an unambiguously pro-western direction, encapsulated by Finland's membership of the European Union in 1995. VAS found itself profoundly disorientated by these changes; its initial opposition to EU membership and subsequent radical reversal of policy on this key issue (and the unresolved internal tensions this caused) perhaps symbolise this most clearly. Moreover, by 1995 electoral support was down to 11.2 per cent – the party's participation within the broad ambit of government was no longer central to political stability, but rather a goal that party leaders saw as vital to rescuing the party from marginalisation and long-term decline.

The decision to offer itself as a coalition partner to the Social Democrats in 1995 has to be set against the background of a perceived lurch to the right in Finnish politics during the preceding four years. In 1991, the SDP moved into opposition and a coalition government of the conservative National Coalition Party (KOK) and the ex-Agrarian Centre Party (KESK) took office. This 'bourgeois' government introduced a number of policies that were seen by both the SDP and VAS as an attack on the policy achievements of the broad left, above all radical cuts to the welfare state and an attempt to reduce trade union power. The main union confederation, SAK, in which the Social Democrats have a majority role but with a substantial VAS minority faction, feared its growing exclusion from collective agreements on wages and prices and also from the management of the unemployment assistance fund (Dunphy, 2007: p. 38). Unemployment in Finland had reached a record 16 per cent by 1994. The two left-of-centre parties feared that the right might attempt a permanent restructuring of the Finnish political landscape, against a backdrop of mounting economic insecurity, similar to that carried out by Margaret Thatcher in the UK during the 1980s. To stop and derail any such attempt at Thatcherisation thus became a shared priority. A series of strikes and demonstrations were organised by SAK in the period leading up to the 1995 general election. That election saw the SDP recapture the position of leading party with 28.3 per cent of the vote (see Table 5.1). Under Finnish political conventions, this allowed SDP leader Paavo Lipponen to emerge as government *formateur*.

Table 5.1 Recent general election results in Finland (percentage of the vote)

Party	1995	1999	2003	2007
Social Democrats (SDP)	28.3	22.9	24.5	21.4
National Coalition (KOK)	17.9	21.0	18.5	22.3
Centrists (KESK)	19.8	22.4	24.7	23.1
Left Alliance (VAS)	11.2	10.9	9.9	8.8
Greens (VIHR)	6.5	7.3	8.0	8.5
True Finns (PS)	n/a	1.0	1.6	4.1
Swedish People's Party (RKP)	5.1	5.1	4.6	4.6
Others	11.2	9.4	8.4	7.2

The trade union block within VAS – more precisely, the block of party members who were SAK leaders – had long been to the fore of those arguing for government participation. Led by Pekka Hynönen,[2] this group visited SDP party offices for talks with Lipponen aimed at convincing him to invite VAS into government. According to Hynönen, they subsequently played a key mediation role between the SDP and VAS leaderships.[3] This, incidentally, would prove both a strength and a weakness. The strength lay in the fact that the strong support for the subsequent coalition agreement by the unions helped 'sell' the deal to many labour activists and older VAS voters. The weakness lay in the fact that this style of negotiation, with its reliance on personal relations and covert deals between elites, meant that party debate was short-circuited and many ideologically motivated party members felt a distinct lack of ownership of the agreement, to put it mildly. After weeks of elite negotiation, in March 1995 VAS finally entered coalition government with the SDP and three other parties – the conservative National Coalition, the Greens and the Swedish People's Party. The party had two ministers in what became known as the first 'Rainbow' government, with Claes Anderson as Minister for Culture, Youth and Sport and Terttu Huttu-Juntunen as Minister for Health and Public Services.

Ideological and programmatic compromises in government

Perhaps the first compromise that coalition politics forced upon VAS concerned the very manner of its entry into government. VAS had always assumed that its 'natural' partners in government would be the SDP and the Centrists (ex-Agrarians). These had been the parties that had governed with the old SKDL on several previous occasions. By contrast, the conservatives of KOK were seen as the traditional 'class enemy' – the very force whose policies had marked Finland's rightwards move in the early 1990s. The inclusion of KOK in the new Rainbow government was a severe blow to the credibility of the government in the eyes of many left-wingers. Many party members were furious. Former party leader Suvi-Anne Siimes observed that the decision provoked 'widespread uproar and dissent' within the party.[4] However, having staked everything upon government participation, the party leaders felt unable to object to the SDP's choice of partners. The SDP, of course, had its own reasons for its choices. One author has argued that the SDP sought to include VAS in order to cover its left flank in anticipation of having to implement harsh economic policies in the years ahead (Jungar, 2002: p. 67). The party may well have included

KOK for a not dissimilar reason – perhaps hoping to offset the burden of responsibility for cutbacks onto the shoulders of the conservatives. The inclusion of both the Greens and the centre-right Swedish People's Party gave the Rainbow government a huge majority in parliament – more than 70 per cent of the seats. This relieved Lipponen of the possibility of any one coalition partner holding his government to ransom, and reduced the bargaining weight of the smaller parties accordingly.

There is no doubt that VAS entered the new government in a defensive manner and with little advance preparation. The party leadership's energies had gone into persuading the SDP of VAS's acceptability as a partner. According to Raunio and Wiberg, there has been a tendency in Finland for coalition Government programmes 'to become longer and more detailed over the decades, with the coalition partners investing considerable resources in bargaining over the programme... which forms the backbone of the cabinet and... is binding on all the coalition parties' (Raunio and Wiberg, 2008: p. 590). Yet VAS had little input into the 4541-word programme for government that they signed and subsequently had to defend. Siimes admits that 'we had no clear idea of what we wanted to achieve' and 'we were so happy to be in government that we failed to put our finger print on the programme.'[5] Moreover, the failure to debate the issue of participation within the party – instead the leadership effectively relied on an appeal to loyalty along the lines of 'there is no alternative' – meant that many members felt a complete lack of involvement.[6] The agreement was approved by a party forum consisting of the 55 members of the party council and the 22 MPs, but with 25 votes against and five abstentions. Three MPs subsequently left the party in protest. Finally, it must be noted that the party's lack of preparation and inexperience showed also in the acceptance of the two ministries it occupied in the first Rainbow government. The Ministry of Culture, Youth and Sports was scarcely of central importance. The Ministry of Health and Public Services was potentially very important, but, as the SDP must have known, this was where painful cuts were to be made. The VAS Minister would subsequently find herself having to defend in public cuts that she and her party had voted against at the cabinet table – and, of course, take the public criticism for such perceived 'U-turns' (Dunphy, 2007: p. 42).

The period of the first Rainbow government (1995–9) involved many painful decisions and compromises on VAS's part. Perhaps the worst experience for the party was finding itself party to a programme of 20 billion Finnish marks of spending cuts (1995–9). VAS could claim, and perhaps with justification, to have fought tirelessly to ameliorate what might have been a more drastic programme of cuts – certainly more drastic if the centre-right had continued in government and possibly even if the SDP and other parties had formed a coalition without VAS. But, as one party leader subsequently admitted (Lindén, 2005: p. 3), the pill was a bitter one to swallow. Many people living on social security payments and on small pensions were badly hit by the cuts in 1996; VAS was unable to prevent cuts to housing benefits in 1997, instead having to content itself with having reduced the cuts from 20 per cent to 7 per cent. To the party's natural supporters, this was a difficult 'achievement' to sell.

One policy area where VAS carried out major change during the time of its participation in government was, of course, EU policy. The party had opposed Finland's EU membership in the past and campaigned against the single currency in particular. Many in the party favoured change to a policy of campaigning for radical change and reform of the EU from within, but many others regarded this as a surrender to social democrat revisionism. Finland joined the EU in 1995, the decision to join having been taken, obviously, before VAS entered government. It was obvious by then, also, that the two main government partners – SDP and KOK – favoured participation in the single currency. A new generation of VAS leaders, epitomised by Suvi-Anne Siimes, pushed through a change of policy in favour of EU membership, arguing that the only alternative in a post-Cold War world was for Finland to sink into national isolation and economic decay – and for the Finnish left to sink into national populism of an increasingly authoritarian and xenophobic kind. Siimes and many others doubtless regarded a change in EU policy as a desirable goal in itself. But the party leadership also sought to portray this to the membership as a necessary part of proving the party's 'government vocation' – of establishing its full credentials as a party that deserved to be taken seriously. Thus Claes Anderson, Siimes's predecessor as party leader, who personally opposed the single currency, believed that the issue should not be allowed to drive a wedge between the party and its coalition partners (Dunphy, 2007: p. 42). By linking policy change to an explicit espousal of the party's credibility as a party of government, the leadership succeeded in winning a referendum of party members in December 1997, but only just: 52.4 per cent voted for the new, pro-'EU reform from within' and pro-single currency position. A very sizable minority remained unconvinced, and they had a charismatic champion in the popular Esko Seppänen, MEP from 1995 until the party's disastrous performance in the European Parliamentary election of 2009 (in which he did not stand), when it lost its EP seat. The decision to allow everyone to maintain their positions on EU policy avoided a split, but did not resolve an acrimonious policy debate that has continued to rumble ever since.

At the time of the 1999 general election, VAS had little to show for its four years in government in terms of concrete achievements. Many of its supporters were hurt and disillusioned. Yet the worst of the spending cuts were now over, the Finnish economy was beginning to grow and unemployment was falling rapidly. Party leaders felt that, having made the sacrifices, they had every right to reap the rewards that a second term in government ought to bring. Having traded short-term minor electoral losses for longer-term gains, and having avoided an outright party split, VAS had some reason for optimism about a new term in office. Even party activists who had opposed government participation in 1995 felt by 1999 that it was their hard-won right – and that a forced return to opposition now, after the sacrifices had been made, would be the worst of all possible scenarios.[7] In the wake of the 1999 election, the SDP was once again in a position to act as government *formateur* (see Table 5.1) and Lipponen appointed the same five-party coalition. This time, a much bigger majority within the party forum approved government participation – 61 votes for, eight against and one abstention (Dunphy, 2007: p. 42).

By 1999, VAS had clearly learned some important lessons. The party had a much greater input into the 6711-word programme of the second Rainbow (or Lipponen) government. It set out a list of 10 key priorities and secured commitments in the fields of employment creation and housing construction. Having identified the Ministry of Finance as the powerhouse of 'neoliberal' opposition to progressive social policies, it demanded and secured a post in that Ministry from which it sought to challenge Finance orthodoxy: Suvi-Anne Siimes (the new party leader) became deputy Minister for Finance and Housing and Martti Korhonen became Minister for Municipal and Regional Affairs. The period 1999–2001 saw what the party regarded as some real achievements: the highest level of job creation in the OECD area, reducing unemployment from 16 per cent in 1994–5 to 9 per cent by 2001; the raising of capital and corporate taxes from 25 per cent to 29 per cent, in place of spending cuts; the lowering of mortgage rates; and the restoration of some trade union powers, with comprehensive incomes policies once again agreed with the unions. However, the government seemed to stagnate during its last two years in office. In 2002, the Greens (VIHR) pulled out of government in protest against a decision to build more nuclear power plants. Siimes forced her party to accept the controversial decision. Many amongst the younger generation of feminist and environmentalist 'red/green' VAS activists privately admired the VIHR decision (even while bitterly critical of the 'right-wing' nature of many in the Finnish Greens), both for showing that it took its anti-nuclear policy seriously and for drawing a 'line in the sand' that it would not cross in pursuit of office.[8] A further issue that caused serious divisions within VAS was foreign and security policy. Although the party in government opposed increases in defence spending and SDP/KOK proposals to send Finnish troops abroad in overseas operations, many activists suspected that Siimes was preparing to change party policy on NATO membership. Time and time again, she argued that NATO membership should not be seen as a matter of fundamental principle but of tactics, and that opposition to NATO should not be allowed to get in the way of participation in a third Rainbow government. But, in the eyes of many members and activists, the NATO question was *indeed* a matter of *principle* – more than that, it was an *existential* issue, for what did VAS stand for and why should it not merge with the Social Democrats if it abandoned even its opposition to NATO?

By the time of the 2003 election, the government appeared both less red and less green. The SDP seemed to be leaning towards the 'bourgeois' wing of the government. VAS seemed increasingly isolated, despite its obvious willingness to compromise. The election campaign was something of a disaster for the party. Not only did it fail to make a dent in the big parties' domination of media coverage or SDP leader and prime minister Lipponen's attempt at a presidential-style campaign, but VAS scored an embarrassing 'own goal' when one of the senior figures on its trade union wing publicly urged voters to back the Social Democrats, arguing (correctly as it turned out) that VAS's chances of being invited to join another government depended on the SDP coming first and having the role of *formateur* (Dunphy, 2007: p. 46). Moreover, the NATO issue surfaced constantly during the 2003 election, and this was a source of endless friction within VAS (Nurmi and Nurmi, 2007: p. 768). The party failed to receive the expected electoral reward for its eight years of government work. Instead, its slow decline continued, with the vote falling again to 9.9 per cent (see Table 5.1). Even worse, by the tiniest of margins, the KESK pulled ahead of the SDP and thus stole the right to act as *formateur* in the new coalition government negotiations. A three-party KESK/SDP/VIHR coalition government subsequently took office, leaving VAS in opposition. Many VAS leaders and members felt angry, even betrayed, that the SDP had not seemingly fought sufficiently hard to have their party included in government.[9] Others took the more conciliatory attitude that, had the SDP pushed too hard, KESK might have rejected it and sought a coalition with KOK and VIHR.

Issues and themes at the core of the Left Alliance's project

In the immediate aftermath of VAS's return to opposition three closely related issues moved to centre stage, in terms of defining the party's future project. The first was the need to find a clear and convincing role for the party in opposition. The second was to prepare for what many leaders felt would be a possible, and desirable, return to government after the 2007 election. The third was to maintain party unity and raise morale by establishing a clearer identity for the party. The first two issues are obviously interlinked: one establishes a clear role in opposition by seizing on certain government policies to which one is strongly opposed and campaigning against these; yet to campaign too strongly against a government made up of the very parties one wishes to be in government alongside requires a difficult balancing act. The third issue lay behind the decision to establish a party commission to prepare a new party programme, which would be presented for approval to the 2007 party congress.

The move into opposition caught VAS by surprise. By this time, three main internal groups – they are certainly not coherent factions – were discernible. These have been dealt with in detail elsewhere (Dunphy, 2007: pp. 47–9), so the briefest of summaries will suffice. First, there is a group that might be described as 'left-populists' and which appeals to many of the older Communist generation (and loyal, if ageing, VAS voters). This group includes such figures as ex-MEP Seppänen and MPs Jaakko Laakso and Esko Juhani Tennilä. They tend to be strongly opposed to EU membership and NATO membership, in favour of protectionist economic policies in the struggle against globalisation, and anxious to win back older voters who have deserted VAS for the extreme right True Finns party, which preaches a policy of 'preferential treatment' of 'native-born Finns'. In the eyes of some party members, they do so by flirting with xenophobia and show a lack of concern for immigrants' or minority rights.[10] This group tends to be most critical of recent VAS participation in government, albeit not universally so. The leadership election that followed the resignation of Siimes in March 2006 showed this group to be by far the weakest of the three.

Second are the so-called 'Modern Leftists', whose ranks include former leaders Claes Anderson, Martti Korhonen and Suvi-Anne Siimes (although she has now turned her back on left politics and launched outspoken attacks on her old party). This group has majority support within the party. They tend to be pragmatic on questions such as EU policy and NATO membership, although most are not as 'revisionist' as

Siimes proved to be. They are strongly supported by members who work in the public sector and by the trade unionists, who benefited most from VAS's spell in government. They favoured government participation in 1995 and 1999 and are committed to an early return to government. One of their number, the current party general secretary Turo Bergman, has stated that 'for us, government participation [in 1995] was a pragmatic solution ... the other option [to remain in opposition] would have been a catastrophe. Many of our members and voters never understood or accepted this but there are situations when you cannot say no'; and, moreover, that 'we have to participate in government again, if possible, at the earliest opportunity.'[11] The trade union 'faction' of the Modern Leftists is closest ideologically to the SDP and most supportive of EU membership, which they see as essential to the health of the Finnish economy.

Third are the so-called 'red/green' activists, feminists and 'new leftists',[12] led by Paavo Arhinmäki. This group proved its strength during the 2006 leadership election when, at a specially convened party conference, Arhinmäki polled 150 delegates to Korhonen's winning 273. They tend to be critical of government participation at any price while supportive of participation in principle. They advocate leadership and cultural renewal, a much stronger embrace of green and gender and racial equality issues, and a move to the left on security and defence policy. The red/greens are strongly opposed to NATO membership and believe in adopting a position clearly to the left of the SDP, while shunning old communist authoritarianism and remaining fairly open on EU policy. Involved in the anti-war movement, they have established links with Europe-wide social movements and movements against globalisation – although it has to be said that these links are weaker in Finland than in many other countries.

Government participation helped maintain party unity and mask these divisions, to an extent, and certainly in the 1999–2003 period. However, the unexpected return to opposition in 2003 brought divisions into the open. In large part, the immediate cause was the inability of the party leadership to define an oppositional role. Suvi-Anne Siimes had been a very impressive Government minister, but was unaccustomed to opposition and seemingly lost in the role of leader of a small opposition party. Wavering between enthusiastic support for the SDP in EU, foreign and security policy fields and increasingly strident attacks on the 'right-wing' and 'neoliberal' drift of the economic policy of the post-2003 government, her leadership became erratic in the eyes of many.

On the 'right' of the party, there were those trade union leaders and others who warned that she risked permanently alienating the SDP and preventing VAS from returning to government in 2007. In February 2005, two prominent trade unionists called for negotiations to be opened with the SDP leading to a merger of the two parties. This was swiftly rebuffed by all 19 of the party's MPs, and one of the union leaders left VAS and joined the SDP subsequently. Morale suffered as a small number of others followed him into the SDP.

On the left, Arhinmäki and others, such as the party's current youngest MP, Merja Kyllönen, argued against any move to a pro-NATO position and criticised any support for nuclear power and for the logic of unfettered economic growth.[13] But the biggest public division was between Siimes and the 'populists', a mutual antagonism that spilled over into increasingly incautious and unrestrained public abuse in 2005 and 2006. The issue of NATO, and Siimes's support for a common EU army, were to the fore as Siimes called publicly for the 'de-selection' of some of her party's MPs, declaring that she did not want to belong to the same party as MPs such as Jaakko Laakso, who led the opposition to her change of defence policy. The damage to the party's image was incalculable. Eight years of government participation was supposed to establish the party as a serious, acceptable party of government, whose democratic credentials were beyond reproach and which had escaped from beneath the 'long grave-shadow'[14] of the USSR. Instead, within two years of leaving office, the party was publicly humiliated by infighting that saw its own leader brand some of its MPs as 'unreconstructed Communists' and condemn the entire party as 'unfit' for government office unless it shed them.

Isolated within the party because of the extremity of her attacks on her party opponents, Siimes resigned the leadership in March 2006. She subsequently resigned from the parliamentary group, whilst remaining an MP until 2007, when she left politics altogether. Siimes had long enjoyed a positive image in the media, as a young, dynamic female leader who had never been tarred with the communist brush. Indeed, at the height of her ministerial popularity, it is fair to say that the party majority had been happy to bask in the reflected glory of her media image. The damage her resignation and public split with the party caused is powerful proof, however, of the danger of relying on a single powerful personality. Some party leaders might tell themselves that a positive side of the subsequent leadership contest was the emergence into the media limelight of numerous contenders, removing the idea that VAS was a one-woman show;[15] but the reality is that endless media speculation about the imminent death of the party caused lasting damage. It was against this singularly unfortunate background that final preparations got under way for the 2007 party congress that was to approve a new party programme.

The new party programme was endorsed by the Party Board in May 2007 and adopted by the Fifth Party Congress in June 2007.[16] Given the setbacks of the previous four years, it is perhaps not surprising that the aim of restoring party morale and defining what the party stood for was now firmly tied up with the need to rebuild at least the appearance of party unity and behind a programme in which (virtually) every member (apart from the small trickle that defected to the SDP) might find something with which to identify. Naturally, this makes for blandness and ambiguities in places, but this is probably true of most party programmes and statements of principle. Nevertheless, the 2007 programme contains some key points that are worth noting – as well as one glaring and prominent omission.

First, on paper at least, the new programme represents a shift towards a more clearly defined left-wing, socialist position. The party, which had been regarded by some observers as one of the least radical of Europe's radical left parties (and even jokingly referred to as such by its leaders in interviews), declared itself for the first time to be explicitly anti-capitalist: 'Left Alliance makes a difference [sic] between capitalism and the market economy. Left Alliance opposes capitalism, which is a politics that one-sidedly favours the capital owners' economic interests and prerogatives.' The party then pledged itself to strong regulation of the market economy to make the market 'ecologically, socially and humanly sustainable'. The programme also included a strong attack on capitalist globalisation, accused of 'chipping away at the goal of an equal society and social trust' and posing 'a threat to every welfare state'. It is painfully short of concrete proposals for opposing and challenging such processes, however. Declaring VAS to be a party that 'identifies itself with socialist thinking', the programme pledged the party to a strong defence of the public sector: 'the realisation of [our] goal calls for a strong public economy, the public production of the basic services and the development of state ownership, investment and subsidies.'

Second, the programme involved a clearer elaboration of the party's EU policy. There was no going back to the straightforwardly anti-EU positions of the 'populists'. Equally, however, there was no uncritical endorsement of all things European such as had been associated with Siimes. Instead, the programme declares that 'with neo-liberal politics the EU does not deserve the trust of the European people.' It calls for a root and branch reform of the EU from within 'in such a way that the EU supports the development of the society on the basis of the Nordic model of solidarity'. Many of the sentiments expressed drew VAS close to the declared policy positions of the European Left party (ELP), to which VAS has now decided in principle to adhere.[17] Yet a glaring omission was any mention of opposition to the Lisbon Treaty. In fact, while polls suggest overwhelming opposition to Lisbon on the part of VAS members and voters, many of the leadership wish to keep a more flexible position, in view of possible future coalition negotiations.

Third, the programme declared VAS to be an anti-militarist party that wants 'to dismantle military alliances, promote universal disarmament, world peace and international security based on the respect of the principles of the United Nations'. Yet this stopped short of an explicit rejection of Finnish membership of both NATO and any EU army. Presumably, it was intended to be sufficiently ambiguous to keep all wings of the party on board.

Fourth, the party clearly and strongly denounced racism, xenophobia and nationalism, calling for Finland to adopt a much more open and welcoming immigration policy and identifying VAS as a party committed to supporting 'Finland's development into a multicultural country... We welcome immigrants to Finland and to full citizenship. Immigrants and refugees bring new life and cultural richness into Finland.' Finally, the programme sought to give a much stronger emphasis to VAS's green credentials, with clear commitments on support for sustainable development, reducing carbon emissions, support for organic farming and animal rights, and strong policies on public transport, biodiversity and reduction of consumption and waste. However, it avoided a rupture with the 'workerist' and trade unionist constituencies by omitting any mention of nuclear power.

In many respects, the new programme represented a compromise between the 'modern leftist' and 'red/green' wings of the party and heralded an attempt to give a clearer left-wing profile to the party in opposition. However, its impact was considerably diluted by the negative outcome of the March 2007 general election.

Conclusion: Future prospects and challenges

Given the fact that VAS had failed to find a convincing role for itself in opposition and had been badly damaged by public infighting, the acrimonious resignation of its media-friendly and popular leader, the defection of some members to the SDP, continuing policy turmoil over

NATO and defence policy in particular, and a seemingly endless barrage of (sometimes gleeful) negative media publicity, it is scarcely surprising that the party's slow decline continued in the 2007 election (see Table 5.1). A further fall to 8.8 per cent – the sharpest single fall since the party was founded – caused considerable worry about its future. VAS only just managed to stay ahead of the Greens, who increased their share to 8.5 per cent. In fact, the decline might well have been steeper – and may yet prove to be, if VAS does not quickly find a role for itself that appeals to younger and new voters, and if the truly horrendous performance in the 2009 European election is repeated in a general election (see below).

The 2007 election result suggested that attempts to reinvent and reinvigorate the party had been too little, too late to reverse the damage inflicted by recent divisions or to halt the seemingly inexorable decline. Ironically, given that so much self-inflicted damage revolved around the issue of NATO membership and Finnish neutrality, the issue featured hardly at all in the overall 2007 campaign (Nurmi and Nurmi, 2007: p. 798). The reason, suggest Nurmi and Nurmi, is that politicians from the big parties sensed that opinion polls suggested little popular support for NATO membership and so sidelined the issue. It is surely a rich irony that the one issue that VAS could have truly made its flagship policy – a strong and clear opposition to NATO that would not only have been popular with its members and traditional voters but fully in line with majority Finnish opinion, and potentially appealing to younger and new voters – was the issue that it was unable to resolve internally and had torn itself apart in public over since 2003.

A major issue the party faces in the aftermath of the 2007 election is that of generational renewal – and of attracting new voters. Past predictions that VAS's ageing electorate would eventually die off, condemning the party to inevitable decline in the absence of replacement voters, now seem alarmingly prescient. Above all, young voters seem more attracted by the resurgent Greens – and even by the Centrists and Conservatives. For some time, the Greens (VIHR) had been positioning themselves as a centrist, liberal urban party (albeit with a leftist red/green minority wing). This strategy has allowed the party to make very considerable inroads with the young educated urban middle classes, precisely the constituency that Arhinmäki and his red/green supporters had identified as essential recruiting ground for VAS. For example, in 2007 VIHR captured 20.1 per cent of the vote in Helsinki (while VAS took just 6.8 per cent). VAS remained strongest in the remote northern

Lapland area (23.1 per cent). VAS lost ground (and a seat) to the Greens in Siimes's old constituency of Uusimaa, where the popular Siimes had polled 16,000 personal votes in 2003 (the Finnish voting system allows voters to award personal preferences to candidates on a list system (see Nurmi and Nurmi, 2007: pp. 797–800)).

A brief consideration of the composition of the new VAS parliamentary group reveals the problem of generational renewal that the party faces. Of the 17 MPs elected in 2007, just two are under the age of 40, while eight are over the age of 60 and a further five in their 50s. Three MPs were elected for the first time; four others had been first elected in 2003, with the majority in parliament since the 1990s (indeed two had been MPs since the 1970s).[18] This was not a line-up that would easily allow VAS to escape the image of being a party dominated by 'grey old men in suits'.[19]

A significant outcome of the 2007 elections is that the SDP fell to third place and was excluded from the new government, a four-party coalition of the conservative KOK, the centrist KESK, the Greens and the Swedish People's Party. The fact that both left-of-centre parties were now in opposition together has considerably eased relations between VAS and the SDP. It has helped VAS, at least in the short term, to find a clear oppositional role, although not necessarily a role that is yet very distinctive from that of the SDP. Nevertheless, given that VAS's prospects of re-entering government depend not only on being able to work with the SDP, but on the SDP coming first in an election and being in the position of government *formateur*, the ability to define a combative role in opposition without being involved in a head-on clash with the SDP is obviously an advantage. That said, support for the combined left-of-centre is now at its lowest level in Finland – 31.1 per cent – in the 100-year history of Finnish parliamentary democracy. Given the decline and isolation of the left in general, and the participation of the Greens in a 'bourgeois' government, it is at present difficult to see how the parliamentary arithmetic after the 2011 elections might support either of the two scenarios VAS most favours – a VAS/SDP/VIHR or a VAS/SDP/VIHR/KESK coalition.

The immediate problems the party faces, moreover, have been considerably compounded by the result of the 2009 European Parliament election. Despite opinion poll predictions of a comforting 9.0 per cent, VAS fell to a catastrophic 5.9 per cent and lost its only MEP. The absence of the popular (and arch-eurosceptic) Esko Seppänen may have contributed to the loss of older voters; low voter turnout (just over 40 per cent), always seen as a problem for the left in Finland, also contributed. Once

Table 5.2 Outcome of the 2009 European Parliament election in Finland

Party	% of vote	Seats won
Social Democrats (SDP)	17.5	2
National Coalition (KOK)	23.2	3
Centrists (KESK)	19.0	3
Left Alliance (VAS)	5.9	0
Greens (VIHR)	12.4	2
True Finns (PS)	9.8	1
Swedish People's Party (RKP)	6.1	1
Christian Democrats (KD)	4.2	1

Source: Finnish Ministry of Justice

again, the SDP also polled appallingly, winning just 17.5 per cent, meaning that the total left vote declined to just 23.4 per cent (see Table 5.2).

VAS was heavily out-polled, not only by the Greens, but by the extreme right True Finns party, which polled 9.8 per cent and won a seat for the first time. The True Finns had combined right-wing populism and xenophobia with some policies – defence of the welfare state, support for high taxes to fund generous pensions, opposition to the EU as a 'capitalist project' – that appealed to older, formerly left-wing voters, and post-election analyses suggested that both the SDP and VAS lost votes to them. If this is so, then the signs for the future are truly alarming. It seems that assumptions about older VAS voters being loyal even if in decline can no longer be taken for granted; the party may be in danger of losing younger voters to the Greens and older voters to the True Finns. Of course, it is foolish to transpose the results of European elections to national elections; frankly, a vote as low as 5.9 per cent in the 2011 national elections seems unlikely, but the party's share could slip again to perhaps 7 or 7.5 per cent.

In the wake of the 2009 European election, the party moved quickly to signal its willingness at last for radical renewal. Party leader Martti Korhonen resigned and an extraordinary meeting of the Party Council on 27 June elected 32-year-old Paavo Arhinmäki, leader of the radical left (or red/green) wing of the party, as his successor. Significantly, his only serious challenger was 32-year-old Merja Sinikka Kyllönen, the other young MP elected in 2007. She was supported by the feminist caucus within the party.[20]

Without question, Arhinmäki is the most left-wing leader VAS has ever had, and his election may mark a radical departure. His power base has always been amongst the party youth – and young Helsinki voters. If he can carry the bulk of the party with him – and it won't be easy – then his leadership may mark a new style and culture of politics for VAS. Although he favours future government participation in principle, he has always criticised those within the party who put office before principle, and has argued that a return to government should be on the basis of clear priorities and agreed commitments, and that VAS should not be afraid to bring down a government that reneges on these. In any case, Arhinmäki's clear priorities now are to rebuild the party and capture young voters, rather than prepare for a return to government in the short term. His priorities include: a vigorous assault on government policies, including reclaiming the radical green agenda from VIHR, which he insists must be held to account for the present government's failure to adopt green measures on climate change; the formulation of clear, alternative policies to distinguish VAS from other parties; and a strengthening of extra-parliamentary political activism, including ties with the social movements.[21]

Arhinmäki has long argued that there is no alternative to this radicalisation of the party's politics, culture and image other than that of continual decline. He may now have a chance to prove that VAS can become a red/green 'new left' party in more than name only – if he can overcome the considerable obstacle of party bureaucratic inertia, and if it is not already too late. In a sense, the even more dramatic decline and crisis of the SDP means that his own proposed 'left turn' for VAS risks fewer defections and splits than at any time in recent VAS history. The group perhaps most likely to defect to the SDP in the face of an 'oppositional left turn' – the moderate trade union tendency amongst the 'modern leftists' – are less likely to be tempted by an SDP in opposition and engulfed in a crisis of its own than if Arhinmäki were directing his fire against a government led by, or even including, a strong SDP.

Notes

I gratefully acknowledge the financial backing of the British Academy, which facilitated an initial research trip to Finland in September 2004.

1. A small group of hard-line Communists, who refused to support the VAS project, continue in existence to this day under the banner of the SKP. They are, however, electorally insignificant, polling less than 1 per cent in national elections.
2. Hynönen was general secretary of the construction industry trade union, a key component of the SAK confederation, as well as a member of the VAS Party Board.

3. Interview with Pekka Hynönen, September 2004.
4. Interview with then VAS leader and MP Suvi-Anne Siimes, September 2004.
5. Siimes interview.
6. Interview with VAS MP Minna Sirnö, September 2004.
7. Interviews with Paavo Arhinmäki, September 2004 and June 2009. Arhinmäki, a former VAS Youth League leader, was runner-up in the leadership elections of 2006 and became MP for the Helsinki constituency in 2007. A radical 'red green', he led opposition both to old 'Stalinists' and to those like Siimes who would compromise on issues such as NATO membership. Following the disastrous result in the European elections of June 2009, he became party leader.
8. Sirnö and Arhinmäki interviews.
9. Interview with VAS MP Mikko Kuoppa, June 2009.
10. Interview with Jarmo Lindén, September 2004, and interview with Paavo Arhinmäki, June 2009.
11. Interview with VAS general secretary Turo Bergman, June 2009.
12. Admittedly, this can be confusing as the entire party claims to be 'red/green' and 'new left'!
13. Interview with VAS MP Merja Sinikka Kyllönen, June 2009.
14. The colourful phrase was used by Jarmo Lindén, 2005: p. 4.
15. Letter from Paavo Arhinmäki to the present author, 8 September 2006.
16. VAS (2007), 'The Left Road to a Just World: the Left Alliance Party Programme', Helsinki, from which subsequent quotations in this section are taken.
17. Bergman interview.
18. All information from the official Finnish parliament website, http://web.eduskunta.fi/ (accessed 23 April 2009).
19. Arhinmäki interview, 2004.
20. http://www.hs.fi/english/article/MP+Paavo+Arhinm%C3%A4ki+wants+greener+shade+of +red+for+Left+Alliance/1135246800318 (accessed 8 July 2009).
21. Paavo Arhinmäki (2007), 'Address to Informal Conference of Left Parties', Oss, the Netherlands, 14 July.

6
The Spanish United Left – The Belated and Troublesome Transition from Policy- to Office-seeking

Tània Verge

Introduction

For many years the Spanish United Left/*Izquierda Unida* (IU) had a low share of parliamentary seats and a radical left-wing profile, and subsequently no governing potential. In the late 1990s, however, the party moved from its traditional role as an opposition party to one with real ambitions for government. The IU managed to establish itself as a governing partner at the regional level from 1999 and it acted as support party at the national level from 2004 to 2008 – and this despite its lack of experience in government, a non-pivotal and non-central ideological position in the party system, and being riddled with factionalism (Ştefuriuc and Verge, 2008). This subsequently represented a big step for a party whose radical programmes and fierce confrontation with the main Social Democratic party (the PSOE) had previously rendered it non-coalitionable. This chapter analyses the strategic choices made by the party in the period 1999–2008 which led it to seize the various opportunities it had to influence national and regional politics and shape policy outcomes. This chapter also reflects on the paucity of change, examining both how the party's organisational structure and dynamics have affected IU's turn towards more office-seeking considerations and the impact that this new strategy has had on the very same party organisation.

History and background of the IU

In 1986 the Communist Party of Spain/*Partido Comunista de España* (PCE) began working with other minor left-wing parties to ultimately form the United Left/*Izquierda Unida* (IU). This was quite patently a means to counteract the electoral crisis of communism by launching a 'red–green project'. The PCE's vote share dropped from 9.3 per cent in the first democratic elections to 4 per cent in 1982 (see Table 6.1). The PSOE's landslide that year left the PCE in a marginal position. Although plans were initially made to dissolve the founding parties of the coalition into the new organisation, the PCE maintained a prominent role that granted the preservation of a clear Communist identity. By the mid-2000s the PCE was the only party to remain in the IU, the rest having gradually abandoned it. Simultaneously, the number of non-communist party members sharply increased. While in 1992 PCE affiliates accounted for 78 per cent of the IU membership, in 2004 the proportion had dropped to 38 per cent. Nonetheless, the PCE is still a very important actor within the IU, and many of its activists remain IU cadres (Ramiro-Fernández, 2004).

The IU experienced a significant gain in votes from the mid-1980s to the mid-1990s, reaching its peak in 1996 (10.5 per cent of the national vote). Since then it has suffered a steady electoral decline, albeit maintaining itself as the third most popular national party. A majoritarian twist in the electoral law works to the IU's disadvantage when transforming votes into seats (Spain uses the d'Hondt method of proportional representation, with medium-sized provincial districts averaging 6.7 seats). Minority parties whose support is spread thinly throughout the country are systematically discriminated against (Montero, 1999: p. 73). It takes about two-and-a-half times as many votes to elect an IU deputy as one from a regionalist party whose votes are concentrated in

Table 6.1 The PCE's and IU's electoral results in legislative and regional elections

	PCE					IU				
Legislative	1977	1979	1982	1986	1989	1993	1996	2000	2004	2008
Seats	19	23	4	7	17	18	21	8	5[b]	2[b]
Votes (%)	9.3	10.8	4.0	4.6	9.1	9.5	10.5	5.4	4.9	3.8
Regional			1980–2[a]	1983	1987	1991	1995	1999	2003	2007
Seats			35	52	46	74	97	36	48	47
Votes (%)			10.9	7.6	6.7	9.4	10.8	5.2	5.9	6.1

[a] Includes results for the Basque Country (1980), Catalonia (1980), Galicia (1981) and Andalusia (1982).
[b] In 2004 two out of the five MPs and in 2008 one of the two MPs belonged to the ICV.
Source: Electoral results archive, Spanish Ministry of Interior.

a few districts. Therefore, the IU has had very little governing potential at the national level.

At the regional level the IU had several opportunities to form governing coalitions with the Socialists in the 1980s and 1990s. However, none of these opportunities was seized upon, as the IU's strategy during that period was based on maintaining a differentiated radical-left profile. On a scale ranging from 1 'extreme left' to 10 'extreme right', the party obtained an average location of 2.3 in public opinion surveys. Despite the fact that the average distance between the IU and the PSOE was not that wide (about 1.9 points), the IU always projected itself in opposition to the PSOE, rather than as its potential partner (Verge, 2007: p. 88). This strategy was pursued as a means to increase its vote share and eventually even overtake the PSOE as the largest party on the left. No trade-offs were envisaged between vote-seeking and policy-seeking goals (Ramiro-Fernández, 2004: p. 20). Indeed, the party's electoral performance in the late 1990s was better than ever, which reinforced the leaders' conviction that the correct strategy had indeed been chosen and the best party goals had been set. Regional federations and minority factions who failed to obey the leadership line of no formal co-operation with the PSOE were severely punished. Sanctions included the expulsion of undisciplined leaders, the dissolution of regional directorate boards, and even the rupture of relationships with the IU's sister party in Catalonia (Paniagua and Ramiro-Fernández, 2003).[1] The existence of several coalition governments at the local level between the PSOE and the IU were exceptions in a general context of sustained confrontation.

However, in the period 1986–2000, the IU did on occasion demonstrate a willingness to work with the PSOE. After the 1987 regional elections, the IU supported the PSOE government in Madrid and Asturias in exchange for concessions on certain policies, although the party stayed in opposition in both regional parliaments. Since 1990 the IU has made sporadic calls to reach agreements with the PSOE if common policy platforms could be found. In 1993, the IU leader Julio Anguita offered legislative support to the first minority Socialist government, but the PSOE preferred to work with the main Catalan regional party (Convergence and Union/*Convergència i Unió*, CiU). In 1997 Anguita proposed increased dialogue with the Socialists, and Joaquín Almunia, Felipe Gonzalez's successor as PSOE's secretary-general, publicly invited the IU to develop a common strategy against the conservative government even though the strong personal incompatibility between the IU's secretary-general and his Socialist counterparts seriously affected the possibility of actually reaching agreements. Within the IU, the attempt at rapprochement was used simply to avoid being accused of sectarianism (Ramiro-Fernández, 2005: p. 303).

Within the PSOE, some influential leaders also disliked this possibility (Chari, 2005). It should also be noted that the Spanish social democrats have traditionally been exceptionally wary of working with their far-left competitors, only choosing to break this convention in very recent times (Hough and Verge, 2009: p. 42). Furthermore, on those occasions in which the PSOE did not have the majority of votes (1993–6, 2004–8, 2008 onwards) the party has considered almost all parties in forming a coalition government or reaching a formal agreement on a comprehensive legislative programme. On top of this, the Spanish constructive motion of no confidence provides the governing party with a degree of insulation and the option of pursuing a strategy of shifting alliances with various parties (Field, 2006: p. 218).

The IU's position towards its main rival was revised only once the disastrous results in the local, regional and European elections of 1999 threatened the party's very survival. One year later, as the polls predicted severe losses for both the IU and the PSOE in the 2000 legislative elections, the two parties signed for the first time an electoral agreement, which IU voters seemed to demand (Ramiro-Fernández, 2004: p. 21). Leadership change in both parties was crucial in crafting this pact.[2] It included a short list of common policies, a commitment to form a coalition government if the Socialists won the election without securing an overall majority and a specific pact for the Senate elections (García Escribano, 2002). However, both parties campaigned separately, and electoral messages were not co-ordinated. The co-operative strategy did not stop IU's electoral decline, which eventually brought change within the party's dominant coalition.

Ideological and programmatic consistency

Programmatic and ideological changes were the primary motive behind the IU leadership moving to make the party more coalitionable. The severe electoral defeat in the 2000 legislative elections, when the IU saw its vote share halved and its representation reduced to eight MPs, led to major change within the dominant coalition. The new leadership sought to de-radicalise the traditional communist discourse by relaunching the organisation as a post-communist, eco-socialist party with an emphasis on new left values and on 'politically solvent and socially reliable' policies as a means to recover votes and to expand the party's electoral niche (interview with a member of the party's Federal Executive Presidency, 26/11/2004. See also IU, 2003: p. 34).

Simultaneously, a more pragmatic position towards the PSOE and, more generally, towards taking office was introduced. However, the shift from the party's long-term status as an opposition party to one that wanted to govern was not a peaceful one and it had significant organisational consequences, namely an increase in factional activity and the loosening of vertical integration within the party. The most orthodox wing of the PCE, which actually had control of the PCE's directorate but remained a minority faction (albeit a powerful one) within the IU's dominant coalition, orchestrated an aggressive opposition towards the new eco-socialist discourse and towards the party-of-government role that IU's dominant faction had adopted.

Divided party dominant coalitions can be seen as coalitions of factions. In this case, the party's 'dominant faction' is the coalition component that usually manages to impose its ideological or organisational preferences (Harmel and Tan, 2003). At a party conference in 2000, the two contending candidates belonged to the core PCE and IU leadership groups: Gaspar Llamazares, the leader of the IU and PCE regional federation of Asturias, and Francisco Frutos, PCE's secretary-general. Llamazares won the internal ballot with only one more vote than his rival, and was thus forced to integrate members of the losing faction into the party directorate. This election interrupted a long-established tradition by which PCE's secretary-general was the IU leader as well. Since then, the PCE leadership has been acting as an opposition or critical faction within the IU's dominant coalition. In the 2003 and 2004 party conferences Llamazares was re-elected, again defeating the PCE base, which increased the level of opposition against the dominant faction.

The IU's new dominant coalition tried to reshape electoral and coalition strategies, as those implemented during the 1990s were perceived to have damaged the party's electoral chances. The attempt to build a new image as a 'coalitionable' partner was most visible at the subnational level, where its vote share had also dramatically decreased from 10.8 per cent in 1995 to 6.1 per cent in 2007 (see Table 6.1). Since 1999, the IU has participated in four regional governments, and not only alongside its natural partner, the PSOE (in Asturias), but also alongside regionalist and nationalist parties (in the Balearic Islands, the Basque Country and Catalonia) – and this despite its non-pivotal position in any of the four regional parliaments, except for the Asturian one (Ştefuriuc and Verge, 2008: p. 160). It also reached a pact with the

PSOE in a fifth region (Madrid), but the PSOE's factionalism in this Autonomous Community hindered the coalition: two of its deputies defected at the investiture vote, claiming that too many concessions had been made to the left party (Hough and Verge, 2009: p. 49).

Later on, in March 2004, after having experienced more electoral decline, when the PSOE won the legislative elections and went back in a minority government, the IU accepted the 'preferential partnership' the PSOE offered it: the IU's five MPs would support the government's investiture, its most important legislative initiatives and the annual budget in exchange for influence on policymaking (interview with member of IU's and PCE's executive boards, 5 November 2004). The new IU leadership had two main goals: pursuing office as a means to implementing policy at the regional level and offering external parliamentary support for the PSOE-led national government in exchange for policy concessions.

As leadership change was only partial, the dominant faction did not exert complete dominance over the rest of the party. As we know from previous research, leadership change is not always a sufficient condition for party change. If the party suffers from factionalism or there is no internal cohesion within the dominant coalition itself, party change may indeed be inhibited (Appleton and Ward, 1997: p. 348). As Harmel and Tan have put it, 'the ability of a newly dominant faction to fully direct the party rests on whether the change in conformation has resulted in complete rather than just partial turnover of dominant coalition and also on whether the party's effective leaders are fully committed to the objectives of the newly dominant coalition' (2003: p. 411).

The new eco-socialist ideological orientations were seen by the minority faction as a threat to the organisation's core ideological identity and a betrayal of the party's communist past (Verge, 2007: 347). According to this critical faction, this shift constituted a threat to the organisation's very soul. Eco-socialism was regarded as the substitution of anti-capitalist stances with quasi-social democratic values. Green parties' moderate policies are considered to privilege 'being a party of government' over being 'a party of struggle and social mobilisation' (interview with a member of IU's and PCE's executive board, 25 November 2004). Resistance to moderation was subsequently defended even though the IU's electorate was, and is, less radical than the party (see Table 6.2).

Beyond ideological stances, alliances with other political forces, and particularly with the PSOE, engendered acute confrontation between the dominant and critical factions. For Llamazares and his supporters, agreeing to a preferential partnership with the national government was a strategy that aimed to force the PSOE to deliver left-wing

Table 6.2 Ideological placement of the IU and the Spanish electorate (scale 1–10)

	1986	1989	1993	1996	2000	2004	2008
IU placement	2.1	2.3	2.4	2.5	2.5	2.4	2.4
Spanish electorate	4.4	4.6	4.7	4.7	4.9	4.6	4.6

Source: Electoral public opinion surveys carried out by the Centro de Investigaciones Sociológicas (CIS) in the period 1986–2008.

policies and at effectively bringing government decisions nearer to IU's policy preferences (Izquierda Unida, 2004). For the dominant faction, a strategy of radical confrontation would only consolidate the transfer of votes experienced in 2004, when about 300,000 former IU voters strategically opted for the PSOE to oust the conservatives from power (Chari, 2005: p. 208). But the opposition faction blamed this strategy for being responsible for blurring the IU's identity, as support for the PSOE has not entailed any specific programmatic agreement (Report to the PCE's Federal Committee, 18 June 2006). Furthermore, the latter saw collaboration as detrimental to the party's chances at the next election. The support party role was regarded as delivering the worst of all worlds, namely 'responsibility without real power' (Bale and Dunphy, 2006: p. 12). This very same reasoning applied to the electoral pacts and government coalitions reached at the regional level.

The IU's MPs in the national lower house endorsed Llamazares's strategy, so support for the PSOE remained stable during the legislative period. In terms of the regional level, the multilayered nature of the Spanish political system became an advantageous factor for the dominant coalition. In multi-level contexts, as Ştefuriuc and Verge (2008: p. 163) argue, dominant factions ridden by deep ideological divisions are actually aided by a further division – the territorial one. The party's dominant coalition turned the party's regional platforms to its advantage and used the party's own organisational meso-level to circumvent ideological factionalism at the centre and promote its own agenda.

The IU's regional federations are also formed by the regional branches of the PCE and other left-wing forces. While the opposition faction was strong at the national level or the centre, it gradually lost the support of party members in several regions. The dominant faction used this decline to implement party change at the regional level, especially in the regions where the IU had some coalition potential. In those regions, the IU adopted an eco-socialist discourse and put emphasis on the party's regional face as an electoral asset (see Ştefuriuc and Verge, 2008: p. 164 for more details on this). At the same time, being in government was framed as helping the party present itself to left-wing voters as a useful and reliable option when compared with the PSOE.

So what has the IU been able to achieve in regional government in terms of policy? The office-seeking behaviour was justified as a means to bring policymaking under the party's direct authority in those areas which are key to defining and developing its profile as a left-wing governing party different from the PSOE, such as basic income, housing, social services, environment or labour. Overall, in terms of both particular ministries and/or policy outcomes the party could claim to have sufficiently placated its electorate (see Hough and Verge, 2009, for more details).

At the national level, however, the possibility of forming a coalition government was never on the table. As has been said, Spain has no tradition of coalition governments at the national level. On top of this, some Socialist activists and cadres are still very suspicious of the IU, and any sort of coalition with it would have caused serious internal strife within the PSOE. Therefore, the IU had to choose between becoming a support party and being cornered in opposition. The conditional support for the Socialist minority government endured from 2004 to 2008. Nonetheless, the IU was only one of the supporting parties and, short of its support, the PSOE could rely on the votes of other parliamentary parties. The IU's bargaining power was thus limited. Some policy gains were made in return for supporting the government but, unfortunately for the IU, they were not particularly visible. Because in many policy areas the PSOE's and the IU's electoral manifestos happened to be very similar (social policies such as support for increased elderly welfare programmes, gay marriage, reform of the divorce law, equality law, withdrawal of Spanish troops from Iraq, etc.), the government did not play fair by giving proper credit to its 'preferential partner'. Asymmetric access to the public media was also crucial in the lack of visibility of the IU's role in the approval of these policies (interview with IU advisor to the parliamentary group, 28 April 2009). Support for the government lessened the party's maximalist positions on various issues such as the temporary contract agencies or the national security law.

In addition, the PSOE could assume that the IU was a 'captive party' unwilling to jeopardise the stability of the government. And, indeed, the IU's support was also justified to its membership in terms of preventing the conservative Popular Party (PP) from benefiting from government instability. Furthermore, the government occasionally threatened to go to nationalist parties in order to pass legislation.

On the benefits side, the PSOE helped the IU overcome the restrictive conditions imposed on minor parties by lower house rules to form their own parliamentary group. Moreover, the PSOE agreed to set up a parliamentary commission to study the reform of the electoral law, which harms minor parties with a countrywide-spread support. However, this commission did not see the light of day during the legislative period, only being created in October 2008. Finally, although the party wanted to negotiate some second-tier positions in the government, in particular, for a couple of IU incumbent MPs who had not been re-elected in 2004, the PSOE refused to give away any offices to its so-called preferential partner.

Issues and policies of the IU

Attitudes to European integration

For Spaniards, Europe has meant above all progress towards democratisation and economic growth (Morata, 1997). This view has been widely shared by all political parties, including the IU and its predecessor. The PCE shared the strategic conviction that democracy could be best protected by being anchored in the European Communities, in tune with the party's alignment with Eurocommunism and the declared autonomy from the USSR. Nevertheless, rooted in its support were demands for democratisation of the European institutions and for the strengthening of the powers of the European Parliament, which still remain a priority (Dunphy, 2004).

Until the Maastricht Treaty, Spanish European politics was based on a nationwide consensus rather than on partisan preferences (Closa, 2001: p. 10). This consensus weakened in the 1990s when the IU mounted an effective criticism of the Economic and Monetary Union project based on the alleged monetarist nature of the Maastricht Treaty, and its potential negative impact on unemployment and social security spending. To some extent, opposition to the Maastricht Treaty was also a tactical strategy to distinguish itself from the PSOE (Benedetto and Quaglia, 2007: p. 492). This strategy was not wholeheartedly supported by the rank and file or indeed by the entire leadership. Indeed, eight of its MPs voted in favour of ratification. Five years later, the IU voted in favour of the Amsterdam Treaty. As Dunphy (2004) notes, the party stressed its support for European federalism but expressed its desire for an alternative Europe, which was economically and socially cohesive, along with a deeper and more rapid progress towards a federal political union, including a constitution with a strong concept of EU citizenship.

In terms of the most recent developments within the EU, the IU opposed many of the key issues raised in the negotiations leading up to the signing of the European Constitutional Treaty. In particular, the party rejected any reference to Christianity, and was in favour of giving the human rights charter the highest juridical relevance by including it in the main body of the text. The IU was critical of what it perceived to be the insufficient democratisation of the institutions that the draft introduced, although it welcomed the simplification of the institutional structure and the strengthening of the European Parliament. The IU also rejected the process by which the constitutional treaty came into being in the first place, pointing out the contradiction of a constitution that was born not out of popular sovereignty but from the state's will. In a nutshell, the Constitutional Treaty was, according to the IU, too conservative, neoliberal, anti-democratic, anti-social and militaristic. The IU believed that it did not protect social and labour rights, or include adequate protection of the environment. It also, according to the IU, meant that European foreign relationships would be subordinated to NATO, as the prospective constitution established a common defensive force not explicitly bounded by UN decisions and urged the EU to increase its military capacity (Verge, 2010).

The Spanish government submitted the draft of the constitution to a referendum on 20 February 2005. The IU was among the 'No' supporters that gathered under the banner of 'more Europe', 'a different Europe' or 'a better Europe' (Torreblanca, 2005). Eventually, the number of positive votes was vast, 76.7 per cent. Practically one-third of the IU followers who turned up at the polling station voted in the opposite way from what the party indicated – only 23.7 voted against the proposed European Constitution (Eurobarometer, 2005: p. 16).

The changes factored into the Reform Treaty that was adopted to overcome the French and Dutch opposition to the original document were not enough for the IU to change its basic position. In tune with European United Left – Nordic Green Left (GUE/NGL) negative vote in the European Parliament, the IU voted against the Lisbon Treaty in the lower house and urged the government to call a new referendum for its ratification. The IU's position is to resume talks on where the EU goes from here through a truly constituent process based at the European Parliament after the 2009 European elections (IU, 2008a). The IU's firm opposition to the Lisbon Treaty is based, on the one hand, on the new democratic deficit of the reform process, which has excluded both national parliaments and the European Parliament as talks have been held behind closed doors. On the other hand, its opposition, as it was for the draft constitutional treaty, is based on federalist maximalism on account of the constitution being insufficiently radical (see IU, 2008b).

Perceptions of globalisation and relationships and attachments to the anti-globalisation movement

The IU defines itself as an anti-capitalist, transformative party and has frequently used the motto of the anti-globalisation movement – 'another world is possible.' The criticisms that the party mounted of the 'neoliberal' character of the European integration process since the Maastricht Treaty have already been noted. The IU has been particularly active against some recent EU policies such as the 'Bolkestein Directive' on the liberalisation of services and the initiative to allow a 65-hour working week, which was defeated at the European Parliament – the IU remains active in defending the 35-hour working week. It also supports initiatives such as the 'Tobin tax' and advocates public control of the banking system; more specifically, it argues that the European Parliament and not the European Central Bank should decide the monetary policies of the EU. The party is also against the increasing restrictions on immigration and against the idea of 'fortress Europe'.

On the other hand, it has also been an active member of the 'Citizens Network for the Abolition of External Debt', aimed at cancelling the debt poor countries have to pay back to the richest nations, and the 'Platform for the 0.7', which urges national governments to devote this amount of the GDP to Third World aid. Its anti-militaristic character is also emphasised by opposition to NATO. The party advocates its dissolution as well as rejecting any European military structure. At the individual level, many IU members participate in, and often lead, different organisations that form the anti-globalisation movement (be it feminist, pacifist, environmental, social forums, NGOs etc.) in Spain. At the party level, the Secretariat for Social Movements has aimed to establish contact with an array of social organisations linked to the anti-globalisation movement. In addition, the IU sends a party delegation to all social forums, at the local, national, European and global levels. The PCE and other internal currents of opinion/structured factions also send their own delegations.

In the last period of severe factional disputes, the party admitted having had a fragmented presence, with no political direction or strategy, which impeded its attempts to bridge demands of the social movements and public institutions. Furthermore, internal disputes were often brought into the anti-globalisation movement, trying to instrumentalise its support in favour of one of the competing factions (interview with the IU's former secretary for social movements, 3 November 2004; see also IU, party conference resolutions, 2003: p. 21).

Links to the centre-left and to other left parties in Spain

The IU was formed as an organisation that aimed to create a political space to the left of the PSOE into which all left-wing parties (communist, democratic socialist and new left parties) and political and social groupings could integrate. Six minor left-wing parties (none of which had ever obtained representation at the national or the regional level), along with the PCE, joined the coalition in 1986. The collaboration among these parties has its origins in the civic platform that rallied for the 'no' vote in the referendum on Spain's membership of NATO. The referendum yielded a narrow victory for the 'yes' campaign, and over seven million voters cast a 'no' vote, which the various groups within the coalition sought to translate into votes in the then forthcoming legislative elections of 1986. Nonetheless, unity of action among the founding members was short-lived, and as they all gradually abandoned it the coalition failed to serve as an attractive common house or *uolivo* for the Spanish non-social democratic left.

The IU has also intermittently sought to form coalitions with green parties. At the national level, this strategy has been unsuccessful. The Spanish party system does not have an electorally relevant green party and there is a high degree of fragmentation between the various green representatives. Besides the fact that green parties might be ideologically closer to the IU than to the PSOE, green parties have sometimes, such as in the 2004 legislative and European elections, formed an alliance with the PSOE, as the latter offered some winning positions for Green candidates in its electoral ticket. Certain regional party branches have managed to form more stable coalitions with the green regional parties, though, nowadays, only a few of them survive.

The behaviour of the centre-left has undoubtedly affected the left party's strategic choices. In the first two democratic elections the PCE did not receive any pay-off for its active role in the underground during the Francoist regime, whereas the PSOE gathered the support of the vast majority of the left-wing electorate. The PSOE's landslide victory in 1982 cornered the PCE in a very marginal opposition role, both within Spain's representative institutions and also across society at large, on account of the social demobilisation imposed by the democratising political elites since the late 1970s, with the resigned support of the PCE, in order to prevent a military intervention (Sastre García, 1997).

By then, a one-sided relationship with the PSOE was already taking shape, wherein the IU's position was always dependent on that of the PSOE. The strategy of totally opposing the PSOE proved moderately successful in electoral terms for about a decade, and the party managed to attract an increasing amount of centre-left voters who were dissatisfied with the government's unpopular policies, such as the industrial restructuring process or tight fiscal policy, as well as with the corruption scandals affecting Socialist public officers during the 1990s.

There has also been an exchange of activists, members and voters between the two parties. Whereas, in the first years after the transition to democracy, some former PCE activists integrated into the PSOE, as the latter was in need of valuable cadres when it assumed office in 1982, some PSOE members and activists joined the IU between the mid-1980s and the mid-1990s because of dissatisfaction with the PSOE's evolution (for example, some left-wingers within the Socialists founded the Party of Socialist Action/*Partido de Acción Socialista*, PASOC, which integrated into the IU). In 1992, a group of former IU national executive members who were more moderate and enthusiastic in their willingness to collaborate with the PSOE sowed the seeds of what was eventually to become a new party in 1996 (New Left Democratic Party/*Partido Democrático de la Nueva Izquierda*). A year later its members were expelled from the IU. This party ended up integrating into the PSOE, and its most visible leaders occupied relevant positions in Socialist (national and regional) governments (Paniagua and Ramiro-Fernández, 2003).

By the mid-1990s, the electorate in general was shifting from the left to the centre-right, but the IU's leadership failed to acknowledge this. In order to weaken the Socialist government, the IU frequently worked with the centre-right Popular Party, a strategy not enthusiastically applauded by either IU members or voters. Once the PSOE became an opposition party the IU not only found it increasingly difficult to attract Socialist voters, but also started suffering a significant decrease in its own vote shares. As Lago (2009) argues, the interaction between low district magnitudes and a fragmented left provides a very appropriate setting for strategic voting. As the races between the PP and the PSOE became more competitive, IU supporters, encouraged by the PSOE's strategic-voting appeals, gradually defected from their party and voted for the Socialists to avoid a right-wing government. For the PSOE, attracting voters from the IU has always been a secondary concern, but the IU was very dependent on former Socialist voters until 1996, when the importance of former PSOE voters in the IU's electorate diminished sharply (Ramiro-Fernández, 2004: p. 15). On the other hand, in the

2008 national election, only 16 per cent of individuals ideologically closer to the IU than to the PSOE voted for the IU. Indeed, 21 per cent of individuals who voted for the IU in 2004 defected to the PSOE in 2008 (Centro de Investigaciones Sociológicas, January and March 2008). So, the IU was not really able to benefit from its collaborative strategy. However, it is also unclear whether an opposition strategy would have prevented, or encouraged to a greater extent, strategic voting by IU voters.

Future electoral and political outlook

For the first time in the IU's history the opposition faction within the party (led by the PCE) forced the election of the candidate for the 2008 general election through a membership ballot. They did this in order to gain control of the party in public office in the national lower house. IU leader, Gaspar Llamazares, accepted the challenge and asserted that the winner would obtain the legitimacy to relaunch the IU in his own way. He thus tried to placate what was a sustained internal opposition. As he put it: 'in this ballot members will evaluate our task in parliament, our constructive opposition to the PSOE government as well as the appropriate political identity the party should adopt' (Gaspar Llamazares, *El País*, 3 December 2007). Llamazares obtained 62.5 per cent of the members' vote, demonstrating that the opposition faction was weaker amongst the rank and file than within the party's dominant coalition. He continued to push for his programme of party change and stuck to the collaborative strategy, even calling for a coalition government with the PSOE if the latter found itself again in a minority position.

In the last general election of March 2008 the PSOE failed to win the majority of seats but the IU suffered a catastrophic electoral result: its vote share (aggregated with that of its coalition partner, the Catalan party Initiative for Catalonia Greens/*Inicitiva per Catalunya Verds*, ICV) slumped to 3.8 per cent. The extreme concentration of the vote into the two main national parties (the PSOE and the PP), which between them gathered 84 per cent of the national vote share and 92 per cent of the seats, negatively affected all minor parties. Although the IU obtained almost a million votes, the majoritarian underpinnings of the Spanish electoral system left the party with only two MPs (and one of them belonged to the ICV). The IU's single seat was won by Gaspar Llamazares, in the district of Madrid. In addition, the IU's safe seat in the district of Valencia was lost because the regional branch split, dividing voters' loyalty among two different party lists.

For the first time in its history, the IU failed to form its own parliamentary group and had to unite with the Catalan left-wing nationalist party Republican Left of Catalonia/*Esquerra Republicana de Catalunya* to meet the criteria established to form a parliamentary group. Decreased representation not only makes the present parliamentary situation more difficult but also constrains future options. Public subsidies to political parties allocated according to the number of votes and seats obtained will be sharply reduced and the visibility of the party in the parliamentary debates will also decrease. These are acute problems for an organisation that is highly indebted on account of a continuous drop in voter support, and cannot count on the sympathy or attention of the national mass media.

Llamazares subsequently resigned from his position and a conference was called to decide on the party's future. By then the more ideologically radical sectors of the party had split and founded their own movements or parties. The so-called Red Current/*Corriente Roja* had already abandoned the party by 2004. On the eve of the November 2008 conference, the faction Alternative Space/*Espacio Alternativo* founded a new party, Anticapitalist Left/*Izquierda Anticapitalista*, which integrated into the European Anticapitalist Left – a conglomerate of communist parties with slightly different outlooks. Yet, open factionalism was well reflected at the party conference.

Five groups put up a candidate for the leadership position and for seats in the national executive committee. The one that best represented the PCE's most critical faction obtained 43 per cent of the delegates' votes, and the one that supported the former party leader 27 per cent. As neither of the two managed to obtain sufficient support from the other three minority candidatures, the conference finished without having elected a new leader. A temporary commission was established in which the five candidates were proportionally represented according to the delegates' votes that they had obtained. It took a month to reach the decision, and it was finally the opposition faction led by the PCE that managed to see its candidate, Cayo Lara, come out on top. Nonetheless, representatives of all five groups got seats on the national executive board, which means that currently the dominant coalition remains very heterogeneous.

The new leader urged the party to distance itself from the PSOE and stepped up a radicalisation of rhetoric seen, for example, in the call for a general strike. This was immediately quashed by the two main trade unions, including the union that used to be closer to the party, the Joint Commissions/*Comisiones Obreras*. In order to put the party at the 'vanguard of left-wing politics' in Spain, Cayo Lara advocated focusing on traditional left anti-capitalist policies, which mainly target workers. In his first meeting as IU's party leader with the Socialist Prime Minister José Luis Rodríguez Zapatero, he refused to offer general parliamentary support to the government. Conversely, support was to be conditional on the approval by the government of social and economic measures addressed at fighting the economic crisis, and especially at helping workers cope with the difficult economic situation ('Cayo Lara niega a Zapatero un apoyo global', *El País*, 20 April 2009).

At the conference all factions unanimously agreed to establish the goal of 'refounding' the IU. The party admits that change is needed as the current political trajectory has come to a natural end. The document approved by the delegates defines the goal to once again 'make credible and necessary a political offer of an anti-capitalist, alternative, and transformative left [...] with proposals that are useful for social transformation and for the improvement of the living conditions of the popular classes from a socialist perspective [...], and bringing politics back to the work place' (IU, 2008c).

This goal is reflected in the party structure. One of the leadership positions of the national executive board will be specifically in charge of the refoundation of the party, and it will monitor the creation of a constituent assembly by mid-2010. In the meantime it will co-ordinate the efforts of the different regional party branches and programmatic committees aimed at elaborating the strategic lines within this constituent process. The party also aims to become more of a 'political and social movement' than a traditional party. All 'political groupings, trade unions, and civil society organisations and movements that oppose neo-liberalism and imperialism' are also invited to put forward their inputs for the renewed project (IU, 2009).

However, the PCE is still clearly predominant, and its structure and organisational procedures mirror those of a traditional hierarchical party, which might well undermine this aim. And we must not forget that the party is still strongly divided. Hence, ending aggressive factionalism and resuming confidence among previously confrontational groups is a necessary, but maybe an insufficient, condition. The updating of the membership registry, which is due in 2009, might also show that IU's social roots are even weaker than suspected, as there has been a gradual defection of members in the past ten years.[3] Furthermore, defection among some high-profile leaders who belonged to the former dominant faction has already started.[4]

The various experiences in office (as a coalition partner at the regional level or as a support party at the national level) were preceded by a de-radicalisation of the party stances and a radical change of strategy towards the PSOE. Nonetheless, these changes were not unanimously supported by the whole organisation, and factionalism has been very acute during the whole transition process from an opposition to a governing party. The party-of-government role has not yielded all the results the former dominant coalition expected, which might well have placated internal opposition. The IU is now seen by an array of different political parties as a reliable coalition partner, but electoral pay-offs have been largely absent and the IU has kept on losing votes and seats. However, one should acknowledge that factionalism has also severely limited the IU's prospects, if not seriously damaged its electoral results, as voters tend to punish divided parties.

In the last decade it seems that the political space to the left of the social democrats has dramatically shrunk. The cumulative effects of an electoral system that leans towards majoritarianism and an increasing polarisation between the two largest national parties has reduced the number of districts in national elections in which the IU obtains representation. At the regional level, the IU is currently present in only 11 out of the 17 regional parliaments (in three of them the party has only one representative).

Strategic voting by the IU's potential voters seems to have become consolidated in the Spanish electorate irrespective of the party's performance and strategies, and unless there happens to be a negative perception of the Socialists the IU will find it very difficult to improve its electoral records. It is too soon to evaluate what kind of results the 'refoundation' process might produce, but certainly the severity of the situation requires immediate action. It is also not yet clear whether the internal reflective process that has just started will bring about significant change or whether it will end up in another dead end. Furthermore, a radicalisation of discourse might not find particularly strong support in the Spanish electorate, which places itself in more moderate ideological positions. Simultaneously, this potential radicalisation may harm the IU's opportunities to enter coalition governments at the regional level, the only level in which office-seeking goals can materialise in the near future. Finally, party strategy will be very much dependent on the electoral results the IU obtains in the forthcoming regional and local elections (Spring 2011), as this constitutes a test for the 2012 legislative elections. If results are again disappointing, the party will find itself at a very critical juncture and the factional struggle might well come to the surface one more time.

Notes

1. IU and the eco-socialist Catalan party Initiative for Catalonia Greens/ *Iniciativa per Catalunya Verds* (ICV) were sister parties, including looser organisational linkages, from 1987 until the rupture in 1997. These parties inherited the relationship between the PCE and the Catalan communist party (the PSUC), which had also led a coalition with other minor left-wing parties in the Catalan party system. Relationships between the IU and the ICV were re-established in 2002 in the form of a coalition for all types of elections.
2. Julio Anguita was hospitalised a few months before the electoral campaign and was replaced by Francisco Frutos. Felipe González resigned as PSOE's secretary-general in 1997 and was substituted by Joaquín Almunia.
3. IU membership is currently 68,000 (Verge, 2007: p. 113). In the membership ballot held before the 2008 national election only 21,900 members cast a vote (37.4 per cent). For such a tight and polarised contest the percentage is very poor, which may indicate that membership is actually much lower.
4. That is the case with Rosa Aguilar, the Mayor of the city of Córdoba since 1999, who has accepted to be a regional ministry in the Andalusian government led by the PSOE. Córdoba is the only provincial capital (out of 54) governed by the IU.

7
Close to, but Still Out of, Government: The Swedish Vänsterpartiet

Michael Koß

Introduction

Sweden can be seen as a testing ground for a new form of coalition government called 'contract parliamentarism'. Tim Bale and Torbjörn Bergman (2006a: p. 422) define contract parliamentarism as follows: 'in contract parliamentarism, what are formally minority governments (formed by either a single party or a coalition of parties) have relationships with their "support" parties that are so institutionalised that they come close to being majority governments.' Next to the Swedish Greens (*Miljöpartiet den Gröna*, MP), the Swedish Left Party (*Vänsterpartiet*, V) was the main support party of Social Democratic governments between 1998 and 2006. As we shall see in the following, the Left Party, after achieving an all-time electoral high of 12 per cent in 1998, suffered badly at the polls during this period and, indeed, afterwards. Even though Bale and Bergman (2006a, b) analysed contract parliamentarism closely, they paid scant attention to the Left Party. This chapter aims to fill this gap and addresses three major questions: first, why did V end up as a support party rather than a coalition partner? Second, which factors caused the collapse of the Left Party's electoral appeal after 1998? Third, how much did this collapse have to do with V's role as a support party? In order to answer these questions, this chapter proceeds as follows. After first discussing V's background as a Communist party, I provide an overview of the (institutional) context of the Swedish party system. Then I trace V's ideological development before, during and after its experience as a support party. The next section discusses the consequences of V's support party experience, while the final section provides a brief analysis of the party's future prospects. As we shall see, a combination of unfavourable institutional factors and unsolved strategic dilemmas weakened V's bargaining power vis-à-vis its support partner (the Social Democrats). More ominously, on account of the structural changes within the Swedish party system the future prospects of V joining a coalition government are anything but rosy.

The Communist legacy as a millstone restricting strategic flexibility: The Left Party's origins

The Left Party, originally called the 'Swedish Social Democratic Left Party' (*Sveriges Socialdemokratiska Vänsterpartiet*), began life as a breakaway party of the 'Social Democratic Workers Party' (*Socialdemokratiska Arbetarepartiet*, SAP) in 1917. In 1921, the party entered the Communist International and changed its name to the 'Swedish Communist Party' (*Sveriges Kommunistiska Partiet*, SKP). By the 1950s SKP began to distance itself from Moscow, with a final rupture in 1964 (Banholzer, 2001: p. 84). Even though SKP's initiatives to negotiate a common electoral platform with SAP began as early as 1966 (Berg, 1982), the party's ongoing relative closeness in ideological terms to Soviet Communism rendered SKP an unacceptable partner for the Social Democrats (Christensen, 1998: p. 59). However, after 1964, the party turned towards the 'New Left', stressing policies such as anti-militarism, solidarity with the Third World, and opposition to many of the developments in the Communist states of central and eastern Europe. Consequently, it was renamed the 'Left Party Communists' (*Vänsterpartiet Kommunisterna*, VPK) in 1967 and thereafter became one of the leading proponents of Eurocommunism. Despite a lack of any formal co-operation with the Social Democrats, the party continuously supported SAP governments from 1958 onwards (Sannerstedt and Sjölin, 1992: p. 102). VPK thus became a 'truly captive party', unwilling to jeopardise the stability of social democratic governments (cf. Bale and Bergman, 2006a: p. 439). Consequently, prior to 1990 SAP was never forced to make any significant policy concessions to VPK. However, things slowly began to change after the breakdown of Communism. After dropping the 'Communists' in its name, V entered new territory by bringing down a Social Democratic government for the first time in 1990 (SAP having linked its survival to an austerity package during Sweden's severest post-war recession). However, following a brief cabinet crisis Sweden's brand of negative parliamentarism (to be discussed in the next section) nevertheless enabled the government to carry on. The growing importance of V was nonetheless reflected by the fact that it has been represented since 1994 in the parliament's foreign affairs committee (where it received a seat formerly held by SAP (cf. Banholzer, 2001: p. 86)).

V's roots in the 'Old Left' are the reason for the permanent struggle between 'reformers' and 'traditionalists' that underlies its history (Christensen, 1998: p. 55). Even after 1990, traditionalists resisted the desire of reformist elements to broaden the party's appeal, remaining strong in the party executive (Arter, 2002: p. 10). Significantly, the ties with Communist parties in central and eastern Europe were frozen as late as the mid-1990s (Aylott, 2008: p. 189). Indeed, V's ongoing association with Communism remained an 'electoral millstone' (Arter, 2002: p. 19) of the party. On account of severe internal disputes, many believed that V would split before its 1993 party conference. According to most accounts, the most important reason why this did not happen was the personality of the successor of Lars Werner (who had led the party from 1975 to 1993) as party chair, Gudrun Schyman. Schyman, charismatic and popular for her openness about past alcohol problems and her feminist and anti-Communist views, was able, if not to unite, then at the very least to lead V in spite of the constant internal tensions. During the 1970s, Schyman was actively involved in the feminist, environmental and anti-nuclear protest movements. In 1996, she managed to gain a party conference's approval for describing V as a feminist and ecologist party (Süssner, 2006: p. 193). As well as broadening the Left Party's ideological profile (to be discussed in more detail in the third section), Schyman also tried to tie V more closely to the governing SAP.

Given that many spectators had predicted that V would die a rapid death, the 6.2 per cent it polled in the 1994 election was a remarkable success, giving the party the opportunity to begin to co-operate more closely with the Social Democrats. This co-operation was, to be sure, not an institutionalised one, despite Schyman looking for an arrangement with the government covering the entire parliamentary term (Arter, 2002: pp. 11–12). Instead, there was an agreement between V and SAP on a series of tax increases in the autumn of 1994. However, the major reason why SAP relied on V rather than the Greens for its budget was that the latter asked for more policy concessions than did the Left Party (Bale and Blomgren, 2008: p. 89). Nevertheless, by the start of the following year, with the need also to make cuts in public spending, SAP turned towards the Centre Party as a legislative ally. This strategic setback had electoral advantages for the Left Party: while SAP deepened co-operation with the Centre, V rose continuously in the polls to become the third largest party in the 1998 election with 12 per cent. This electoral success opened the door for V to become an institutionalised support party of the Social Democratic government.

Significant constraints on office-seeking (at least until recently): Contextual factors

Before discussing the ideological development of V before, during and after the support party episode, it will be helpful to discuss the context and the dynamics of Swedish party politics. Two features are of major importance for the discussion here. First, the Swedish system provides considerable institutional constraints on office-seeking. As well as its Communist past, this is another important reason why V did not fully enter government in 1998. A major institutional barrier to purely office-seeking strategies of small parties in Sweden is its 'negative parliamentarism'. Under Sweden's constitution, governments merely need to be tolerated by parliament rather than actively supported. Whereas '"positive" parliamentarism requires that an incoming cabinet demonstrate explicit parliamentary support, typically by a simple majority, in an investiture vote., [...] in negative parliamentarism, the coming to power of a new cabinet requires only toleration by a parliamentary majority, not active support. Typically, the head of state appoints the new prime minister and no investiture vote is held' (Bergman, 2004: p. 206). This makes it comparatively easy for SAP, which traditionally attracted the median voter, to form minority rather than coalition governments. Since SAP is one of the most successful parties in the world (having been in government for 69 out of 89 years between the introduction of universal suffrage in 1921 and the 2008 election), it was culturally preprogrammed to govern alone (Bale and Bergman, 2006a: p. 439). Additionally, this long history of single-party government led to a certain reluctance of the public and the media towards the idea that the government formation process could take time to work through (Bale and Bergman, 2006a: p. 437). The fact that parliament's committees have considerable powers in the policymaking process (Sannerstedt and Sjölin, 1992: pp. 112–19) also renders office-seeking strategies less important than in many other countries (Bale and Bergman, 2006b: p. 193). Recently, however, there have also been intitutional incentives for office-seeking strategies: according to Bale and Bergman (2006a: pp. 438–9), the budget procedure introduced in 1996 probably made it harder for a cabinet that loses a vote on the budget (which is now voted upon as a whole rather than in many different sections) to stay in power. This might well serve as an incentive for minority governments to seek closer co-operation with support parties in order to secure a majority on the state budget.

The second important feature of Swedish party politics is its bloc dynamics and (perhaps even more importantly) recently increased tensions between these blocs. Traditionally, Sweden had a five-party system comprising a socialist – SAP and V – and a centre-right bloc – the Centre Party, the liberal People's Party (*Folkpartiet*, FP) and the conservative Moderates (*Moderaterna*, M). After 1988, two additional parties were able to establish themselves in the Swedish party system: the Greens (which can be considered a part of the socialist bloc despite their self-image as neither left nor right (cf. Burchell, 2001: pp. 243–7)) and, in the centre-right bloc, the Christian Democratic Party (*Kristdemokraterna*, KD). Whereas traditionally, not least because of social democratic hegemony, these blocs have been rather permissive (with the Centre especially often willing to support SAP governments), levels of bloc confrontation have increased significantly since the mid-1990s. Even more importantly, the centre-right bloc was able to electorally defeat its socialist counterpart both in 1990 and in 2006. The reasons for this are twofold: on the one hand, unity among the centre-right parties (largely facilitated by the Moderates, who toned down their neoliberalism) and, on the other, an increasing exchange of voters between party blocs on account of a favourable contemporary *Zeitgeist*. Whereas neither the winners of the 1998 nor of the 2002 election (the Moderates and FP, respectively) were able to attract left voters (cf. Madeley, 1999: p. 190; 2003: p. 170), the surprisingly stable (and ideologically modest) 'Alliance for Sweden' of the centre-right parties was able to do exactly that in 2006, rendering it 'an unseen and major contender of the left bloc' (Aylott and Bolin, 2007: pp. 626–7). This development had a direct impact on V, which was less able to attract disaffected SAP voters, who instead increasingly voted for the centre-right parties. This was especially true for union voters, a core pillar upon which V had built its electoral success during the 1990s (cf. Johnsson and Pettersson, 2009).

Biting the Social Democrats, but not too hard: V's ideology before, during and after contract parliamentarism

It is hard to disagree with David Arter's (2002: p. 18) claim that V is still searching for an ideology. Possibly the best description of V's inconsistent ideological profile comes from Tim Bale and Torbjörn Bergman (2006a: p. 426): '*Vänsterpartiet* is strident in its rejection of a "neo-liberal", "consumerist" and "globalised" capitalism and in its support for state action to achieve full employment, protect working people's rights, redistribute wealth and provide welfare through non-market mechanisms. Internationalist in outlook, expressing solidarity with oppressed people all around the world, attempting to put itself in the vanguard of opposition to both "globalisation" and "imperialism", it also champions feminism and, at the very least, pays lip service to environmental perspectives.' Thus far, at least, there seems to be no innovative synthesis of socialism and environmentalism discernible here. However, before assessing the ideological roots of V, let us first have a look at the reasons for its electoral appeal during the 1990s.

After SAP's turn towards the Centre Party in 1995, V increasingly appeared to be the only party defending the values of the 'people's home' (i.e. the Swedish welfare state). In particular, its 1998 election success can be traced back to voters dissatisfied with the 'neoliberal' economic policies of SAP government (Möller, 1999: p. 266). About 30 per cent of V voters came from SAP, with the party able to break into Social Democratic core groups such as trade unionists,[1] women, the unemployed, and public sector employees. Under Schyman's leadership, V was also able to play on fears of women working in the public sector that they would lose their jobs if SAP continued its austerity programme (Arter, 2002: p. 11). This illustrates the impact of Schyman's appeal on the Left Party's electoral success among women (and intellectuals (cf. Spier and Wirries, 2007: pp. 87–9)).

Another ideological factor explaining V's electoral success during the 1990s (which should come as a surprise given that the party's core ideology – Communism – was anything but popular after 1990) can be found in Sweden's unique attitude towards European integration (shared possibly only by Britain). The 1994 EU referendum introduced foreign policy as a permanent cleavage in its own right in Swedish party politics (Christensen, 1998: p. 56).[2] Since Sweden still remains a Eurosceptic country today (Aylott, 2008: p. 181) – even if with diminishing intensity, as we shall see below – the Left Party significantly profited from this sentiment. As early as the late 1950s, V condemned both the EC and EFTA as the building up of new capitalist blocs in Europe. Consequently, it was the only party to oppose the Swedish free trade agreement with the EC in 1972. After the breakdown of Communism, V favoured the Council of Europe as the major European institution (Christensen, 1996: pp. 533–4). The Maastricht Treaty was seen as the construction of a new capitalist bloc and thus a threat to the security of Europe. Therefore, the 2008 party programme states that both

EU military operations and NATO expansion are a 'threat' to Sweden's national autonomy (Vänsterpartiet, 2008: p. 19). Dag-Arne Christensen (1996: p. 540) holds that the main rationale for V to oppose Sweden's EU membership was vote-seeking. V has, by any account, been very successful in attracting former SAP voters critical of European integration, largely profiting from the fact that SAP's electorate has effectively been split on this issue (Aylott, 2008: p. 191). Therefore, it comes as no surprise that the majority of those who switched towards V in the 1998 election were also opposed to EU membership (Möller, 1999: p. 266).

Before turning to V's relationship with the Greens and the Social Democrats, it will be helpful to give an overview of the support party contracts V agreed to with these parties in 1998 and 2002. Scholars have assumed V to be the loser in these negotiations: 'Sweden, where the left party supported a social democratic minority government between 1998 and 2006, is widely regarded as the paradigmatic example of what not to do' (Bale and Dunphy, 2006: p. 12).[3] Through institutionalised co-operation, SAP has been able to 'wrest [...] the populist weapon from the Left Party' (Möller, 2007: p. 40). V effectively remained a captive party; and this significantly limited its freedom of action (Bale and Dunphy, 2006: p. 16).

In line with its vote-seeking ambitions, V demanded no ministerial offices in 1998. On 5 December 1998, a support contract covering five specific areas was signed (Bale and Bergman, 2006a: p. 433) dealing with the economy, employment, distributive justice issues, gender equality and the environment. In a joint statement published in the newspapers (with all party leaders stating their intention to work together for the full electoral period), SAP, V and the Greens summarised their project as building a 'green, gender-mainstreamed people's home' (Persson et al., 1998). The contract remained as vague as the announcement; according to one Green party official 'it was very broadly formulated: it contains everything and nothing' (Bale and Bergman, 2006b: p. 196). SAP made only marginal concessions towards V; most importantly, it agreed to increases in grants to local authorities and on pensions and family benefits (Madeley, 1999: p. 193). However, SAP kept its previous overall spending limits. In contrast to the Left Party, the Greens, who also entered coalition talks with the bourgeois parties in 1998, were able to strike a much better deal with SAP (Süssner, 2008: p. 68). Furthermore, co-operation between the three parties was hampered by insufficient formal and informal meetings of party officials – SAP was obviously neither used to sharing, nor willing to share, power (Bale and Bergman, 2006b: p. 197).

Despite (or perhaps because of) these marginal policy concessions, Schyman tried to change V's strategy after 1998. In a newspaper column in 2000, she advocated changing V's strategy from support party to full coalition partner (Schyman, 2000). In April 2000, V's party board demanded a common V–SAP platform during the 2002 general election campaign and a coalition government thereafter. However, neither the party on the ground nor SAP was happy with Schyman's turn towards office-seeking. The Social Democrats flatly rejected V's demand, and so did a V party conference the following month, although V delegates did approve a subsequent coalition with SAP. The conference also rejected Schyman's quest to agree on a new party programme. Four conditions were attached to a potential coalition with the Social Democrats: there had to be no privatisation of state companies and no reduction in the rights of trade unions; additionally, the Left Party asked for a reduction in the working week and a change in the budget process that would in practice abolish the ceiling on expenditure (Arter, 2002: pp. 12–13). However, V clearly shifted towards office-seeking. In April 2001, a joint article of Schyman and the SAP prime minister, Göran Persson, in the daily newspaper *Dagens Nyheter* stressed the joint efforts of both parties in raising the social security ceiling in 2003 (Arter, 2002: p. 13).

However, the Social Democrats showed no willingness to grant V formal cabinet representation after the 2002 election. They argued that, due to its foreign policy positions (i.e. a rejection of both the EU and NATO), V could not become part of a formal coalition. According to SAP, the Swedish constitution requires that the entire cabinet takes responsibility for government policy (cf. Aylott, 2008: p. 193). However, there is good reason to assume that SAP was keen to keep V out of government for two other reasons: first, because it could afford to (due to its traditional hegemony in Swedish party politics and its good electoral result) and, second, because SAP and V had similar electorates. For this latter reason, SAP was not willing to increase V's legitimacy by accepting it as a coalition partner (cf. Eriksson, 2002). Due to its disappointing electoral result, V in any case dropped its demand to fully join government after the election.

Despite its electoral setback, V was able to strike a better deal in 2002, widely regarded as being equally good as the deal that the Greens struck (Süssner, 2008: p. 68). In October 2002, a second support contract was signed: the so-called '121 points programme'.[4] As opposed to the five areas covered in the previous agreement, the new and much more detailed one comprised 11 broad headings, including sound public finances, gender equality, a green and sustainable Sweden, promoting the welfare of children, improving working life, fairness in housing, improvements for the elderly and regional economic survival (cf. Bale and Bergman, 2006a: p. 433). The three parties also agreed to disagree in several policy areas such as EU policy and foreign policy. Additionally, the contract specified several measures to ensure better co-ordination between the parties. For example, a 'co-ordination office' was set up in the finance ministry. Up to three representatives from each party, paid for from the government budget, could be appointed to this office. Furthermore, both support parties were allowed to second political advisers to other ministries. V received three posts in the finance ministry, 2.5 in the economics ministry, one in the environment ministry, one in the education ministry and half a post in the justice ministry (Konstitutionsutskottet, 2003: p. 133). According to the contract, party leaders' meetings were to be held every month. The parties also agreed on a system of joint press conferences to prevent unfair credit-claiming by the Social Democrats (Bale and Bergman, 2006a: p. 433). As opposed to the preceding legislative period, the impact of V on government policies was considerable. For instance, the party could claim credit for a new asylum law and moreover held a de facto veto position in economic policy (Brors, 2006). However, V remained less visible and less successful than the Greens after 2002. A possible explanation for this is V's character as a captive party whose space for policy manoeuvres still remained quite limited. Unlike the Greens, V could never credibly threaten to leave the support agreement and strike a deal with the bourgeois parties.

Interestingly, the impact of V's support party status on its policies was less significant than in the case of the Greens. This is especially true for foreign policy. V is still opposed to Sweden's participation in military operations led by NATO, EU or even the United Nations. The party remains opposed to any weapon exports and military co-operation with Israel due to the country's unlawful occupation of Palestinian territories. During the second support period, V consequently opposed the American invasion of Iraq, whereas the Persson government supported the War on Terror. Indeed, Schyman's successor, Lars Ohly, called Sweden's 'unlawful occupation' a 'shame' (Ohly, 2004). Even though the EU cleavage has declined considerably in importance,[5] V still wants Sweden to leave the EU. However, there is good reason to believe that the Left Party has now lost the second biggest electoral trump card it held besides Schyman's charismatic personality – its Euroscepticism. V polled only 5.6 per cent in the 2009 election to the European parliament, a loss of 7.2 percentage points compared with 2004. The party itself admitted that it failed to mobilise anti-EU sentiments among voters in the 2009 European election campaign (Hamrud, 2009). In welfare-state and economic issues, V continued to present the image of being the only Swedish party which still embodied the vision of the 'people's home'. For instance, V remains opposed to any reform of the pension system. Indeed, rather than de-radicalising during its period as a support party, V seems to have re-radicalised after Schyman's departure in 2004. One of V's core demands became the six-hour working day without a decrease in wages. Furthermore, V has asked for a tax hike of 5.4 billion Euros (Brors, 2008). It was largely this re-radicalisation that, in the run-up to the 2006 election, rendered a three-party coalition unthinkable for SAP (Aylott and Bolin, 2007: p. 624).

This leads us to V's relationship with the Greens and the Social Democrats. Since the Swedish Greens are similar to V, their relationship is hardly uncomplicated. Not only is V quite 'green'; the Greens are, despite their bloc-transcending image, really a party of the left. This is illustrated by the fact that it was only when they gave themselves a pronounced leftist image that the Greens could ensure their election to the Riksdag in 1994 after they had lost representation in 1991 (Arter, 2003: p. 80). There is a deep mistrust and virtually no communication between the two parties. Even while they supported the Social Democrat government, MP and V communicated almost exclusively via SAP (Karlsson, 2007). As has already been mentioned, SAP still has not come to terms with the fact that V is an independent party, and treats it instead like a captive one. Even during the support party period, the Social Democrats regularly tried to explore opportunities for legislative co-operation with the Centre Party rather than with V. The Centre's turn towards the other bourgeois parties after the 1998 election is one of the most important reasons why the support contacts between the socialist parties were negotiated in the first place. The Centre Party was the biggest loser of the 1998 election. Since it felt punished by voters, the party had no incentive to sustain any co-operation over the bloc divide (Madeley, 1999: p. 193). However, in the run-up to the 2002 campaign, SAP nonetheless considered a more institutionalised coalition with the Centre; yet the latter rejected this offer and chose to co-operate with the bourgeois parties instead (Madeley, 2003: p. 166).

Due to their differing electorates and the Greens' more modest policy platforms, SAP has a much bigger interest in entering an exclusive two-party coalition with MP rather than a red–red–green, three-party coalition (cf. Aylott, 2008: p. 193). In 2002, SAP ruled out a three-party coalition not because of the Greens, but because of V. Talks about a red–green two-party coalition started as early as 2004 (cf. Eriksson, 2004).

According to Nicholas Aylott (2009), SAP and MP leaderships currently get on 'like a house on fire'. This might be due to the fact that the Greens have become a much more clear-cut office-seeker than V. Indeed, MP abandoned its claim that Sweden should leave the EU in 2008 as an explicit condition for coalition government (cf. Brors, 2009b) following an ultimatum by SAP towards both MP and V (Kjöller, 2007). In October 2008, they announced a would-be coalition between themselves only. However, only two months later SAP had to change its coalition plans and accept V as a third partner. Apparently, SAP's rank-and-file had pushed its leader, Mona Sahlin, to include it. According to one commentator, V has now become an 'equal partner' in Swedish coalition politics (*Dagens Nyheter* 18 December 2008a). The three parties of the left aim to present a common budget for 2010; additionally, they created working groups in areas such as the economy, welfare and the environment to develop a common policy platform, just as the bourgeois parties did before the 2006 election. There are indeed a considerable number of policies on which the three parties still have to find common ground: apart from Europe (and foreign policy in general) and economics, nuclear power remains an obvious example of this. Both the Greens and the Left Party are deeply anti-nuclear. The Social Democrats (who are not anti-nuclear) accordingly declared their continued support for decommissioning nuclear plants. However, this is currently not particularly popular among voters (Aylott, 2009).

Decline or normalisation? The consequences of V's support party status

Electorally, V's experience as a support party can only be termed catastrophic (cf. Table 7.1). A loss of 3.6 percentage points in 2002 was followed by another defeat in 2006, when V only polled 5.6 per cent and lost another 2.5 percentage points. It appears as if V's inroads into the SAP's electorate were only possible in the times of economic recession and rampant Euroscepticism that existed in the early 1990s. As we have seen, discontented SAP voters are increasingly willing to switch blocs, not least because they reject V's anti-European platform (cf. Johnsson and Pettersson, 2009). The development of V's membership is also not encouraging. When Schyman became leader in 1993, V's membership had dropped to a post-war low of 10,691 members, only a fraction over one-fifth of its all-time record high of 51,090 in April 1948 (Arter, 2002: p. 22). After that, the membership steadily grew to 14,000 in 2002, only to fall to 11,000 again in 2008 (Süssner, 2008: p. 69).

Table 7.1 Electoral results of the Left Party in national elections, 1982–2006

	1982	1985	1988	1991	1994	1998	2002	2006
Votes (per cent)	5.6	5.3	5.8	4.5	6.2	12	8.4	5.9
Seats	20	19	21	16	22	43	30	22

What role did V's support party status under contract parliamentarism play in V's electoral decline? David Arter (2002: pp. 18–22) holds that this experience significantly damaged V's electoral appeal. According to Arter, the quasi-coalition with the Greens reduced the Left Party's opportunities to present itself as a green party. Furthermore, the pro-coalition strategy undermined V's credibility as a radical anti-establishment force. This verdict is in line with Tim Bale and Torbjörn Bergman's (2006a, b) assessment of Swedish contract parliamentarism discussed at the beginning of this chapter. In these authors opinion, V's support for the SAP government between 1998 and 2002 nevertheless only partly explains its deteriorating electoral results. I would argue that V's electoral success during the early 1990 was the exception, not the rule. In other words, what needs to be explained is V's electoral success in the 1990s, not its recent electoral failures. Its success can largely be explained by two factors: Gudrun Schyman's extraordinary charisma (which enabled V to attract two completely heterogeneous electorates to its cause) and the virulence of the EU cleavage in Swedish party politics. Once Schyman left the party and the EU issue lost its resonance, V fell back to its normal electoral share of about 5 per cent of the vote – the share of the vote it regularly received between 1948 and 1991. In this respect, it seems more appropriate to speak of a normalisation rather than a decline of V.

The re-radicalisation that kicked in after Schyman's departure was thus caused as much by unsolved internal conflicts (or rather trade-offs between different goals) as old as the party itself as by its flirtation with being a support party. The Left Party can be described as a loose association of left socialists, nostalgic Communists, environmentalists, former Social Democrats and feminists. The looseness of its supporter base became clear after Schyman's departure in 2004, prompted by allegations of tax fraud, when there was no longer a charismatic leader to unite the disparate factions. The more traditionalist image of Schyman's successor Ohly reintroduced the 'electoral millstone' of the Left Party – its Communist past. Indeed, a counterproductive debate began around whether it was acceptable (or, for some within the party, desirable) to call oneself a 'Communist'. Ohly himself had defended Stalinist repression against Swedish guest workers in the USSR as late as 2002, and only distanced himself from these statements when he eventually became party leader. This cost V both members and votes (cf. Spier and Wirries, 2007: pp. 82–6). In 2004, the progressive opposition within V created an intra-party platform 'Decisive Vote (for) the Left' (*Vägval vänster*), which the Greens immediately started to court (cf. Carlbom, 2005). A considerable number of (mostly progressive) local and national office-holders left V. Schyman also left the party to found a (largely unsuccessful) feminist party.

The disappointing results in the 2002 and 2006 elections have thus been attributed to problems other than V's support party status (cf. Carlbom, 2002). In 2002, V mainly lost those voters it had attracted in 1998 from SAP (Blomqvist and Green-Pedersen, 2004: p. 607). According to the former Left Party MEP (and progressive dissenter) Jonas Sjöstedt (2006), the 2006 defeat had much to do with the internal struggles both within the party and among the parties of the left. This is not to say that these internal struggles were not prompted by the constraints of being a support party, most importantly the fact that V was made responsible for SAP's economic policies without being able to significantly influence them (cf. *Dagens Nyheter* 5 June 2008). However, the fact that, under Schyman, V tried to attract completely different electorates with differing agendas and beliefs that were subsequently very difficult to reconcile posed problems irrespective of V's coalition politics. Put differently, the major emphasis on vote-seeking gave rise to a fundamental contradiction between a traditional working-class appeal and a 'new politics' environmental orientation, which eventually caused internal warfare once V's focus shifted from vote- to office-seeking. However, the conflict between 'traditionalists' and 'progressives' is as old as V, or, indeed, SKP that preceded it.

At the moment, it is unclear whether the Left Party's aim is to reverse Schyman's strategic change from vote- to office-seeking. It is clear, however, that V's erratic behaviour neither increases the party's credibility as a future coalition partner nor its standing among voters. Ohly gives the impression that he is not really pursuing a clear-cut strategy at all: after he took over from Schyman, for example, he made it clear that he did not strive for ministerial office in return for policy support for SAP. However, in the run-up to the 2006 campaign, Ohly demanded a ministerial office despite the re-radicalisation of his party. He announced that his party would prevent the formation of another centre-left government unless it was asked to join a coalition by the

Social Democrats. Directly after the 2006 election, V promised to focus on extra-parliamentary action rather than any co-operation with the other parties on the left (Karlsson and Wijnbladh, 2006). Indeed, the 2008 party conference ruled out an electoral platform with SAP and MP (Carlbom, 2008c) – but also toned down the party's resistance towards co-operation.

Recently, internal tensions seem to have decreased significantly (Carlbom, 2008a). This might explain V's renewed willingness to co-operate more closely with SAP and MP. According to an internal strategy paper, V 'clearly' considers itself a future party of government despite its refusal to enter a fully-fledged electoral alliance with SAP and MP (Cullberg, 2008). The price V paid for the current de facto electoral alliance with the Social Democrats and the Greens included concessions on economic and especially fiscal policy. V agreed to follow the other parties' policy on budget discipline and modest rather than significant tax rises. According to Lars Ohly, the Left Party 'made a big sacrifice to get this co-operation going' (Carlbom, 2008b). Although a radical, unattached position might be the best solution to pursue votes and preserve the party's ideological purity, three factors are in favour of the Left's reorientation towards office-seeking – the internal armistice, the decreasing importance of the EU cleavage, and the current financial crisis. 'In what is likely to be a really miserable couple of years for the Swedish economy, they may have guessed that Swedish voters – or a good deal of them, anyway – will by 2010 prefer a party, even a radical party, to show that it is prepared to shoulder responsibility and make compromises with others when necessary, rather than standing in glorious isolation' (Aylott, 2009). Whether the Left Party is really ready for the policy concessions necessary for this strategy remains to be seen – even more so since the dynamics of Swedish party politics are not currently favourable for the parties of the left.

Double marginalisation? V's prospects in the new Swedish party politics

Strategically, V followed a rather erratic course after the breakdown of Communism: whereas vote-seeking (with an emphasis on anti-EU positions and attempts to attract electorates as diverse as socialists, feminists and ecologists) led it to be a support party in contract parliamentarism, problems began when the shift towards office-seeking (with the ultimate goal of entering a formal coalition) met serious internal conflict in the wake of a leadership change in 2004. Since then, V does not seem to pursue any coherent strategic goal; the party rather oscillates between vote- and office-seeking. The good news, however, is that V now seems to be accepted as a potential coalition partner by the two other parties of the socialist bloc – possibly a lesson learned by SAP from the catastrophic 2006 election (Süssner, 2008: p. 67). The bad news is twofold: not only does V face the threat of becoming marginalised within the socialist bloc of the Swedish party system, but the socialist bloc itself also never looked so weak in comparison with its bourgeois counterpart. The left remains significantly divided over issues like Europe, nuclear power and economic policies. Education minister Jan Björklund said that Ohly (whom he called a 'Communist') would be 'the Alliance's best campaigner' (*Dagens Nyheter* 18 December 2008b). Voters indeed do not seem to appreciate the disunity of the socialist bloc: after a lead of the left parties of 20 percentage points in February 2008 (*Dagens Nyheter* 18 February 2008), the latest poll in April 2009 showed a lead for the Alliance over a potential red–green coalition (Brors, 2009a).

Furthermore, the historically unprecedented unity among the bourgeois parties and left voters' readiness to cross bloc borders contribute to a potential change in patterns of competition of the two blocs: the 'cannibalisation' effect of mere intra-bloc voter switches (which traditionally weakened the right) could easily kick in on the socialist side, severely damaging the three parties' prospects of winning a majority enabling them to form a coalition. In this case, the Left Party's newly gained coalition potential would become useless. Even worse, V runs the risk of being marginalised itself. Strategically, its attempt to simultaneously pursue votes and office can only be called a failure. Additionally, the party lost its biggest electoral trump card: whereas the advent of the EU cleavage made it possible for V to hide its internal confusion and instead campaign against EU accession (cf. also Christensen, 1998: p. 59), this opportunity seems to have passed, as EU membership becomes less disputed in Sweden. V now faces the task of shaping its profile as a distinguishable party of the socialist bloc and a reliable coalition partner of the Social Democrats and the Greens. The threat of a double marginalisation (both of, and within, the socialist bloc) has never been bigger.

Notes

1. The share of union members who voted for V rose from 4 per cent in 1991 to 20 per cent in 1998 (Möller, 1999: p. 266). The indirect prerequisite for this success was the abandonment of an automatic institutional affiliation of all union members with SAP in 1990 after years of criticism by all other parties (cf. Aylott, 2003).

2. This has led to a distinct Swedish way of dealing with EU issues, termed 'compartmentalisation' by Aylott (2002). At the core of this approach is a tendency to decide EU-related questions through referendums, that is, to quarantine the issue from 'normal' electoral, parliamentary and intra-party politics. Traditionally, norms of party unity are thus suspended when it comes to EU policies. Sweden's 2003 decision to stay outside the European Monetary Union also came about through a referendum.
3. Tim Bale and Richard Dunphy even go so far to generalise this verdict. According to them, support party status 'is regarded as delivering the worst of all worlds, namely responsibility without real power' (Bale and Dunphy, 2006: p. 12).
4. A summary of this contract can be found in the proceedings of the Committee on the Constitution (Konstitutionsutskottet, 2003: pp. 128–9).
5. Despite the rejection of the Euro in a referendum, there is evidence for an emerging consensus on accepting European integration among Swedish voters (Lindahl and Naurin, 2005).

8
The Danish Socialist People's Party: Still Waiting After all These Years

Dag Arne Christensen

Introduction

Like its counterparts in Sweden and Norway (see Koß and Olsen in this volume for more on those parties), the major left-socialist party in Denmark, the Danish Socialist People's Party (*Socialistisk Folkeparti* – SF), has traditionally been considered non-coalitionable. In the Danish case, this has largely been on account of its opposition to both NATO and EC/EU membership, as these stances would naturally have caused significant problems between Denmark and these institutions if the SF had ever entered national government. In recent times, however, the Scandinavian left-socialist parties have gone down different paths in terms of their attitudes to government participation. Despite its NATO opposition, the Norwegian Left Socialist Party entered a red–green alliance together with the agrarian Centre Party (*Senterpartiet*) and the Labour Party (*Arbeiderpartiet*) after the 2005 general election (see Olsen in this volume). In contrast, the Danish Socialist People's Party, although more willing to become a government party over time, has filled the role of a support party to social democratic minority governments. The principal focus in this chapter is on how the SF has balanced its strategic options between policy, office and votes (see the introductory chapter about different party goals for more details). How has the party redesigned its policy in order to become an acceptable coalition partner? Which coalition alternatives have been available to the party? Why has SF, despite its willingness, not been able to become a fully fledged member of government?

The analysis of how the SF has tried to handle these issues is divided into four parts. The first part briefly sketches the party political setting in Denmark and traces the origins of the SF. In the second part we look at the key institutional features that have defined the opportunity structure available to the SF in the parliamentary arena. Then we analyse SF's electoral performance and identify the different coalition options discussed within the party. Finally, the last section takes a closer look at how SF has redesigned its EU policy in order to become an acceptable coalition partner.

The party political setting in Denmark and the origins of SF

The historic Danish parties were born between the adoption of the first constitution in 1849 and the implementation of a proportional electoral system in 1915 (Bille, 1989; Goul Andersen and Jensen, 2001). The original cleavages in the Danish party system were economic and social, and rested on four divisions. The Social Democratic Party (*Socialdemokratiet, SD*), founded in 1871, aligned with the trade unions and the working class. The Left Socialist Party (*Venstresocialistiske Parti*) was founded as a splinter party from the SD in 1919 (renamed the Communist party of Denmark (DKP) from 1920). The Radical Liberal Party (*Det Radikale Venstre, RV*), established in 1905, had smallholders and city intellectuals as its electoral base. RV grew out of a group of MPs within the Liberal Party (*Venstre*) who were expelled after a disagreement over the issue of defence spending. RV separated itself from Venstre in its anti-militarism and its orientation towards issues of social justice. By the 1930s SD and RV had joined forces, paving the way for an alliance between the two parties that has played an important role in Danish parliamentary politics ever since. Venstre (founded in 1870) was a straightforward liberal party, oriented towards economic liberalism and the class interests of farmers. Finally, the Conservative People's Party (*Det Konservative Folkeparti*) based itself around employers and business associations. These four parties dominated Danish politics until the early 1970s. The only new party established in this period was the Socialist People's Party (SF), which entered parliament for the first time in the general election in 1960 with the support of 6.6 per cent of the voters (Arter, 1999).

The formation of SF indicated a fragmentation of the traditional Nordic five-party model that emerged around 1920. As part of the 'New Left' of the 1960s, the SF represented a break with what until then had been labelled leftist politics. The old paradigm of the materialist left, represented by what Seymor Martin Lipset and Stein Rokkan termed the owner–worker cleavage, was subsequently challenged (Lipset and Rokkan, 1967; Markovits and Gorski, 1993). The New Left placed itself between the Social Democrats and the old communist parties and gave priority to issues beyond the traditional class cleavage. Anti-militarism, anti-hierarchy, solidarity with the Third World and opposition towards the developments in the socialist states of central and eastern Europe became the ideological backbone of the movement (Tarschys, 1977; Einhorn and Logue, 1988). Amongst other things, this ideological platform made adherence to the EEC impossible in the 1970s. In addition, the issue of NATO membership divided the left into two distinct blocs. Traditionally, the Left-Socialist parties in Scandinavia have been opposed to European integration. As we shall see, however, the SF advised its followers to vote 'yes' to the agreement between EU and Denmark at the European Council meeting in Edinburgh in May 1993 after the Danes, one year earlier, had shocked the political elite by turning down the Maastricht Treaty in a referendum held on 2 June 1992 (Svensson, 1993). The agreement granted Denmark four exceptions to the Maastricht Treaty, and was eventually ratified by Denmark.

The SF was established in 1959 when several prominent members of the Communist Party either left or were excluded. The split was a result of a major conflict within the Danish Communist Party (DKP) after the Soviet invasion of Hungary in 1956. Ultimately, the Communist party's loyalty towards Moscow, the lack of internal party democracy and the lack of co-operation with the Social Democrats eventually split the party (Bille, 1992). The foundation process was led by former Communist Party leader Aksel Larsen, who was expelled after taking an autonomous stand vis-à-vis Moscow. The DKP (founded in 1919) lost its representation in the 1960s and did not return to the *Folketing* until after the 'earthquake' election of 1973. It has recently resurfaced as part of the Red Green Unity List (Enhedslisten-de Rød-Grønne), composed of the DKP, the Left Socialist Party (VS) and the Socialist Workers Party (never represented in parliament).

SF's relationship with the Social Democrats was troublesome from the start. When, for the first time, the election results in 1966 opened up the possibility of a socialist majority in the *Folketing* between the Social Democrats (SD) and SF, SF decided to support a minority SD government from the outside. The government became known as the 'red-cabinet' and lasted until 1968. However, the role as a support party led to internal conflicts within SF. An extraordinary party congress was held on the issue in 1967, with a majority ending up supporting the government. The minority wanted to bring the government down and in an attempt to do that they formed the VS, but the new party did not pass the 2 per cent electoral threshold in the 1968 election. Later the VS entered the Red Green Unity List. Hence, the crowdedness on the left is further complicated by the existence of a number of smaller parties.

Left-wing positions on the highly salient security dimension were heavily altered in the aftermath of the 1989 central and eastern European revolutions. Pro-Sovietism was wiped off the political agenda at the same time as the background to both pro-Americanism and 'bridge-building neutralism' lost their historical meanings. The one-dimensional communist/anti-communist cleavage pattern was subsequently replaced by a more complex security scenario and the left was confronted with new policy dilemmas – security was becoming more than simply nuclear threats. The East–West axis, however, remained an important dividing line. Social Democrats aimed at enlarging the European Union, a solution whereby the EU could fuse security and economic dimensions in an integrated Europe. Yet the SD (much like its Norwegian sister party) remained committed to NATO, while constrained by an EU-sceptical national electorate. SF, on the other hand, envisioned alternatives to these in the form of the OSCE (The Organization for Security and Co-operation in Europe), the European Council, and the UN. As a true 1960s party, however, SF had no ideological baggage to shed when communism collapsed in 1989. The next chapter will shed light on the institutional surroundings within which SF tried to develop its parliamentary strategy.

SF's opportunity structure: Key characteristics of Danish multiparty politics

Institutions matter, especially in multiparty systems. They limit the range of options open to party strategists; thus, they produce different results from those implied by a theory of purposive choice. Hence, parties must be treated as constrained actors in the process of government formation. As pointed out by Strøm et al., (1994: p. 307), 'the real world of coalition politics is one of constraints, in which it is quite definitely not the case that everything is possible.' Not everything is possible because parties are institutions that apply rules and procedures for their own conduct. Parties put internal constraints on their own behaviour when they confront other parties. Given this, it is not accidental that SF remains devoid of governmental experience.

Four factors have defined SF's opportunity structure in the parliamentary arena. First, the Danish Social Democratic Party has not performed as well as its Norwegian and Swedish sister parties. This has (as we shall see) made cabinets across the socialist and non-socialist party boundary more common in Denmark. Second, increased fragmentation of the party system has made coalition formation more complex. The landslide general election in 1973 dramatically changed the structure of the party system. The four old parties dropped from 84 per cent to 58 per cent of the votes (Bille, 1989), three new parties entered the *Folketing* (The Christian People's Party, The Progress Party and the Centre Party), and an additional two made their comeback (DKP and the Single Tax Party). Since 1973, there have never been fewer than eight parties in the parliament. Third, RV has played a pivotal role as a bridge-builder between left and right. RV is the only non-socialist party in Scandinavia with an explicit background in foreign policy opposition. The party even voted against Danish NATO membership in 1949 (Larsen, 1994). RV has a history of close co-operation with the Social Democrats and did not accept NATO membership until it entered a coalition with SD in 1957. RV has functioned as a pivotal party in economic policy, while simultaneously breaking with the traditional left–right cleavage in foreign policy (Schou and Hearl, 1992). Fourth, the EU issue has been more or less permanently on the political agenda in Danish politics since the 1970s, both within and between parties (Worre, 1992). So far, six referendums have been held on the issue. According to Bille (1989), Europe has taken on such significance that Denmark has two party systems: one for general elections and one for European elections or referendums on EU issues. In the latter the SF has played a pivotal role in policymaking (see discussion below).

These four features have defined the coalition alternatives open to SF and structured the parliamentary arena. In addition, Danish governments are in a position to respond to a vote of no confidence by dissolving parliament and calling a general election. In Denmark, the right to dissolve parliament has been used frequently; the *Folketing* has seldom sat for the whole of its four-year term. The combination of a strong referendum institution, the government's right to dissolve parliament and the unstable situation of governments has shaped the SF's parliamentary scope of action. In the next section we look more closely at how SF and its potential coalition partners have performed both in elections and in the parliamentary arena.

SF: Electoral and legislative performance

The formation of SF did not prompt any sort of immediate electoral dividend for the new party. However, it experienced a slow but steady upturn in its electoral fortunes in the 1980s (see Table 8.1). Voter support grew from 5.0 per cent in 1979 to a peak of 14.6 per cent in 1987.

Table 8.1 The Danish SF's electoral support, 1960–2007 (per cent)

Year	Per cent
1960	6.1
1964	5.9
1966	10.9
1968	6.1
1971	9.1
1973	6
1975	5
1977	3.9
1979	5.9
1981	11.3
1984	11.5
1987	14.6
1988	13
1990	8.3
1994	7.9
1998	7.6
2001	6.4
2005	6
2007	13

However, in the three elections in the 1990s, the party's support fell back to around 7.5 per cent. In the general election of 2007 SF again gained support, with 13 per cent of the votes. Indeed, the SF became the fourth largest party in the *Folketing*. The election of Villy Søvndal as party leader in 2005 appeared to be an important short-term factor behind SF's electoral gains. The party also doubled its membership figures between 2004 and 2009 (from 8,213 members in 2004 to 16,518 in 2009).[1]

In Danish politics, possessing relevant policies is not enough for a party when communicating with voters. SF has faced the challenge of demonstrating its relevance for government and policymaking. This has proven to be problematic. On the one hand, co-operation has been necessary for SF in order to influence policy; on the other, co-operation has required compromises that have brought the risk of reducing its credibility among core supporters. SF has concentrated on two coalition alternatives – 'Red-Bloc', comprising SD and S (favoured in the 1960s and 1970s), and a 'Red-Centre' alliance between SF, SD and RV. This last alternative was favoured from the 1980s and currently seems more relevant than ever before.

Prior to the general election of 1973, the Danes were confronted with a two-bloc system with governments consisting of either the centre-left (SD, RV and other small parties) or a coalition consisting of the two major right-wing parties (the Liberals and the Conservatives). The landslide election of 1973 changed this situation. Despite a large majority for the centre-right, the non-socialists now had to rely on the support of the extreme right Progress Party (Green-Pedersen, 2001). However, two years later, in 1975, opposition from other non-socialist parties made it impossible to form a government with the support of the Progress Party. As shown in Table 8.2, this led to the formation of several Social Democratic minority governments in the 1970s.

Table 8.2 Governments in Denmark since 1973

Year	Type of government	Member parties	Majority/Minority
1973–5	Right-wing	L	Minority
1975–7	Social Democratic	SD	Minority
1977–8	Social Democratic	SD	Minority
1978–9	Broad Coalition	SD-L	Minority
1979–81	Social Democratic	SD	Minority
1981–2	Social Democratic	SD	Minority
1982–4	Right-wing Centre	L, C, CD, CPP	Minority
1984–7	Right-wing Centre	L, C, CD, CPP	Minority
1987–8	Right-wing Centre	L, C, CD, CPP	Minority
1988–90	Right-wing Centre	L, C, RV	Minority
1990–3	Right-wing	L, C	Minority
1993–4	Social Democratic Centre	SD, RV, CD, CPP	Minority
1994–6	Social Democratic Centre	SD, RV, CD	Minority
1996–8	Social Democratic Centre	SD, RV	Minority
1996–8	Social Democratic Centre	SD, RV	Minority
1998–2001	Social Democratic Centre	SD, RV	Minority
2001–5	Right-wing	L, C	Minority
2005–7	Right-wing	L, C	Minority
2007–	Right-wing	L, C	Minority

Source: Green-Pedersen (2001: p. 55) and the *Folketing* website (address?). http://www.ft.dk/Demokrati/Regeringen.aspx Key to the different parties: SD=Social Democrats, CD=Centre Democrats, CPP= Christian People's Party, RV= Radical Liberals, L= Liberal Party, C=Conservatives.

Table 8.3 Socialist parties' performances in Denmark

Year	Seats (per cent) and parties
1973	36 (SF, DKP, SD)
1975	41.7 (SF, DKP, SD, VS)
1977	48 (SF, DKP, SD, VS)
1979	48.5 (SF, SD, VS)
1981	48.5 (SF, SD, VS)
1984	46.8 (SF, SD, VS)
1987	46.2 (SF, SD)
1988	45.1 (SF, SD)
1990	48 (SF, SD)
1994	46.3 (SF, SD, UL)
1998	46.4 (SF, SD, UL)
2002	38.9 (SF, SD, UL)
2005	36.6 (SF, SD, UL)
2007	41.1 (SF, SD, UL)

Source: Christensen (1998: p. 61), own calculations. Key to the Socialist parties: SF=Socialist People's Party, SD= Social Democratic Party, VS= Left Socialist Party, UL= Unity list.

Table 8.3 depicts the left's parliamentary strength and its fragmentation. Note the short period between elections in Denmark, and the electorally weak and fragmented nature of the left's representation in the *Folketing*. In Denmark the socialist parties have not been in a majority position since the 1966 election. Consequently, it has been necessary for both the Social Democrats and the SF to include one of the centre-right parties as a prospective coalition partner. The inclusion of the Radical Liberals was a natural one for the SF based on the party's previous co-operation with the Social Democrats and its foreign policy stances.

In the 1982–8 period SD, SF and RV converged in the area of foreign policy. Damgaard (1992: p. 294) argues that in this period the Danish parliamentary system developed a new form of 'minority rule' in foreign policymaking. The Conservative-led 'Four-leaf clover' government composed of Conservatives, Liberals, Centre Democrats and the Christian People's Party faced a united opposition on foreign policy issues. It survived for eight years despite weak representation in parliament, and governed on the basis of agreements with the Radical Liberals on social–economic policy (Damgaard and Svensson, 1989; Green-Pedersen, 2001).

Indeed, the government made it clear that it would not accept the opposition altering socio-economic policy. The Social Democrats, Radical Liberals and SF pushed through several issues: Denmark vetoed the stationing of nuclear missiles in Europe and advocated a nuclear arms 'freeze', and the opposition ordered the government to work for the creation of a Nordic nuclear-free zone. The 'alternative majority' also made joint proposals on environmental issues and cultural policy. Hence, the government found itself having to implement decisions it opposed. This strategy worked so well that SF started to believe in a formal governmental co-operation based on this 'alternative majority'. RV, however, was not willing. Divisions in both economic policy and European integration ruled out such a coalition in the eyes of RV.

The 2001 general election, however, represented yet another 'landslide' in Danish politics as things changed once again. For the first time since 1924 the Liberal Party replaced SD as the largest in the *Folketing*. Only 29.1 per cent supported SD, the party's lowest share of the vote since the other watershed election in 1973 (Skidmore-Hess, 2003). Again, the fall of SD was associated with rising support for the extreme right in Danish politics. The election resulted in a right-wing government led by the Liberals, supported by the Danish People's Party, which gained support on a strict anti-immigrant campaign. For SF it was more important that RV lost its pivotal position in Danish politics, and had to redefine its parliamentary strategy. In April 2009 RV party leader Margrethe Vestager declared for the first time that it was not unthinkable that RV could enter a coalition that, in addition to the Social Democrats, included SF. While SD is positively inclined to the idea, several high-ranking RV party members ruled out such a coalition, claiming that RV does not belong in the 'Red-Bloc' (see Informationen 27 April 2009).

The 'alternative majority', SF and Europe

The permanent political relevance of the EU in Danish politics led the 'alternative majority' to develop a common platform in their attitudes towards European integration. Among other things, they confronted the government in the debate over the Single European Act in 1986. A parliamentary majority opposed the Act, which led the government to propose a referendum on the issue. A comfortable majority of 56.2 per cent of voters supported the Act. However, policy disagreements still existed among the three opposition parties. The Social Democrats and the Radical Liberals did not share the SF's view on EU membership. They both saw the EU mainly as a question of economic co-operation, but they rejected any move towards a political union (Petersen, 1994). The Social Democrats re-evaluated their attitude in the aftermath of the revolutions in central and eastern Europe. The party chairman at the time, Svend Auken, declared in a speech in 1990 that the party had given the conservative forces in Europe too much space, and it was time for the party to strengthen the EC in its own image (Haahr, 1993). In the 1990s, SF followed.

SF's leadership hoped that the EU issue could help to reshape the 'alternative majority' into a coalition government. The Danish 'No' to Maastricht on 2 June 1992 was followed by intense negotiations between the political parties. The three parties united in the so-called 'national compromise', which became the solution to the political crisis created by the Danish veto on Maastricht. The compromise was initiated by SF in May 1992 before the Maastricht referendum. The compromise involved seven of the eight parties in the *Folketing* – the right-wing Progress Party being the only outsider. The document, entitled 'Denmark in Europe', contained three main parts: one on issues of common interest between the EU and Denmark, one on particular interests for Denmark and one on the Danish position in the discussion of enlargement of the Community. The proposal included several areas where Denmark should be exempted: the defence policy dimension (WEU), the single currency, union citizenship, and co-operation in judicial and police affairs. The Edinburgh summit accommodated the Danish claims. On 18 May 1993, the National Compromise was brought to a referendum with the SF's blessing and accepted by 56.7 per cent of the Danes. Although only 20 per cent of its voters went along with the SF leadership in the 1993 referendum, the party was for the first time in a position to shape the direction of Danish EU policy. An extraordinary EU party congress decided to acknowledge the leadership's decision in 1993. The party stated that a precondition for its EU membership approval was 'that the basis for Danish policy towards Europe is the national compromise' (cited in Christensen, 1998: p. 58).

The period of strong EU policy agreements within the 'alternative majority' corresponds directly with weak bargaining constraints on the SF's leadership (see Table 8.4). The SEA referendum in 1986 resulted in immediate changes in the party's coalition strategy. In 1986 the National Congress accepted the leadership's view that withdrawal from the EC would no longer be an ultimatum determining potential governmental co-operation with the Social Democrats and RV.

If the SF were to be involved in government then, up to the June 1997 Amsterdam summit, the 'national compromise' was to determine the

Table 8.4 SF's formal constraints on coalition bargaining, 1973–95

Year	EC/EU constraints on government participation
1973–84	EC withdrawal
1984–5	EC membership referendum within a year after government declaration
1986–92	Government should present alternatives to the EC Govern without considering the EC
1993	National compromise basis for governmental EU policy.

Sources: 1984: Congress statement on the 'workers' majority (SF-Status, 1984: p. 84); 1986: EC statement at the 1986 party congress (SF-Status, 1986: p. 78); 1993: National Executive meeting January 1993 (SF-Status, 1993: p. 76).

direction of the government's EU policy. By 1998, Denmark was facing its fifth EC/EU referendum on Europe, this time on the Amsterdam Treaty. The SF entered the campaign with strong internal conflicts brewing. Before the party's extraordinary EU congress in September 1997, the debate between its different EU fractions was intense. 'Euro-optimists' and 'Euro-realists' came out with the smallest possible majority in the parliamentary group (seven against six), while the 'Euro-opponents' dominated where it really mattered, in the National Executive and at the local party level. Confusion at the elite level was preordained. The party Chairman, Holger K. Nielsen, opposed the Amsterdam Treaty; the vice-chairman, Christine Antorini, supported it along with the parliamentary leader, Steen Gade (Christensen, 1998). At the local party level, 'Euro-opposition' prevailed. A clear majority (28 against 10) in the National Executive recommended that the extraordinary congress reject the treaty. In a newspaper survey of local party chairmen, two out of three were opposed (Christensen, 1998: p. 67). At the extraordinary congress, 67 per cent of the delegates rejected the Treaty, but the congress statement opted for a 'Yes' on the basis that there would be improvements in a renegotiated treaty in the future. Prior to the congress, divisions were so intense that key party members proposed that the party should refrain from taking a decision. The idea was inspired by the Finnish Left Party, which, before the 1994 EU membership referendum, could not agree on the membership issue and thus decided not to take a stand.

It turned out, however, that the party leadership miscalculated when it believed that the 'national compromise' could be used as a springboard to a common government declaration with RV and SD. RV had no intention of forming a coalition government that included the SF, and in 1993 SD took the initiative to form a majority government with the parties at the centre of the political system (the Christian People's Party and the Centre Democrats). While SD in 1987 had opted for a possible governmental co-operation with SF, the door was closed in 1990, and, after more than 10 years in opposition, SD headed instead for a 'broad majority coalition' (Bille, 1991: p. 40). Even in 1987, scepticism prevailed among the SD leadership with regard to including the SF in the government, as many thought it would be difficult to formulate a coherent NATO policy with the SF as a government party (Boel, 1988: p. 228).

The Danish case underlines the huge difference between decisions to enter government coalitions and decisions to form parliamentary alliances. Parliamentary coalitions usually rally around specific policy areas, while government coalitions have to deal with a wide range of issues. The RV's key argument against any co-operation with SF has been made on traditional left–right grounds. This is hardly surprising, since the SF usually turned against all budget proposals in parliament. With the notable exception of the 1996 Social Democratic-led minority government's budget plans, it opposed all budget proposals from 1981. However, in 2008 SF voted in favour of the Liberal-led government's budget for the first time. In the given parliamentary situation the party needed to show that it was 'economically responsible'. In addition, a coalition between the two parties divided on European integration (Social Democrats and Radical Liberals) would make EU negotiations difficult if the SF held to its opposition to full EU political integration. Finally, SF declared itself as the 'watchdog' for the Danish opt-out included in the Edinburgh Agreement. Eurosceptics among the Radical Liberals and Social Democratic grassroots could also lean towards the SF in order to ensure that the 'national compromise' became government EU policy.

Yet another compromise, this time on the EU's Constitutional Treaty, was negotiated among the Danish parties in 2004 (Bille, 2005). Again SF played a pivotal role. The Liberals, the Conservatives, the Social Democrats, the Radical Liberals and SF agreed on a platform called 'Denmark in the enlarged EU'. The parties wanted to see the EU making majority decisions on environment, energy taxes, discrimination, minimum rates for indirect taxes, financial planning and collaboration on the evasion of taxes and duties (Bille, 2005). The SF demand of a veto was accepted, and the parties also agreed that the constitution should be subject to a referendum. The four Danish opt-outs could be put to vote after such a referendum. The SF even arranged its own membership ballot on the agreement, and 66 per cent of the membership approved.

SF in Europe

Studying SF's policy on European integration not only reveals the leading role played by the party in setting the agenda for Denmark's relationship with the EU, but also reflects the party's general policy development. The referendum on the Single European Act (SEA) in 1986 removed the membership issue from the political agenda and placed developments in the EU at the centre of the political debate. The traditional membership cleavage was played down and replaced with a conflict over degrees of integration in different policy areas (Worre, 1992). This required an alternative strategy for the SF. Institutional experience within EC institutions set in motion political behaviour that encouraged political innovation and competition for issue-leadership.

The SF's attitude towards Europe falls into three phases:

1. 1973–86: Towards Euro-realism, with a focus on substituting the conflict over membership with that over the degree of integration;
2. 1986–8: Euro-realism, marked by a withdrawal of the claim that Denmark should leave the EC; and
3. 1988–94: Euro-realism and Euro-optimism, with an increased focus on a multi-speed Europe.

The party remains sceptical of further political integration in the EU but, as we shall see, this does not extend to all policy areas.

The first phase concerned whether or not the SF should take an active part in the parliamentary work within the EC. Since the EC in 1975 agreed to constitute the European Parliament through direct elections, the SF was troubled by how to take part in the elections. The first dispute was whether the SF should allow the 'People's Movement against the EC' to organise the selection of candidates to the 1979 EP elections. The SF feared that the Communist Party would use the movement for its own interests. In 1980 a new anti-EC committee was established outside the SF, a committee critical of the People's Movement focus on withdrawal from the EC and its attitudes towards Danish national interests. The anti-EC committee claimed that it was important for the SF to strengthen its contacts with the Socialist forces in other European countries, even if they, such as the Italian Communist Party, were pro-EC. The National Committee in the SF found it unwise to take part in creating such a committee and claimed that it would make co-operation with socialists and other opponents to the EC difficult (Folkesocialisten nr.3 1980, nr.5 1980).

Following the election of the SF's first Euro-MP in 1979, a confrontation broke out over the party's parliamentary strategy. Different interpretations of the party's programme led to discussion with the party's EC committee over whether the party's representative could originate proposals or support other proposals in the European Parliament (Christensen, 1996). After a long and intensive debate, the National Committee, with a majority of one vote (18–17), decided that the delegate could support and originate proposals, but only in the 'area of international solidarity'. An extraordinary party congress in 1983, deciding on the 1984 EP election programme, agreed that SF should only support proposals in the EP that could weaken further integration and those that were in accordance with the party programme. The acceptance of an active role in the EP was finally acknowledged at the 1986 party congress. It stated that the party still 'opposes the EC but at the same time we do not suffer from Euro-phobia when it comes to acting within EC institutions' (Folkesocialisten nr.10 1986). The SF's acceptance of membership in the late 1980s was part of a continuous adjustment process, not a radical change of EU policy.

When the SF doubled its representation in the EP in 1984, the party moved towards Euro-realism. The aim was no longer to get Denmark out of the EC, but to prevent Denmark promoting a policy that would lead to further political integration within the EC. Flemming Sørensen, a member of the party's EC Committee, claimed that it was not possible to 'even imagine that we can withdraw from Brussels without the bottom falling out of our national economy' (cited in Christensen, 1996: p. 531). The party's parliamentary group in the *Folketing* echoed this view. Now, the leadership wanted to set in motion a discussion of the potential reactions of the EC if Denmark should withdraw from the EC, and the possible consequences of such a reaction.

The controversy over the Single European Act in 1986 strengthened the 'Euro-realist' camp within the SF. SF opposed the package, and feared that 'the mix of economic and political co-operation within the EC would weaken Danish foreign policy independence' (Christensen, 1996). SF argued that a 'No' to the Single European Act could halt the centralisation with the EC and thereby result in a reasonable Danish withdrawal from the EC. When it turned out that a comfortable majority of 56.2 per cent of the Danes supported the Act in the February referendum, SF immediately changed its EC policies. Søren Keldorf, a member of the EC Committee, announced a proposal to the next national congress that the party should withdraw the claim of a Danish withdrawal from the EC, and that the National Executive should set in motion a debate over SF's

EC policies. The SF's EC policy was seen as unrealistic after the Danes, for the second time (and after 13 years of Danish membership), had confirmed their faith in membership. Instead, the SF should turn its attention towards what kind of Europe it wished to be a part of. The National Congress in 1986 held on to the opt-out strategy, but acknowledged that after the acceptance of the Single European Act it would be difficult to get a majority of the Danish electorate to support a withdrawal from the EC. 'Euro-realists', however, came to the fore when the congress decided that withdrawal from the EC would no longer be a barrier to potential government co-operation with the Social Democrats.

The 'Euro-optimists' won an additional victory when the congress accepted EC institutions as an arena for party activity. Environmental policy in particular was introduced as an issue in need of further integration and co-operation in Europe. It also pointed out that SF no longer agreed with the strategy of the People's Movement Against the EC, which deviated 'from real political life and only sees the EC-membership as a problem of national sovereignty' (Christensen, 1996: p. 532). The 'Euro-realists' were further encouraged by the breakdown of Communism in central and eastern Europe and the increased interest of the other Nordic countries and Austria in EC membership. Bjarke Larsen, a member of the party's International Committee, argued that this development had opened up new possibilities for the left in Europe. The party's new EC policy in the EP elections of 1989 would be an 'open and committed co-operation within and outside the EC' (Christensen, 1996). In 1990 the SF published its own Rome Treaty, and among other things aimed to strengthen both the environmental and social dimensions in the Treaty and to commit the EC to welcoming newcomers into the Community (Christensen, 1996). SF also launched a campaign for an 'Open Europe', aimed at engaging the rank and file in starting local committees for discussion about the future of Europe. However, the local party branches showed very little interest in the idea and the campaign subsequently fizzled out.

The 1991 congress advanced a policy aimed at changing the EC. The developments in eastern Europe and the new potential applicants to the EC had already delayed work on the party's new programme of principles for a year. The programme was completed in November 1991 and was a compromise that tried to include the interests of the different Euro-camps. The 'Euro-oppositionists' won a victory with the programme's statement that the 'SF is against the Rome Treaty as the core for the co-operation within the Community'; the 'Euro-realists' were pleased that the 'opt-out' option was out of the question; and finally the 'Euro-optimists' were satisfied with the vision of an open and multi-speed Europe. Democratisation of the EC by strengthening the EP's ability to control the Commission was put in the forefront. Even if the SF opposed the Maastricht Treaty in 1991, the party stressed that 'this does not mean that a "No" in the referendum will lead Denmark out of the EC' (Christensen, 1996). A widening of the EC towards Eastern Europe, concessions to the Third World and more integration in the fields of the environment, social policy and working conditions were among the policy stands advocated.

When SF initiated the 'national compromise' to RV and SD in case of a 'No' vote in the 1992 referendum, the party downplayed its criticism of Maastricht. SF's National Executive decision to accept the Edinburgh Agreement (with 33 approving and only four rejecting) had, according to the party, helped put the questions of openness and democracy on the top of the European political agenda. Since the National Compromise the SF's attitude towards integration has been dominated by a critical view of the so-called United States of Europe even while the party strives to open the EU to new applicants. The party championed flexible co-operation within the EC, 'a Europe of all you can eat' (*Economist*, 16 September 1994), where the different countries' needs and wishes should be key to the efforts of integration.

If political strategy deals with what Schattschneider (1975) describes as the exploitation, use and suppression of conflict, the only viable strategy for SF was 'Euro-realism'. The conflict over membership itself had been made irrelevant by the Danish electorate. Holding on to the minority view of 'Euro-opposition' would have kept the party outside the dominant debate over Denmark's attitude towards growing integration. SF lost faith in the possibility that 'Euro-opposition' could be the winning platform in the long run. The party developed organisational structures to keep the party leadership updated on European policy. As early as 1977, the party established a committee to handle questions of European integration, in the beginning only composed of people from the capital, Copenhagen. In addition, there was a change in SF's priority of international contacts. First, SF gave priority to co-operation at the Nordic and European levels. SF saw co-operation with other leftist and green forces in the EC countries as important to secure social rights and the environment from what it called the EC's blind policy of growth (National Congress statement, 1991).

Conclusion

Under what circumstances do parties redefine their self-imposed policy constraints? What are the motives when parties reformulate their policies? As pointed out in the introduction to this book, political parties change from a co-operative to a competitive strategy when 'heartland' issues become salient. In addition, parties are often internally constrained when they enter bargaining processes. Policy distance and ideology matter to party members, and they (through party congresses) usually take the final decision. Internal constraints are important, precisely because policy positions are closely related to the very identity structures of political parties. External constraints can also be added to the list, the most important being the numerical strength of potential coalition parties. We have highlighted three important factors that have defined the SF's opportunity structure: the content of the EU issue, foreign policy distance and the structure of government.

The SF confronted a conflict over Europe where the question was to what extent Denmark should integrate into EC/EU structures, a question that was highly salient across all parties. SF followed a co-operative strategy and involved itself in the policy formation process. Foreign policy issues have not only been high on the agenda in Danish politics; they have also led to a convergence among the opposition parties. Convergence along the security dimension among the SD, SF and RV has made government coalitions possible, at least in the minds of the SF leadership. Post-2001, when RV lost its pivotal position in Danish politics through the 1980s, SF's government ambitions seem to be more realistic than ever before. Indeed, the three parties have experience with close co-operation in parliament. They joined the 'national compromise' in order to renegotiate the Maastricht Treaty in 1992 and did the same on the European Constitutional Treaty in 2004. Even if RV's foreign policy has become acceptable to SF, it remains an issue whether SF's economic policy is palatable to RV's rank and file. A weak Social Democratic Party and frequent minority governments have forced SF to reformulate its parliamentary strategy. It aimed at office and convinced the party membership that it had to soften its foreign policy demands if it were to head for political power. Currently, the obstacle in the way of government participation for SF is not its own party members, but those of the Radical Liberals.

Note

1. http://www.sf.dk/default.aspx?func=article.view&topmenuID=10964&id=10963 (accessed 18 August 2009).

9
From Pariah to Prospective Partner? The German Left Party's Winding Path towards Government

Dan Hough

All parties have unique histories, but the history of the German Left Party (LP) is more unique than most. One of its predecessors, the Socialist Unity Party (SED), ruled the German Democratic Republic for all but the last few months of its inglorious history (1949–90) before giving up power and watching from the sidelines as German unification steamrollered past it. The new SED leadership quickly realised that unified Germany would have no place for a (post-)communist party that did not make at least some effort to recant for its past failings; hence the SED changed its name to, firstly, the SED/PDS (Party of Democratic Socialism) in December 1989 and then simply to the PDS in February 1990 (Barker, 1998; Oswald, 2002). Through the early 1990s the PDS struggled gamely for its political life, and, had the process of German unification gone smoothly, there is a fair chance that it would have lost this struggle and vanished off the political map.

By the mid-1990s the PDS had metamorphosed into an eastern German regional party, articulating specific eastern German sentiment in a largely western German-dominated political process (Hough, 2000). Quirks of the electoral rules allowed the PDS to enter the federal parliament in both 1990 and 1994 (Bastian, 1995), but by 1998 it was preserving its status on the back of its strong performance in the eastern states, where it managed 21.6 per cent – just enough to see it over the 5 per cent hurdle nationally. Achieving 5.1 per cent of the vote nationwide in 1998 was to be the high point of PDS electoral success, enabling the party not just to form a fully-fledged parliamentary party (and with this to enjoy all the parliamentary rights that other parties had long since had), but also to receive state funding for such things as a political foundation (namely, the Rosa Luxemburg Foundation). The PDS's Lazarus-like revival appeared complete.

Come the 2002 election, things looked a little different; the party had largely been ignored by its political rivals and there was a feeling of drift amongst party activists. Factional disputes prevented the party from agreeing on anything more than a rudimentary programmatic outline, and the PDS subsequently suffered at the polls, slipping out of parliament and – it was again presumed – towards oblivion (Bortfeldt, 2003). Yet, once more, the PDS – if in a different guise and in a way that very few could have predicted – bounced back again (Hough et al., 2007; Spier et al., 2007). The PDS became the *Linkspartei* (Left Party) in mid-2005 and by 2007 it had been renamed again, this time to *Die Linke* – again best translated as the Left Party. It did this as it sought to merge with another left-wing movement, the newly formed and predominantly western German Electoral Alliance for Labour and Social Justice (WASG) (Olsen, 2007). The successful candidature of former Finance Minister and SPD leader Oskar Lafontaine on a Left Party open list in 2005 enabled the party to poll 4.9 per cent of the vote in western Germany – by far and away its best performance in the 10 'old' *Länder* to date – and 25.3 per cent in the eastern states, surpassing the Greens as the fourth largest party in the *Bundestag*. This was followed by major successes in the five *Land* elections in western Germany between 2007 and 2009, in each of which the LP achieved parliamentary representation. Indeed, the LP in the Saarland not only managed 21.3 per cent of the vote in the 2009 poll; it also came seriously close to being a part of a western German *Land* government for the first time.

Although the LP has never been close to taking on governmental responsibility at the federal level, it is worth discussing within the context of this volume for three reasons. Firstly, it has now accumulated significant experience as a support party at the regional (*Land*) level (from 1994 in Saxony Anhalt) and later as a coalition partner of the Social Democrats in Mecklenburg Western Pomerania (from 1998 to 2006) and in Berlin (from 2001) to be taken seriously as a party of government. These ventures into power at the *Land* level are not likely to be its last, as the recent strong performances, and subsequent discussions about coalitions that they brought with them, in Thuringia, Saxony, Brandenburg and – most interestingly – the Saarland in 2009 have illustrated. Regardless of the respective policy successes and failures of the coalitions that the party has been involved in to date, the PDS/LP certainly did *not* prove to be an untrustworthy opponent of democracy that had no future as a party of government. In fact, the LP's dullness as a government actor was one of the more surprising criticisms that were voiced. The LP will take on more governmental responsibility, and this is likely to be sooner rather than later. Secondly, the LP's programmatic profile is now much closer to that of the Social Democrats than it ever has been in the past. LP politicians can indeed still articulate biting criticisms of both the capitalist system and the Social Democrats, but there have also been constructive attempts to move the party towards stances that could prompt a coalition at the national level, at some point in the medium term, to be a viable option.

Finally, Germany's party system is broader and more diverse than at any time since World War II. Six parties are represented in parliament, and five of them – the LP being the exception – are unambiguously coalitionable. The LP has established itself as an anti-capitalist, pacifist, protest party to the left of the Social Democrats (SPD), who are stuck between the need to appeal to centrist voters who are repelled by the LP's radicalism and attempting to cling on to other supporters who have a degree of sympathy for the LP's agenda. The Greens further squeeze the SPD's vote, and since 2002 left-of-centre majorities have only rarely appeared mathematically viable without the LP. The maths, in other words, is forcing the SPD to take the LP seriously. The main party of the centre-right remains the Christian Democratic Union (CDU), supported in Bavaria by its sister party the Christian Social Union (CSU). The 'Union', as it is known, would ideally like to govern with the Free Democrats, a libertarian party with a clear neoliberal economic profile. Again, however, the arithmetic does not always add up, and it is this that prevented the parties from governing in 2005. This has left the unloved Grand Coalition of the two biggest parties – SPD and CDU/CSU – as the most likely structural outcome; unless, of course, the SPD and Greens bring the LP into the coalition equation.

This chapter proceeds by initially mapping out the development of the LP and its predecessors in the period since German unification. It then carries on by outlining the ideological and programmatic stances that the party has developed over the recent past. The LP remains a diverse party, incorporating a rich mosaic of communists and Marxists (in the so-called 'Communist Platform' and 'Marxist Forum' respectively), modern socialists, western German trade unionists, anti-globalisation protestors and a bedrock of members who have remained true to the party since its GDR days. Finding a coherent programmatic narrative has therefore not been a straightforward task. The chapter then moves on to discuss how the LP has behaved in office in the two eastern German states where it has governed, before speculating on what this is likely to tell us about any prospective SPD–LP alliance at the national level. It concludes by analysing the party's likely future strategy.

Background

The Left Party as we now know it was officially founded on 16 June 2007 when its two predecessors – the PDS and WASG – merged. These parties had very different pre-2007 existences. The PDS, as noted above, was a largely eastern German protest party. Through the early to mid-1990s it was much maligned and in many ways much derided, but it nonetheless transformed itself from an undemocratic, authoritarian 'Staatspartei' into a broad church of leftward-leaning opinion. Although it regularly polled 20 per cent plus of the vote in eastern Germany, it was always very conscious that this was barely 5 per cent of the vote nationwide; the trapdoor out of parliament was therefore always too close for comfort, as the 2002 election illustrated starkly when all but two of the party's MPs left parliament and the PDS only registered 4.0 per cent of the vote.

The PDS's failure to expand westwards was not for want of trying (Weis, 2005). Yet in the minds of the vast majority of western Germans the party remained very much an eastern actor talking an eastern language, and prospects of this ever changing appeared, even for the most optimistic PDS activist, to be pretty slim. It kept its head above water because it began to mobilise support around issues of territorial difference. It did not seek to roll back the process of unification, but – crucially – it did begin to seek a better deal for eastern Germans in both economic and sociocultural terms in the newly unified state. Through the 1990s the PDS's voters saw something in the party's rhetoric and criticisms of other parties (and politicians) that rang true with their own dissatisfaction at post-unification German politics. The PDS was seen to speak for eastern Germans, who were (so they perceived) being largely ignored by everyone else. The PDS did not shirk from doing this; in the run-up to the 1998 election, for example, it published the 'Rostock Manifesto' (which aimed to present the party as an explicit defender of east German interests; see PDS Parteivorstand, 1998) as well as specific proposals aimed to revitalise the eastern German economy. These proposals ranged from decentralising power further in Germany so as to empower eastern Germans, to developing 'publicly funded employment programmes' that were specifically tailored to getting Easterners back to work (PDS Parteivorstand, 1998: p. 31).

The PDS's 5 per cent dilemma at the national level was not replicated at the regional level. In western Germany the PDS never got near entering any of the 10 *Landtage*, and its presence on the ground was thin at best. In some places (such as Hamburg), far-left activists – often with their roots in the *Bund Westdeutscher Kommunisten* (Association of West German Communists, BWK) – took over individual *Land* branches, making the task of building any sort of serious party machine even more difficult (Meuche-Mäker, 2005: p. 63). Even in *Landesverbände* where extremists were not dominant membership numbers remained low and resources minimal, ensuring that the PDS was scarcely able to keep its organisational head above water (Olsen, 2002). The situation in the East was very different. The party had no worries about maintaining a parliamentary presence – it did this everywhere, polling between 9 and 28 per cent of the vote (see Table 9.1) – and the question soon became whether, and if so under what conditions, the PDS should look to become a party of government.

The WASG, on the other hand, originated as an interest group in 2004, opposing many of the SPD's labour and welfare reforms (the so-called 'Hartz Reforms') implemented by Gerhard Schröder during his second term in office (2002–5). Its roots were very much in western Germany, and its supporter base was in the (disillusioned) trade union movement as well as former members of the SPD. It became a party, with a membership of around 5,000, in early 2005 and ran in the North-Rhine Westphalian *Land* election of May 2005. The WASG did not do enough to cross the 5 per cent barrier, but it did show intent to compete with the PDS on the left of the political system in the forthcoming national election. Although the two parties appealed to different clienteles and for very different reasons (westerners vs. easterners, and disillusioned social democrats/socialists vs. disillusioned 'unification losers'), and were sceptical of one another at the beginning, a general opposition to the government's alleged neoliberalism united them – and subsequently

Table 9.1 The PDS's electoral performance in eastern parliaments, 1990–2005

	Mecklenburg Western Pomerania	Brandenburg	Thuringia	Saxony	Saxony-Anhalt	Berlin
1990	15.7	13.4	9.7	10.2	12.0	9.2
1994	22.7	18.7	16.6	16.5	19.9	–
1995	–	–	–	–	–	14.6
1998	24.4	–	–	–	19.6	–
1999	–	23.3	21.3	22.2	–	17.7
2001	–	–	–	–	–	22.6
2002	16.4	–	–	–	20.4	–
2004	–	28.0	26.1	23.6	–	–

prompted talks of how they might work with rather than against each other in the 2005 poll.

Once former finance minister Oskar Lafontaine, the former chancellor candidate of the SPD and long-time Minister-President of the Saarland, signalled his interest in the idea of a unified force to the left of the Social Democrats, the project took on a whole new dimension. Lafontaine was the doyen of the SPD's left wing and therefore ideologically close to many in the WASG. He was also on very good terms with the PDS leadership (and especially parliamentary leader, Gregor Gysi) and as early as 2003 rumours surfaced that Lafontaine and Gysi were hatching plans for co-operation between anti-Schröder SPD rebels and the PDS – and even, perhaps, the founding of a new left-wing party (*Der Spiegel*, 29 September 2003).

By mid-2005, when it became clear that co-operation was indeed on the agenda, things moved quickly. At their initial meetings, the leaderships of the two parties were faced with having to sort out not only ideological and policy disagreements, but also legal and technical questions about what was (and was not) permissible if the two were to run together in the forthcoming federal election (September 2005) – and all of this in an extremely short period of time. In essence, co-operation in the election could assume three forms: the founding of a new party (and a disbanding of the two existing parties), a quick merger of the two parties, or the placement of WASG candidates on a PDS 'open list'. The first option was politically impossible, while there was not enough time for the second to have taken place. The WASG and PDS knew that discussions surrounding a merger would be complicated and detailed, and the best (indeed only) time to do this would be immediately following the federal election; this despite the fact that both parties saw a future merger as a realistic (if not uncontroversial) development. This left the third option. The end result of the negotiations was what Gysi termed a 'co-operation agreement with a perspective for a merger' signed on 10 June by Klaus Ernst, representing the WASG, and Lothar Bisky, representing the PDS (*Der Spiegel*, 30 May 2005: p. 57). According to the new agreement, discussions on a 'new project for the Left in Germany' would proceed further, the PDS executive board would examine the possibility of changing the party's name (which it would later do), neither party would put up candidates against the other, WASG members would submit themselves as candidates on the open lists of the PDS, and the PDS would strive to include them (leaving the actual decision-making process on this to the individual PDS state organisations). Although the final agreement and 'roadmap' for the merger met with much criticism from the membership of each party, WASG and PDS party conferences approved the agreement with decisive majorities.

Through the summer of 2005 the new 'Left Party' subsequently became one of the most intriguing stories of the federal election campaign. The party generated enormous interest – despite, or perhaps because of, its unknown potential – and rode high in the polls (recording as much as 12 per cent in pre-election opinion surveys). Despite legal challenges to the running of WASG candidates on the Left Party's open lists, as election day approached the 'new' party continued to gather momentum. And, even though enthusiasm for the party dampened somewhat in the early autumn as voters began to more carefully consider their choices, the Left Party nevertheless garnered 8.7 per cent of the vote on election day – far more than the PDS ever received, and undoubtedly far more than the WASG and PDS together would have managed had they run as separate parties. Furthermore, this success was repeated in 2009 when the Left Party increased its vote share to 11.9 per cent, enabling it to send 76 MPs to the federal parliament in Berlin and to further stabilise itself in the German party system.

The Left Party's ideological make-up

The 2005 and 2009 election successes should not deflect from the fact that the political project of the Left Party is a surprisingly difficult one to pin down. And, in truth, it has always been thus. Through the 1990s there were two broad groups fighting for the PDS's ideological heart and soul: traditional Marxists keen on programmatic purity, as well as adherents of radical but unorthodox ideologies on the one hand and less dogmatic reforming socialists on the other. To further complicate matters, the reformers were also internally split; 'pragmatists' were keen on enhancing the party's parliamentary base while 'modern socialists' were more occupied with strategic and programmatic questions. To produce an even more complex and confusing picture, these conflicts were overlapping (Brie, 1995: p. 28; Brie, 2000; Land and Possekel, 1995). The divide in the reform-orientated camp is significant, as, although both sides support government participation in principle, they do so for very different reasons. The pragmatic reformers tend to use their ideological base as nothing more than a compass to guide them in their everyday activity. They are predominantly to be found in the eastern branches of the party and see themselves primarily as practical problem-solvers. Their emphasis tends to be less on 'big picture' issues and more on the local, the practical and the doable. The modern socialists are more interested in proving the party's reliability and want to stress that the LP is a serious actor doing serious things. Their goals are more long-term than those of the pragmatic reformers and their aim is to become a reliable part in left/centre-left coalitions.

Over and above ideological differences, a generational cleavage was (and to an extent still is in the Left Party) clearly evident within the PDS. Originally, those who created socialism in the GDR (the so-called 'Aufbaugeneration') and the Perestroika generation faced each other down (Gerth, 2003: p. 184), the former dominating the party's rank and file, the latter its leadership. Recently, the advent of a third generation socialised almost exclusively in reunified Germany has added a further internal tension line to the existing variety of intra-party conflicts, the so called 'emancipated left' promoting a far more libertarian policy approach than elder generations of PDS/Left Party politicians. However, the basic conflict between reformists open to parliamentary politics and coalition-building on the one hand and fundamentalists who focus on extra-parliamentary politics on the other remains clearly evident, even within the new LP.

In terms of policy platforms, the PDS differed from the other German parties with regards to its anti-capitalist, overtly eastern German, political platform. The PDS attempted to develop socialist alternatives to what it described as the neoliberal hegemonic consensus, basing its agenda on a commitment to social justice (including a strong commitment to redistributive tax policies), a commitment to the international peace movement (including such things as the dissolution of NATO and forbidding German soldiers to be active overseas) and a strong defence of 'eastern German interests'. Despite its radical positions clearly challenging the mainstream consensus, the PDS entered a coalition with the SPD at the regional level in Mecklenburg-Western Pomerania in 1998 and three years later it did the same in the city state of Berlin. Indeed, it was returned to power in both of these states, in the elections of 2002 and 2006 respectively.

Yet the fact that the 'new' party (still) does not have a party programme is strong evidence that the merger of the WASG and PDS has done little to generate ideological and programmatic clarity. Indeed, finding *any* consensus on programmatic issues can be a tortuous process. Long-standing groups such as the Communist Platform, Anti-Capitalist Left and Marxist Forum have been strengthened by the merger, and they enjoy both a significant public profile and a considerable presence in the *Linke*'s executive committee; former members of (other) communist groups (namely the German Communist Party, DKP) such as Wolfgang Gehrcke and Harald Werner sit alongside radical leftists such as Christine Buchholz and Janine Wissler, while Sahra Wagenknecht and Thiess Gleiss of the prominent anti-capitalist *Antikapitalische Linke* are also members (Jesse and Lang, 2008: p. 188). These groups enjoy an institutionalised status that prevents the leadership from ignoring them, and ensures that neo-Marxist voices (in all their diversity) still get a hearing. The new LP continues to have a small but vociferous 'alternative' wing, which has, if anything, also been enriched during the merger process. This group is quite disparate in itself, with anti-globalisation protestors mixing with left-wing libertarians. They are not, however, without influence; six members of the 2008–10 executive have links, for example, with globalisation critical movement ATTAC.[1] Of all the groups, they, perhaps curiously, nonetheless tend to have the lowest profile in the party (Hough et al., 2007: pp. 19–21).

The WASG's legacy is also noticeable in that two other predominantly western German factions are evident within the party, and they exert considerable emphasis on the LP's programmatic direction. They also have a not inconsiderable presence in the party's executive committee (where 23 of the 44 members of the 2008–10 committee stem unambiguously from the western states).[2] The first is made up of experienced political activists who have spent many years working in the trade union movement and/or within the SPD. They support what were, in essence, social democratic themes of the 1970s, stressing protectionist policies based largely around Keynesian economics. Alongside them exists another group of predominantly western German activists that is ideologically diverse and, for the most part, politically inexperienced. Its members may well have been active in communist party groupings before they joined the Left Party, although many of them have had little or no experience of working within larger political entities. This group's political naivety has recently led the LP into embarrassing situations, as some of their members either articulate off-message policies or simply behave in politically inopportune ways. Examples include a member of the Lower Saxony state parliament claiming that Germany should introduce a secret service along the lines of East Germany's fearsome Stasi (*Der Spiegel*, 14 February 2008), while others have openly compared the behaviour of German soldiers in Afghanistan with those at the Berlin Wall (*Der Spiegel*, 23 August 2008). A text message scandal in Bremen also did little for the LP's standing there (*Der Spiegel*, 16 January 2008).

Alongside these strategically minded groupings, the LP is also home to a myriad of other voluntary organisations that all push slightly different agendas; some are officially sanctioned, while others continue to wait to hear whether they have met the LP's criteria for achieving 'official' status. They have the right to shape their own programmatic profile and to decide upon their own organisational structures and, provided that they do not contravene any of the core principles of the party's statute, they enjoy considerable autonomy. In August 2009 there were 24 officially sanctioned groups, including the reform-orientated Forum of Democratic Socialism (*Forum Demokratischer Sozialismus*), the Socialist Left (*Sozialistische Linke*) and the Communist Platform (*Kommunistische Plattform*). There were also 15 that had applied to be granted this status (including the *Marxistisches Forum*).[3] There are also some groups who have not yet sought it at all (such as the Anti-Capitalist Left (*Antikapitalistische Linke*)) (see also Jesse and Lang, 2008: p. 176). Even the most cursory of glances through these groups' lists of demands, claims, wants and needs illustrates the ideological and programmatic diversity with which the party leadership is consequently confronted.

This disparate base is the principal reason behind the Left Party's lack of genuine programmatic substance. During the early 1990s the mosaic of AGs (working groups) and IGs (interest groups) used to work as programmatic think tanks, churning out ideas and proposals that the PDS's leadership would then take up and consider. But by as early as the mid-1990s parliamentarians and their staffs in the *Bundestag* and the eastern *Landtage* were taking on more prominent policy-drafting functions. The 'programmatic guidelines' published in 2007 – and this is the nearest document that the current LP has to a programme – nonetheless talk of a 'strategic triangle' of aims that the party should be pursuing (Programmatische Eckpunkte, 2007). The triangle is formed of societal protest on the one hand, ideas for developing alternatives within contemporary capitalism on the other and, finally, the creation of future socio-economic paths over and above current capitalist constraints.

Indeed, the LP's political project appears to be based on three sets of convictions. Firstly, there is a strong, consistent and rigid criticism of Germany's social market economy and, over and above this, of the rather nebulous concept of neoliberalism. Secondly, the LP stresses – much as the PDS did before it – a radical pacifist agenda, emphasising the importance of withdrawing German troops from conflict zones around the globe – no matter why they are there. Finally, the third core tenet of the LP's self-understanding is very clear denunciation of 'bad guys' (namely managers, economic elites, big businessmen) and 'good guys' (the labouring classes in Germany, the poor and downtrodden in the Third World and left-wing movements everywhere) (Hough and Koß, 2009). The 'Guidelines' are more anti-capitalist than the PDS's last party programme (the so-called 'Chemnizer Programm', published in 2003) and they are in many ways more radical in the demands that are made. Indeed, as Jesse and Lang point out, the programmatic demands in the 'Guidelines' are 'more social than the SPD, more green than the Greens and – in the area of inner-German security at least – more liberal than the FDP!' (Jesse and Lang, 2008: p. 176). The list of demands made ranges from free education and nursery places to a guaranteed basic income for all; from national minimum wages to sweeping increases in tax rates for companies and high earners.

Marching through the institutions; The LP's governing experiences thus far

The radical and disparate nature of these programmatic claims did not prevent the PDS, and latterly the LP, from taking part in coalitions with Social Democrats at the regional level. Indeed, although it was the PDS that began this trend back in 1998, recent regional elections in Thuringia and Saarland (both in August 2009) have illustrated that the LP's lack of programmatic clarity has not prevented it from wanting – almost at any cost – to take over the reins of power. This was evident not just in Oskar Lafontaine's claim that he wanted to be the next Prime Minister of his home state of Saarland (something that was never likely because of his own complicated relationship with the SPD there), but, more tellingly, in the LP's keenness to form a government with the SPD in Thuringia. The LP's leader there, Bodo Ramelow, went as far as claiming that the LP was quite prepared to think out of the box in terms of how this co-operation might be engineered; the LP, for example, would not demand – even though it was the largest party in the prospective coalition – that Ramelow automatically become the next state PM, stressing that the project of red–red and removing the CDU from office was too important to fall on the basis of personalities (*Welt*, 3 September 2009). To say that the LP in 2009 was an office-seeker at the *Land* level would be truer than ever before.

Pro-government activists were nonetheless pushing for the pre-2005 PDS to at least consider the idea at the *Land* level by as early as the mid-1990s, even if it remained well and truly out of the equation in the federal arena. Germany's institutional framework clearly facilitated this too; many of the issues on which the PDS held its most dogmatic stances were in areas where the states had very few competencies. Although Article 74 of the Basic Law specifies a range of so-called 'concurrent' legislative competencies (including the regulation of the economy and labour law) where the *Länder* are theoretically free to legislate, in practice these areas have seen a gradual encroachment of federal law over the past decades. By the beginning of the new millennium, the only significant areas of public policy to remain in the sole competence of the *Länder* are education, law enforcement and public broadcasting – not issues that are especially controversial for an LP looking to work with the SPD. To put it another way, *Land* administrations have no say over when and where German troops are sent abroad, for example, and other high-octane foreign policy issues need not affect governing arrangements in the sub-state arena. The *Länder* also do not set tax rates, and they have a constitutional obligation to implement federal laws, no matter how much the governing parties may dislike them (as was the case with the much maligned set of labour market and welfare reforms that the SPD pushed through in the early-2000s). The institutional barriers to SPD–LP co-operation were therefore not as significant as they might have appeared.

Indeed, both the Social Democrats and the Greens started to toy with the idea of bringing the PDS into positions of responsibility at the *Land* level during the mid-1990s. The personalisation of local politics meant that PDS politicians there had long since been brought into everyday political affairs, and PDS mayors – tacitly supported in some places by politicians from other parties – were not an uncommon sight across eastern Germany. Social Democrats in the eastern states had realised that ostracising the PDS was doing the SPD no good at all at the polls; the PDS could portray itself as the victim of western German bullies, and consistent claims that the PDS was either extremist or too linked to the GDR (or both) were not electoral trump cards. Rejecting the PDS outright also limited the Social Democrats' strategic options, and ensured that the CDU maintained the upper hand in issues of coalition formation. The exclusion strategy of the SPD and the Greens therefore needed overhauling.

The first fruits of this came in 1994, when the SPD in Saxony-Anhalt took the PDS up on its offer of acting as a support party to the SPD/Green coalition. Reinhard Höppner, the SPD's leader, had expressly ruled out such an option in the election campaign, but the closeness of the results – and the PDS's position as the third largest parliamentary party – prompted him to take the plunge. Höppner did insist that his government would, on occasion, seek support from the CDU in crafting majorities – in truth, more of his programme appealed to the pragmatists in the PDS than to the centre-right parties. Contrary to the dire warnings of the Christian and Free Democrats, Saxony-Anhalt did not lurch into chaos. Political life continued on very much as normal. Whether the SPD/Green, PDS-tolerated government was successful in its aims is a moot point; what is beyond doubt is that political life continued much as it had done before.

These events were watched particularly keenly in Germany's north-east, in Mecklenburg-Western Pomerania (MWP). The publication of the Erfurt Declaration in January 1997, calling for a working alliance of all parties to the left of the SPD, illustrated that the SPD had not ruled the PDS out as a prospective coalition partner (*ZSPW*, 1997). And, sure enough, post-1998 the coalition came into being. PDS activists in MWP did not take the decision to enter government because they felt it was sending any sort of signal out to the nation at large. It was much more a case of wanting to develop and implement specific policies that might help to solve the (many) socio-economic problems that exist in Germany's economically weakest state. The PDS in MWP subsequently entered the coalition with the SPD in 1998 with a clear set of programmatic aims and concrete proposals. It knew what it wanted to do and it had a pretty good idea of how it intended to do it. This was not replicated in Berlin when the PDS entered government there three years later. Naturally, the PDS had to revise a number of its original aims when it began negotiations with the SPD, but its clearly defined plan of attack left it in a much more advanced bargaining position than was the case in Berlin in 2001, illustrating the preponderance of pragmatic, practical thinkers in the party leadership (Hough and Olsen, 2004: p. 129).

Ultimately, and after eight years in power in MWP, it was the PDS's policy-seeking agenda that also saw it leave government. Although its vote actually increased from 16.4 per cent in 2002 (where it suffered a slump compared with 1998) to 16.8 per cent in 2006, and despite the fact that another red–red coalition was mathematically viable, too many members of both the parliamentary party and the rank and file were unhappy with the progress made during eight years in office. The LP (as it now was) needed to rethink its strategy and to work out new ways of meeting MVP's not inconsiderable challenges, and a spell in opposition seemed the best way to do this.

The PDS's experiences thus far in Berlin have been slightly different. For many in the PDS – and above all party talisman, and Berliner, Gregor Gysi – the importance of the party's long-term strategic vision came into play and there was a real stress on the importance of being reliable and serious in carrying out governmental tasks. Participating in government with the aim of establishing – however slowly – the PDS in western Germany appeared to be the overriding long-term vision of the leadership in Berlin, and such thoughts prevailed within the party as a whole. The PDS skilfully managed to avoid being forced into any major consensus-threatening compromises (Reißig, 2005: p. 13). The same can also be said of the SPD, largely as the PDS was well aware of specific demands that were likely to prove untenable to the social-democratic rank and file. The lack of a coherent socialist programmatic profile was abundantly evident both to PDS insiders (Beikler, 2003: p. 14; Richter, 2003b: p. 20) and to those (both critical and sympathetic) looking in from the outside (Reißig, 2005: pp. 47–50), and it facilitated what has been a surprisingly smooth relationship.

Policy problems in the international arena

Alongside the differences alluded to above, the SPD is well aware that there are at least two more areas where national-level coalitions could run into problems in the way that *Land* level ones have not; attitudes to the European Union and, to a lesser extent, attitudes towards globalisation. This is not to say that everything else would be straightforward; battles over tax rates, levels of welfare spending, the introduction of minimum wages and attitudes to creating jobs would clearly be very fiercely fought. The pivotal position that office-seekers, the namely modern socialists, within the LP have manoeuvred themselves into nonetheless gives plenty of reason to believe that, ultimately, compromises could be found. The office-seekers in the LP may ultimately find common ground on issues of EU policy too, but this will take a lot of hard negotiation and will involve the LP in particular slaughtering some of its own holy cows.

The LP has always been vehemently critical of the EU's alleged neoliberalisation, and it has voted against (if not unanimously, then certainly with a convincing majority) such things as the Amsterdam and Lisbon treaties. The SPD has always supported ratification of these treaties. The 2009 programme for the election to the European Parliament also saw the LP demand an 'economic government' for Europe, illustrating how it sees the EU level as a vehicle through which it can inject more control and planning into the European economy (Die Linke, 2009a: p. 7). The different approaches of the LP and SPD to economic policy in the national arena are subsequently replicated, if in slightly different ways, at the EU level. The LP is, however, quick to stress its own commitment to the European idea and thus to the process of deeper European integration; it is the LP's understanding of what form this integration should take that is the problem (Die Linke, 2009a).

Over and above economic policy, the key differences between the LP's positions and those of the Social Democrats are primarily twofold. Firstly, the LP demands a fundamental change in European military and security policy. Indeed, the LP claimed that the economic interests that were seen as underpinning the development of the Lisbon Treaty went hand in hand with an aggressive foreign policy and Europe's militarisation (Die Linke, 2009a: p. 1). All military missions under the rubric of CFSP should therefore be immediately stopped, and this alongside the abolition of NATO (Die Linke, 2009a: p. 23). Secondly, the LP rejected the EU's Constitutional Treaty, and is unlikely to agree to any future set of institutional reforms that do not encapsulate its own very particular (radical democratic) ideals. The Left Party made it clear that it wanted its MEPs to refrain from being drawn into these structures by effectively sacking two of its more consensual (and widely respected) MEPs (Sylvia-Yvonne Kaufmann and Andre Brie) in the run-up to the 2009 poll, largely on the basis of the less rejectionist positions that they took on integration issues. All further treaties, furthermore, should be passed by referendum in all 27 member states, another stance that the SPD refuses point blank to countenance. The one saving grace here is that the EU itself is likely to have little stomach for high-profile, institutional reform, and European issues – already of marginal significance to the average German voter – are likely to take an even less significant role than normal in the medium term.

The same can be said of the anti-globalisation movement. The LP does possess a vocal body of anti-globalisation protestors, and events such as the 2007 G8 summit in Heiligendamm were used by the LP to try to showcase its radical anti-capitalist character. The LP's rhetoric is unambiguous. It claims in its 2009 federal election programme that its parliamentary party 'will be open to the views of the anti-globalisation movement' (Die Linke, 2009b: p. 57) and in practice it had supported the blocking of roads and other forms of public disobedience around major international conventions (Die Linke, 2007). It clearly wants to be seen as a party that understands the criticisms of these protestors and is loath to criticise the movement in public. But this does not necessarily mean that the LP will balk at working with the SPD on account of this. The processes that underpin globalisation are deep-rooted and inherently difficult to rein in. If the ability to make compromises that has been shown by LP politicians elsewhere is anything to go by, then LP may well seek to maintain an anti-globalisation profile while stressing that it is making small steps – as they are the only steps it can make – towards alleviating some of its worst excesses. If, in other words,

LP politicians want to nod diplomatically to the anti-globalisation parts of its supporter base while trying to work alongside the SPD, this is more than likely to be possible.

Edging closer or treading water?

Despite the existence of various groups of recalcitrants, the LP is closer to the corridors of power in Berlin than it ever has been before. Although its experiences of governing in the *Länder* have been mixed, they have certainly not been disastrous. Life has gone on in MWP and in the Reichstagsgebäude, and further SPD–LP coalitions in the eastern states would be unremarkable; the thought of LP–SPD coalitions, as was mathematically possible following the Thuringia election in August 2009, no longer scares significant portions of the German electorate, and it is only a matter of time before a Left Party *Ministerpräsident* is elected to office. It will take longer before the LP is taken as seriously in the western states, but the LP now polls more votes, and appears to generate less extreme reaction, in western Germany than was ever the case before. Again, a coalition – most likely between the SPD and the Greens – involving the *Linke* is a question of when rather than if.

The fact that pragmatists and traditionalists struggle to find any meaningful programmatic consensus – the LP knows what it does not like, but finds it virtually impossible to agree on what it does support – curiously assists the LP in moving towards government at the national level. Programmatic discussions in the future will undoubtedly be heated and controversial, but for as long as the modern socialists remain predominant it is likely that they will be able to keep the governing option open. This curious balance is nonetheless challenged in the national arena on account of two factors. Firstly, the very existence of current party leader Oskar Lafontaine is a barrier to closer SPD–LP links in Berlin. For many in the SPD, Lafontaine remains a traitor who cannot and should not be trusted; they do not dispute his talismanic status within the LP, but they are not prepared to work with someone who has done so much to undermine the work of the SPD since his resignation as Finance Minister and party leader in 1999. Secondly, there are clear and significant policy differences, and these are of an underlying nature. While the SPD and LP can agree on many competences that fall into the remit of the states, as well as the parameters of much socio-economic policy, there are problems in terms of EU policy, and the two parties are diametrically opposed in terms of foreign and security policy. Attitudes to sending German troops abroad, NATO, the USA (the SPD being much more friendly than the LP) and various other security issues ensure that there is very little common ground between the two actors.

These policy discrepancies cannot, however, disguise the fact that the LP has become a more attractive, and acceptable, proposition for the SPD of late. Germany's party system is now more fluid than at any other time since the end of World War II. The left–right blocs have not become so porous that they have no relevance, but the notion of coalitions involving three parties (i.e. Christian Democrats, Liberals and Greens; Social Democrats, Liberals and Greens; Social Democrats, Greens and the LP) have become more than just dinner-party discussion topics. The electoral weaknesses of the catch-all parties are forcing them to be more promiscuous with their coalition choices – and this cannot help but bode well for the LP in the future.

Notes

1. For more details see http://die-linke.de/partei/organe/parteivorstand/parteivorstand_20082010/ mitglieder/ (accessed 15 November 2008).
2. Some members of the LP's Executive either have backgrounds that genuinely straddle the east/west divide or were born abroad and have only joined the LP in relatively recent times.
3. For more information on all of these groups, see http://www.die-linke.de/partei/zusammenschluesse/ (accessed 15 November 2008).

10
Ready to Get Their Hands Dirty: The Socialist Party and GroenLinks in the Netherlands

Dan Keith

The Netherlands is one of the few western European countries where a left party has not recently entered national government.[1] This last happened when the small Christian-environmentalist Political Party of the Radicals (PPR) played a junior role in a progressive coalition in the 1970s. The absence of left parties from government is not for want of trying. Indeed, two left parties – GroenLinks (GL) and the Socialistische Partij (SP) – have made hard choices with the aim of doing this, sacrificing policy commitments in pursuit of electoral and office goals, and the prospect of these parties entering government is no longer a flight of fancy. GroenLinks and the SP have increasing experience of local government and are now taken seriously in discussions on prospective coalitions. However, electoral successes such as that by the SP in 2006, when its representation in the Tweede Kamer grew from nine to 25 seats, have not, as yet, brought government participation with them.

Given their genuine wish to do so, it is therefore puzzling that neither the SP nor GroenLinks has been able to enter government. The recent upheavals in Dutch politics (most noticeably the 'de-pillarisation' of traditional social cleavages and increased electoral volatility) have also spawned further opportunities to do just this. The three largest parties – the Christian Democrats (CDA), Social Democrats (PvdA) and (right-wing) Liberals (VVD) – have seen their share of the vote fall, naturally benefiting the smaller parties in terms of both vote share and political influence (Lucardie, 1994). Nonetheless, it has been the left-wing liberals (D66), the right-wing populist List Pim Fortuyn and the conservative Christian Union party (CU) that were included as junior partners in governing coalitions.

GroenLinks and the SP's preference for a left-wing coalition between themselves and the PvdA is generally unrealistic on account of the CDA's strength and its presence in every post-war government other than 1994–2002. Not that GroenLinks and the SP rule out governing with the CDA, and occasionally they work together at the local level. However, ideological differences mean that at the national level the left parties are largely reliant on the centre-left PvdA including them. During the 1980s, Dutch left parties were generally too small and radical to contribute to a coalition, and the PvdA's centrist path acted to isolate them. A de-radicalisation of the left since the 1990s has not prevented the PvdA from continuing to seek alternative partners.

This chapter explains why this is. The first section shows that the left parties' historical roots meant that they entered the 1990s with policies that hindered their inclusion in government. The second section analyses their attempts to downplay programmatic goals with the aim of becoming coalitionable. It points to significant similarities in the causes of their transformations and the steps that they took – most importantly, it shows that both parties recruited pragmatic leaders who were willing to make hard political choices. The third section shows that the SP and GroenLinks occupy different niches, particularly on issues of European integration and globalisation. The final section focuses on the parties' failure to enter government in 2006. It demonstrates that this did not occur because of their incompatibility with government *per se*, but because of situational factors that will not always apply. GroenLinks and the SP have not re-radicalised after failing to enter government in 2006, and they are no longer necessarily permanent opposition parties. Being more than interested onlookers, they remain serious contenders for government in the future.

Historical origins

GroenLinks began life in 1990 as a merger between four small struggling radical-left parties: the PPR, the Communist Party of the Netherlands (CPN), the Pacifist Socialist Party (PSP) and the largely insignificant Evangelical People's Party. The merger was aimed at survival, ideological renewal and uniting the forces of the radical left in an effort to increase their influence on the PvdA. The SP, on the other hand, was formed in 1972 out of a Maoist splinter group from the CPN. Through the early 1970s it remained a tiny sect of around 500 members.

Their historical starting points initially presented GroenLinks and the SP with five obstacles to participating in government. First, the parties lacked prior experience in government, making it appear somehow out of reach, and only the PPR had any previous experience of entering national government. Second, this experience of government was traumatic. The PPR's anarchist tendencies and increasingly new-left profile triggered an internal backlash when it governed. The ecologist and left wing of the PPR subsequently took over when it left government in 1977, radicalising policy positions and prioritising grass roots activism (Lucardie and Ghillebaert, 2008: p. 72).

Third, large groups within the parties rejected governing on principle because it threatened to downgrade programmatic commitments and extra-parliamentary activism. The PSP's reluctance to get its hands dirty in government was particularly notable (Voerman, 1995: p. 112). Its leader, Fred van der Spek (1981–5), opposed any participation in government even at the local level, instead preferring principled opposition until a socialist revolution occurred. Even after he left in 1985, the PSP's new leaders prioritised working with radical social movements above governing. The SP also revelled in radical activism. It began providing its own doctors and legal services for workers in cities such as Oss. Participation in parliament (or governing) was a secondary priority and simply a propaganda tool to publicise grass roots activism and a revolution by the masses (SP, 1974, 1987).

Fourth, the parties' firebrand policies were too radical for potential mainstream coalition partners. The PPR was the most flexible but it still called for comprehensive environmental regulations, a redistribution of wealth as a reward for unpaid work, establishing a maximum income, reducing working hours to 25 a week and democratising the economy (PPR, 1977, 1986). The CPN, PSP and SP's proposals included withdrawal from NATO, disarmament, nationalisation (or 'socialisation') of the means of production, abolishing the free market, and massive reductions in unemployment (Koeneman et al., 1988; PSP, 1981, 1986; CPN, 1984; SP, 1974, 1987). The CPN had broken with Stalinism but now incorporated feminism and environmentalism in multifaceted calls for revolutionary change (CPN, 1984).

Finally, the parties could be very fussy in choosing coalition partners. PSP congresses consistently asserted that it would only enter national or municipal coalitions with left-wing parties. The PSP's national executive resigned in 1983 after losing congress votes aimed at taking a positive approach towards government and building coalitions with mainstream progressive parties including D66. In contrast, the CPN and PPR found room to work with progressive Christian Democrats.

Ideological and programmatic consistency

GroenLinks and the SP began the 1990s as outsiders whose programmes opposed the established political system. GroenLinks promoted a mix of its founders' policies, including opposition to NATO and the monarchy. It did not call itself socialist, but continued many of the CPN and PSP's revolutionary social policies and the PPR's radical environmentalism (Lucardie and Voerman, 2003). Political scientists subsequently considered GroenLinks as part of the radical left (March and Mudde, 2005). GroenLinks also inherited its founders' ambivalence towards national government. It believed that the responsibility and discipline of government threatened its radical reformism (GroenLinks, 1992). GroenLinks's leaders had more experience of extra-parliamentary protest than administration. Governing was not likely, or a priority, and was rarely discussed. The SP still remained outside parliament and did not, and could not, spend time discussing the merits of government participation.

The leaders of GroenLinks and the SP have made great efforts to overcome their outsider status. A high degree of ideological and internal change has taken place. What changed the parties' approaches to government so radically? Election defeats provided pressure to change, while, secondly, the emergence of new pragmatic leaders willing to break with past commitments pushed the process on.

The parties' practices of elite advancement were particularly significant. Young functionaries with experience of direct action campaigns rose up the SP's hierarchy. The younger elites were less dogmatic, largely on account of their experiences of providing local services and working in local councils. They soon came into conflict with the SP's founding leader, the domineering activist Daan Monje. In particular, they questioned Monje's strategy of sending aid to the British miners in the mid-1980s even after their strike had collapsed. Their calls for a more vote-maximising strategy in response to the SP's electoral failures resonated in the party executive and Monje's influence waned. The charismatic Jan Marijnissen, an influential local councillor, hitherto excluded from the leadership, became the new face of the SP.

Ongoing participation in local councils was a good training ground for the SP's new leaders. They saw the benefits of swapping theoretically appealing policies for practical ones and they began to accept the need for compromise with other parties. The SP's new leaders, used to exerting influence at the local level, increasingly began to prioritise electoral success over ideologically minded goals. Marijnissen and Tiny Kox, or 'The Rat' as he was known within the party elite, obtained extensive control over the SP through its structures of democratic centralism, which they initially used to change the party. Their attempts to induce change doubled following failure in the 1989 election.

A similar development occurred in GroenLinks. Its (former CPN) leader Ina Brouwer resigned after GroenLinks's 1994 election loss, being replaced by the charismatic Paul Rosenmöller. When GroenLinks was founded in the early 1990s, 'renewers' demanded a fresh start while another group argued for policy continuation. The renewers were generally unsuccessful, although they did secure the inclusion of several non-party members on GroenLinks's list for parliamentary elections, including Rosenmöller. Rosenmöller's rise to the leadership symbolised the new beginning that the renewers had desired. Rosenmöller had once been a radical Maoist but had shown the capacity to revise his beliefs; as a trade unionist he encountered a need for compromise and realistic policies and as a journalist he recognised the importance of presentation. He was unencumbered by the burdens of the past that haunted his predecessors and drew on his experiences to remodel GroenLinks by broadening its appeal.

The new leaders started by moderating their parties' oppositional politics to achieve electoral expansion. Kox and Marijnissen strengthened the SP's central office and formulated a new party programme, Charter 2000 (SP, 1991). This recognised the need for freedom of expression and jettisoned Marxism–Leninism and the nationalisation of the means of production. Instead, a vague notion of 'socialism' (not Communism) became the SP's ideology: 'socialism' was a 'guiding set of morals' rather than an objective blueprint for society (Voerman, 2007a). It involved preventing privatisations, implementing economic planning, full employment and 'socialising' the economy (SP, 1991). The SP also appeared to democratise by reducing restrictions on membership, expanding the size of the leadership and holding more congresses (Voerman, 2008: p. 31).

The SP's leaders professionalised party communications by introducing PR experts who were free to repackage and reformulate policies. A 'Vote Against!' slogan and the image of a tomato now symbolised the SP's oppositional role, replacing its 'Honest and Active' theme (van der Steen, 1994). After entering parliament in 1994, the SP's leaders continued to moderate the party, exchanging socialism for vaguer concepts of human dignity, equality and solidarity (Voerman and Lucardie, 2007). The SP's new programme, *Heel de Mens* (1999), abandoned 'socialising' and planning the economy, and replaced criticisms of Dutch capitalism with attacks on the neoliberalism imported from Britain and the United States.

GroenLinks originally committed itself to the 'socialisation' of the economy, socio-economic planning, state control of the financial system and land nationalisations. It soon began to moderate these demands, and calls for land nationalisation quickly disappeared (GroenLinks, 1994). After the 1994 election failure, GroenLinks's leaders criticised its election programme for being too left-wing, and Rosenmöller promoted a less socialist, less radical agenda. By 1998, the idea of economic planning had been dropped altogether and egalitarian social policies were watered down (Lucardie and Voerman, 2003). The changes broke with much of GroenLinks's socialist and anti-systemic heritage. Rosenmöller also professionalised communications by increasing the use of PR agencies who created campaigns emphasising being in government (Hippe et al., 2002).

Rosenmöller aimed to provide a more effective style of opposition. He instructed GroenLinks's parliamentarians to criticise the PvdA–D66–VVD 'Purple-Government' (1994–2002) only when they had an alternative, with the aim of investing more energy in new policies. Furthermore, Rosenmöller promoted the idea of making compromises with other parties, to the detriment of GroenLinks's own programmatic goals. GroenLinks also found room to use the powers that Dutch MPs have to present draft legislation. These institutional mechanisms were a third factor contributing towards changing its approach to government, giving incentives to make moderate policy proposals and working with other parties. Rosenmöller made increasing use of these powers between 1994 and 1998 in order to practise making realistic legislation and to show that GroenLinks could work responsibly in a governing coalition.

The dynamics of the party system were a fourth factor shaping the parties' changing priorities. However, GL and SP did not moderate because of offers of inclusion from the PvdA but rather because of the break in tradition presented by the Purple-Governments. With their rivals on the left in government, and pursuing apparently neoliberal policies (including privatisations and welfare cuts), it was an opportune moment to change themselves. The parties' pragmatic leaders seized the initiative, repositioning their parties as a credible alternative for disaffected PvdA supporters (Voerman, 2008: p. 35). GroenLinks aimed to unite the forces of the radical left, but its leaders (and members) increasingly sought to carve out a left-libertarian niche emphasising environmentalism and multiculturalism. It yielded its founders' socialist territory to the SP, allowing it to become the clearest 'left' alternative to the PvdA and the main beneficiary of its electoral difficulties.

A fifth factor was the success that the SP and GroenLinks achieved. Both parties attracted PvdA voters, while GroenLinks also attracted D66 supporters (Voerman and Lucardie, 2007: p. 140). GroenLinks increased its number of parliamentary seats from five to 11 in 1998. The SP achieved the milestone of parliamentary representation with two seats in 1994 and expanded spectacularly to five in 1998 and nine in 2002. Moreover, the CDA's leadership was in disarray, effectively making Rosenmöller the leader of the opposition in parliament (Lucardie, 1999: p. 156). Electoral success was a situational factor that made governing realistic, prompting both leaderships to reassess their priorities after the 1998 election.

Growing memberships also affected the parties. The swathes of PvdA voters joining the SP (which increased from 15,000 members in 1992 to 43,000 in 2004) presented further pressures to moderate and to become positive about governing. GroenLinks's new members also lacked its radical heritage (GroenLinks expanded from 12,500 in 1993 to 25,500 by 2004). Its members became less socialist, less committed to state ownership of the means of production, increasingly moderate on green issues, increasingly libertarian and less 'left' on a left–right scale (Lucardie and Voerman, 2008). This strongly affected GroenLinks's approach to government. In 1992, only 6 per cent of GroenLinks's members believed that forming a progressive government should be its main priority; this rose to 53 per cent by 2002 (Lucardie and Voerman, 2008).

Expansion in municipal politics also helped knock the radicalism out of the parties. GroenLinks expanded from 16 (1989) to 62 (1998) representatives in municipal government (some in broad-based coalitions with the CDA) and from 254 to 480 local councillors. The SP increased its number of councillors from 70 (1990) to 188 (1998) and gained its first representatives in local government. The experience of municipal government gave the parties confidence and showed that they could be effective and responsible coalition partners. It helped to convince their leaders that national government was feasible. Ideological change was also a consequence of governing. Ever more politicians who had experienced the constraints of elected office and the need to make administrative compromises entered the parties' elite, providing additional pressures to downplay policy goals. GroenLinks's new councillors often encountered pressures for realistic spending plans and increasingly favoured liberal policies, which they thought would make GroenLinks more attractive to mainstream coalition partners.

Rosenmöller contemplated governing from the beginning of his leadership. The success of the 1998 election made this plausible, and thereafter he tried to show that GroenLinks was genuine coalition material. The SP's leaders came round to the idea in 2001, when polling data showed that target voters doubted whether voting SP was a realistic way to achieve change. Accordingly, both parties' leaders made additional changes as they prioritised governing and continued electoral growth. The SP introduced the slogan 'Vote For!' to replace its previous oppositional message. Both parties' leaders also made statements to convey their desire to govern. Furthermore, they held meetings with other parties to discuss coalition possibilities. GroenLinks spoke with the CDA in 2002 and both parties met with the PvdA in 2006. The SP's leaders also put outsiders on its parliamentary list in 2006 to introduce more expertise in preparation for government and to broaden the SP's appeal.

The party leaders continued to ditch ideological baggage to show that they were moderate and capable of handling government responsibility. Commitments to withdraw from NATO were dropped from GroenLinks's manifesto in 2002 and the SP's in 2006. GroenLinks's parliamentary group also supported NATO intervention in Kosovo (1999) and in Afghanistan (2001), a painful break with its pacifist roots. The SP moderated its proposals on tax rates for high earners and for egalitarian mortgage tax-relief reforms so as to appeal to middle-class voters and to appear less authoritarian. It also sacrificed calls to abolish the monarchy.

GroenLinks's leaders continued to broaden their appeal by parachuting outsiders into its parliamentary group. This has had a profound effect on GroenLinks's programmatic direction. Femke Halsema, a former PvdA functionary, was fast-tracked in 1998. She became party leader in 2003. Halsema has further liberalised the party, partly for strategic reasons on account of her belief that moderating socio-economic policies would increase GroenLinks's ability to participate in government. As a result, GroenLinks toned down its support for an expansive welfare state and labour-market regulation. It also dropped its long-standing commitment to a 32-hour working week (GroenLinks, 2006, 2007). Under Halsema, the party leadership has continued to professionalise GroenLinks's campaign machine and GroenLinks's campaigns now present it as a party seeking power. They have also tried to appear responsible by breaking with the occasionally illegal nature of GroenLinks's activist past and disciplining parliamentarians with murky backgrounds.

Issues at the core of the left party project

The SP and GroenLinks are very different types of left party. The SP has appealed more to the working-class and unemployed, while GroenLinks generally attracts middle-class, public-sector workers. The parties' names were fitting in the early 1990s. The SP was genuinely socialist and provided a radical critique of capitalism, while GroenLinks sought to reconcile green and left issues. It did not provide a theoretical critique of capitalism, but promoted the radical new-left policies of its predecessors (GroenLinks, 1989, 1994). Now the parties' names are not so fitting. The SP has lost its revolutionary zeal, while GroenLinks increasingly resembles the left-libertarian PPR more than the CPN or the PSP and its activism has dwindled (Voerman, 2008: p. 20). Despite such changes, both still promote ideas expected from left parties. Furthermore, they have always taken polarised, left positions on issues of European integration and globalisation.

Political scientists have noted that European left parties have mutated and de-radicalised (March and Mudde, 2005). The Dutch left parties fit this trend. March (2008) still classifies the SP as meeting the requirements to be discussed as a left party, but not GroenLinks, which he claims is now 'non-radical'. Indeed, GroenLinks once wanted an ecological economy with market elements that was 'at odds with the current capitalist market-economy', but soon reined in such rhetoric (GroenLinks, 1992). It now accepts more space for the market (GroenLinks, 2006). However, if a narrow definition of the 'radical left' is used then the SP should no longer be included either. Those seeking a far-reaching theoretical analysis of capitalism in its programmes will be disappointed. Even criticism of neoliberalism appears only intermittently (SP, 2006a). The SP is now more social democratic than classically socialist.

Both parties campaign on policies designed more to deal with the consequences of capitalism rather than unearthing its roots and replacing it with something else. They both accept the need for private property and do not express anti-capitalism by demanding a planned economy. SP policies address goals of limiting working hours, maintaining full employment, capping salaries for company executives and politicians, limiting cheap migrant labour to defend the position of Dutch workers while increasing social provision for migrants, and bringing about a 'fairer distribution of wealth'. The party also aims to end segregation in education, tackle child poverty, strengthen social services, reverse the marketisation of public transport, and balance the economic cycle (SP, 2002, 2006a). In 2002, the SP planned to increase spending by €15 billion (SP, 2002).

GroenLinks has drifted far from the 'drastic simultaneous levelling of incomes' and workers' councils it initially wanted (GroenLinks, 1992, 2006). Nonetheless, its (fading) socialist heritage still informs policies including increased investment in public services and transport, increasing provision for migrants, and massively lowering unemployment.

Moreover, GroenLinks wants free childcare, and government intervention where price mechanisms fail, such as in rewarding unpaid/care work, and it aims to halve poverty rates through increasing state benefits (GroenLinks, 2006). GroenLinks opposes most of the privatisations made by the Purple-Governments. It would invest an additional €13 billion in 'a green and socially sound Netherlands' from slashing defence spending and taxing high incomes (Hippe et al., 2003; Lucardie et al., 2006).

It is hard to tell whether anti-systemic beliefs about the underlying socio-economic structure of capitalism inform these policies and how much of the moderation is window dressing to broaden the parties' appeals. Nonetheless, both parties still meet March and Mudde's broader criteria for classifying 'radical left parties'. They seek to implement more direct democracy and to include marginalised groups (the unemployed and migrants) in the socio-economic system, and identify economic inequity as the basis of existing social arrangements (SP, 2006a; GroenLinks, 2006). Moreover, many of their policies aim for a major redistribution of resources, constraining profit motives and opposing neoliberalism, even if they are increasingly hesitant to play this up. This sets them apart from the type of social democracy pursued by the PvdA.

These parties illustrate the problems involved in classifying 'radical left parties'. Some do not openly call for 'root and branch' change or overthrowing capitalism (criteria used in the typology discussed in the introductory chapter) because they are more electorally minded. For these parties the notion of 'radical left' has changed, meaning that political scientists need to broaden their frame of analysis to encompass parties that hold on to more loosely defined radical left goals.

The parties' policies on Europe and globalisation reflect radical left concerns with structural economic processes, international power relations, redistribution and solidarity with the oppressed. Both parties want a different EU. The SP takes an oppositional approach, wanting a shift of power away from the EU, and criticises the creation of a European super-state, while GroenLinks wants a larger, federal, stronger EU (SP, 2006b). The SP has consistently opposed European integration and campaigns on the slogan 'Send a watchdog to Brussels!' (Lucardie and Voerman, 2005: p. 1,126). It rejected the Euro and was a part of the successful 'no' campaign in the 2005 referendum on the European Constitution, attacking its neoliberalism (Harmsen, 2005: p. 5). This strategy brought many PvdA and GroenLinks supporters to the SP (Lucardie and Voerman, 2006: p. 1,202).

The SP has two MEPs in Brussels but rejects joining the Party of the European Left. It opposes the EU's wasteful agricultural policies, overproduction and the subsidisation of large corporations such as Heineken and Nestle. It also wants to restrict the size of the EU budget and limit EU powers on social issues and foreign policy. It wants to stop the creation of a European defence force and to prevent EU expansion in the Balkans. Furthermore, it criticises unrestricted migration from new member states for displacing Dutch workers and resulting in the exploitation of migrant workers (SP, 2006b). The SP envisages a role for increased EU action on cross-border issues such as terrorism, the environment, energy and asylum. It also supports the implementation of a Tobin tax on capital transactions and regulating investments by pension funds at an EU level (SP, 2004).

GroenLinks emphasises the EU's progressive potential much more than the SP does. GroenLinks's leaders believe that environmental sustainability requires action at the EU level and they joined the European Green Party (Lucardie and Voerman, 2005: p. 1,124). GroenLinks also embraces the EU's potential for left politics. Its left wing can be critical of the EU but remains largely enthusiastic because of its ability to promote peace and socialism. GroenLinks criticises the Europe of 'markets and money' and seeks to strengthen the social dimension of EU policy – promoting human rights and demanding an 'employment pact' to tackle unemployment, poverty and social exclusion (Harmsen, 2002: p. 4; GroenLinks, 2006). It also calls for the EU to tackle global illiteracy and poverty. Promoting EU defence policy is a convenient way for GroenLinks to advocate the replacement of NATO without directly calling for withdrawal (GroenLinks, 2002). Unlike the SP, GroenLinks supported the European Constitutional Treaty, although a majority of its voters rejected it (Hippe et al., 2004: p. 54).

GroenLinks and the SP believe that globalisation requires a progressive response. Both seek to democratise global institutions, including the IMF, World Bank and UN, to empower developing nations. They also seek an expansion of the UN's powers, while the SP calls for resolutions on NATO actions. Meeting the Millennium Development Goals, cutting global poverty and expanding international aid are priorities for both parties. The SP participates in European and World Social Forums and GroenLinks maintains relations with 'globalists' in the fields of international trade, finance and ecology, with whom it published *Progressive visions of a different globalization* in 2005 (*ring* onder redactie van MHippe et al., 2005: p. 54). However, GroenLinks has not engaged with 'anti-globalisation' movements, and is generally more positive about the opportunities globalisation offers than is the SP.

The SP and GroenLinks have struggled to forge links between themselves or, indeed, with the centre-left. Occasionally there are calls for the SP and GroenLinks to merge, but differences in party culture, membership and ideology prevent this (Voerman, 1997). The SP rejected Rosenmöller's proposals in 2002 for joint electoral lists and the PvdA's calls for a progressive opposition bloc (Hippe et al., 2002: p. 153). Nonetheless, in 2004 Marijnissen unexpectedly proposed drafting a short programme to establish the priorities of a PvdA–SP–GroenLinks shadow cabinet (Hippe et al., 2004: p. 82). Before the 2006 parliamentary election, the three parties were riding high in the polls and a left-wing majority in parliament looked credible. In response, they tentatively investigated the possibility of a left-coalition. Pioneering discussions entitled 'Another Netherlands' took place between their politicians and members.

Articles by leading politicians from the parties were also published in the SP's journal *Spanning* (2005). These showed that the PvdA's leaders had little preference for any of its prospective coalition partners and that it recognised similarities in the parties' votes in parliament. Nevertheless, the PvdA feared that support for left-wing policies might disappear, and they found the SP's Euroscepticism troublesome. An article by SP parliamentarian Ronald van Raak was the most sceptical about an alliance, mainly as the SP still rejected the other parties' support for the market (van Raak, 2005). Bart Snels, from GroenLinks's Research Bureau, called for the PvdA to back a left-wing coalition before the election and for a common plan on social policy (Snels, 2005). All in all, the parties recognised their differences in this debate, but showed that they believed a left-majority coalition could still get off the ground.

The SP and GroenLinks's attempts to institutionalise contact with the centre-left failed, largely on account of the intransigence of the PvdA. Halsema and Kox met with their PvdA counterpart Wouter Bos in 2005, and, although Bos signalled that he might prefer a left-wing coalition, he refused to set the PvdA's coalition plans in stone. He would not endorse joint policy proposals (Hippe et al., 2005: p. 47; van Holsteyn, 2006: p. 1,142) and he also ignored GroenLinks's open letter demanding co-operation. Furthermore, he refused to endorse the work of the 'Another Netherlands' discussions.

When polls indicated that the 'Left Spring' was evaporating, the SP's leaders declared that they would not rule out a CDA–PvdA–SP coalition. Vote-maximisation concerns were prioritised as the PvdA lost ground to the SP and the battle between them intensified. Despite Halsema's efforts to bring the party leaders together for comprehensive pre-election talks, all that was possible was a symbolic cup of coffee. This highlights how strong, office-seeking left parties pose a dilemma for social-democratic parties, who can react defensively and subsequently block co-operation.

Electoral and political performance

Both the PvdA and GroenLinks lost seats at the 2006 election, ultimately scuppering hopes of a left majority in parliament. The SP and GroenLinks nevertheless experienced their first realistic opportunity to enter government in a broad-based coalition, ultimately failing to do this largely on account of a combination of situational factors. However, the SP's rise continued in the 2006 election, when it won 16.6 per cent of the vote, up from 6.3 per cent in 2003, making it one of Europe's largest left parties. It won over a large number of PvdA voters, becoming the third largest party in terms of both members (with over 50,000) and now parliamentarians (Lucardie et al., 2006: p. 79). There were calls to include the SP in an oversized coalition with the PvdA and CDA, but the SP ran into one of the 'sacred rules' of Dutch politics, that one of the big three is always relegated to opposition (Fronteers, 2009).

Unfortunately for the SP, the centre-right CDA emerged as the largest party, gaining a position of strength in coalition negotiations. Initial discussions showed that little common ground was evident (de Volkskhrant, 8 December 2006). Despite their fierce rivalry, the PvdA nonetheless tried to include the SP and seemed to listen to calls to blunt the SP's appeal by burdening it with administrative responsibility (Voerman, 2007a). Even so, having lost badly at the election, the PvdA lacked the strength needed to bridge the gap between the SP and CDA (Elseveir, 13 December 2006). The CDA blocked the SP's inclusion to avoid being outnumbered (in terms of seats) by left-wing coalition partners (Lucardie, 2007: p. 1,046). This paved the way for the CDA and PvdA to seek another partner.

GroenLinks's national board expressed an interest in entering coalition negotiations, but its leaders' inexperience in the game of coalition formation meant that they made a series of serious mistakes. Behind the scenes, they informed the PvdA that they were interested in governing, but did not want to seem too eager to do so. They asked the PvdA to pave the way for GroenLinks's inclusion by ruling out an alternative coalition with the conservative CU. GroenLinks's leaders then made the strategic mistake of bluffing that GroenLinks did not actually want to enter coalition talks at all. Halsema declared that GroenLinks would not replace the SP, whom she accused of ruling themselves out too easily despite being an 'election winner' (NRC, 29 November 2006a; van Holsteyn, 2006: p. 1,146). GroenLinks's leaders had calculated that it was unlikely the SP would return to talks and that the PvdA could not coalesce with the CU because of ideological differences. The GL leadership had therefore expected to be brought into discussions.

GroenLinks's strategy of playing hard to get backfired badly. PvdA leader Bos did not react as anticipated, and went into coalition with the CU (NRC 16 December 2006b). GroenLinks overplayed its hand and placed too much trust in its contacts with the PvdA. The SP and GroenLinks struggled to cope with the fallout from failing to enter government, and internal criticisms quickly erupted in GroenLinks. First, officials in municipal government publicly criticised Halsema for blowing a historic opportunity. They dismissed arguments that GroenLinks should not govern when it loses elections or that it was too small to negotiate effectively with the CDA (NRC 28 December 2006c). Second, several of GroenLinks's founders criticised the failure, and left-wing critics argued that Halsema failed to enter coalition talks because her liberalism was incompatible with the policies of the CDA (Lucardie et al., 2006). GroenLinks's left wing was galvanised by the failure and formed a new faction called 'Kritisch GroenLinks'.

Kritisch GroenLinks argued that GroenLinks had become increasingly undemocratic as its liberal parliamentarians marginalised formal decision-making bodies, downgraded socialist commitments and used the party's 'permanent campaign' team to focus exclusively on parliamentary rather than activist politics. Kritisch GroenLinks used the decisions made on entering government – largely taken in a small, unaccountable 'Strategic Council' instead of GroenLinks's national board – to illustrate this. This rebellion has had some impact. GroenLinks's congress agreed to their demands for a far-reaching review of policy, organisation and electoral strategy. This 'Future Committee' has recommended a redistribution of power to strengthen the role of GroenLinks's party board and party council in decision-making and to restrict the unaccountable role of the Strategic Council. A host of proposals for strengthening internal democracy are on the agenda for GroenLinks's 2009 congress.

The future committee's report (*Score in the Upper left Corner*) reaffirmed GroenLinks as a left-libertarian party. However, some ideological rebalancing between the party's liberal and socialist wings occurred at GroenLinks's 2008 Congress, when the committee's proposals were subject to many amendments from Kritisch GroenLinks. Although the changes did not re-radicalise GroenLinks, they added a touch more socialism, including assurances that the market must exist alongside control by the state, trade unions and workers in a mixed economy. The future committee also ensured that GroenLinks drafted a constitution formally committing it to being in government and entering coalition negotiations if these opportunities arose.

GroenLinks's organisational structures have been more conducive to debate, as well as a degree of inner turmoil and general dissidence, than the SP's. Notwithstanding recent complaints, GroenLinks's statutes and party culture have guaranteed plurality and openness. Proposals are well debated, lively discussion groups are encouraged and its website provides a venue for open discussion (GroenLinks, 1997; Ward and Voerman, 1999; Lucardie and Voerman, 2008). These organisational factors have meant that, although Rosenmöller and Halsema's strategies have repositioned GroenLinks, they were (and are) contested and remain incomplete.

Rosenmöller's reforms encountered resistance from a strong network of ecological-socialists and local branches. The leadership lost congress votes on vote-maximising moves to accept more military spending and the monarchy. Disobedient parliamentarians also broke ranks by opposing the defence budget and NATO action in Kosovo and Afghanistan. The split in GroenLinks's national board, party council and parliamentary group forced the leadership to demand the suspension of military action in Afghanistan after initially backing it. This resulted in condemnation from mainstream parties, undermined parliamentary cohesion and tarnished the image of governing responsibility that Rosenmöller craved (Hippe et al., 2002).

Unlike GroenLinks, the SP did not encounter a major internal backlash over failing to enter government in 2006. It did not trigger the organisational time bomb of a lack of democracy and an influx of new members that exists inside the SP (van der Steen, 1994; Voerman, 1998). The SP's incompatibility with the CDA appeared to be largely accepted by the rank and file. However, the SP's organisational structures gave little room for soul-searching or for criticism to develop. Although the SP claimed to have broken with democratic centralism, it retained a highly centralised organisation (Keith, 2010). Troublemakers are not promoted or allowed to challenge the authority of the SP's leaders and their vote/office-driven strategies. Attempts to re-radicalise the SP by Marxist–Leninists and Trotskyist groups were subsequently crushed. Although many western European left parties were keen to learn the key to the SP's electoral success, they were no doubt disappointed by the lack of democracy behind its apparent transformation. Nonetheless, this has not seemed problematic for the SP's prospective coalition partners.

The main problem that the SP encountered came from the electorate. In the 2009 election to the EP (European Parliament) it received only 7.1 per cent of the vote. This was a marginal increase on its 2004 performance but a massive reverse after the 2006 national election result. The SP did not benefit from a 'credit crunch bounce' as might have been expected for a party favouring the nationalisation of banks. Its poll ratings even fell below those of a resurgent GroenLinks to 10–12 per cent in mid-2009, suggesting that the SP may be heading for a massive electoral shock (Peil, 2009). Part of this decline is due to the replacement of parliamentary leader Marijnissen, who stepped down for health reasons. Nonetheless, SP politicians lay the blame for disillusionment on those who voted SP in 2006 believing it could achieve power and initiate social change, only to be let down when it failed to deliver the goods.

Developments in the PvdA have thwarted the inclusion of the SP and GL in government. PvdA leader Wim Kok favoured another Purple-Government in 1998 and included D66 even though it was not necessary for a parliamentary majority. The PvdA's ideological direction precluded GroenLinks's inclusion. Moreover, in 2002 polls predicted that GroenLinks could win 16 seats, and a coalition with the CDA and PvdA was expected (Lucardie, 1999: p. 157). However, the sudden rise of right-wing populist Pim Fortuyn shattered Rosenmöller's hopes of governing. Fortuyn's assassination by an environmental activist stunted GroenLinks's growth and the huge gains for List Pim Fortuyn prevented its inclusion in a coalition (Lucardie and van Schuur, 2009: p. 2).

GroenLinks's elite have embraced de-radicalisation, whereas this is the SP's greatest challenge. Impressive direct action and 'social-populist' contacts with 'the common man' legitimised its outsider status and criticisms of the political elite (March and Mudde, 2005). As long as this continues, it occupies a space that other parties cannot fill (Voerman, 2008). The SP's leaders recognised this and established a free phone line in parliament in 1994 to keep in touch with people's concerns. The SP also has stringent rules compelling its representatives to give most of their salary to the party and to maintain levels of activism, even when in local government. Local sections losing touch with the 'common man' are abandoned. The SP's leaders envisage a need to expand activism if it enters government to avoid de-radicalisation. This looks unlikely given that its membership is now falling, many die-hard veteran activists have left following recent policy sacrifices and the PvdA supporters it recruited are less active.

Conclusion

Certain conditions would improve the parties' chances of entering government. Judging by the experience of 2006, a strong PvdA would make left party inclusion in a broad coalition with the CDA more likely. Further participation in municipal governing coalitions would also strengthen credibility. The SP remains under-represented in local government. It has 345 local councillors but no mayors or members in provincial executives. Differences between the SP and PvdA on spending plans still block the SP's inclusion in important city executives such as Amsterdam and Arnhem. A perception remains that it avoids getting its hands dirty by only participating in local-level coalitions when it is one of the largest parties. GroenLinks must prove its reliability as a coalition partner. Too many of its representatives withdraw from municipal executives over administrative mistakes and policy disputes (Lucardie et al., 2001: p. 55).

Would the parties make substantial policy changes if they were included in government? This is more likely in a left-wing coalition in which they might be able to force back privatisations and expand public services. On forming a governing coalition, GroenLinks would seek commitments on green issues and restricting carbon emissions – although it would not require control of the environment ministry. The SP's leaders are more guarded on what they would require, but progressive social policies would be essential. Where the parties have been in local government they have tried to expand social services, public transport and recycling, though their achievements have been modest (Spanning, 2005a). There are left-majority coalitions in around 40 municipalities. The alliance in Nijmegen, the 'Havana aan de Waal', is the prototype for co-operation. It began by making unwanted spending cuts, but spread them out over the long term to ensure that services for the disadvantaged and public transport could be expanded (Spanning, 2005b). The success of this coalition will be an indicator as to the parties' ability to offer a left alternative.

Both parties still seek inclusion. Rather than re-radicalising, they became more committed to governing after failing in 2006. GroenLinks in particular is increasingly used to administrative responsibility, being in over 100 municipal executives and two provincial executives. Its surveys show that 95 per cent of its members want to enter national government. GroenLinks's elite have also learnt lessons from letting government slip through their fingers. They will not say no again. If the large parties do not want GroenLinks in the government, they will have to say so. The SP's leaders have also assured supporters that it will seek to enter government next time.

The leaders of the SP and GroenLinks envisage opportunities to ally with the PvdA when the current cabinet ends, but poll ratings in 2009 make a left-majority coalition seem unlikely. GroenLinks is more in favour of developing left-wing co-operation. The SP blocked its proposal of joint lists for the Senate in 2007. Participation in a broad coalition with the PvdA and CDA has not been not ruled out. However, obstacles remain, including the parties' opposition to the Netherlands' support for the invasion of Iraq and calls for a parliamentary investigation. GroenLinks seems better placed to reach agreement with the mainstream parties. Nonetheless, the SP's astonishing adaptability persists. It has begun to soften hostility to the CDA, and Marijnissen has signalled a willingness to talk with it about coalition formation. In recent years leading SP politicians have rediscovered Christianity – even though the SP was historically secular – providing room to attract CDA supporters and to converge with it (Voerman, 2007b). The differences between GroenLinks, the SP and their potential mainstream coalition partners are consequently no longer necessarily insurmountable.

Note

1. I would like to thank the ESRC (Economic and Social Research Council) for funding the research for this chapter, as well as the 25 interviewees from the SP, Groenlinks and affiliated organisations interviewed in 2007–9. A list of interviewees is available on request.

11
Conclusion: Left Parties in National Governments
Jonathan Olsen, Dan Hough and Michael Koß

Given their position as key players in their respective party systems – not to mention their growing importance in the coalition formation process – it is perhaps surprising that political science has only reluctantly given left parties serious scholarly attention or, as Bale and Dunphy (2006) have put it, brought these parties 'in from the cold'. Doing just this has been the major purpose of this book. As is clear from our case studies, a considerable number of factors come into play in shaping the behaviour of these parties. Institutional factors, for example, have clearly impacted on left parties in Norway, Denmark and Sweden (owing to their traditions of minority government and negative parliamentarism), in Finland (with its special rules concerning the government *formateur*) and in Spain (with an electoral law that works heavily against minority parties without heavy regional concentrations). Leadership and organisation issues, meanwhile, have also affected left parties' strategic choices in most of the countries considered here (perhaps most especially in the Netherlands, Sweden, Norway and Finland), while situational factors (including 'external shocks') have forced left parties to reconsider their strategies in several cases (above all in Germany, Italy, Norway and the Netherlands). Finally, party system factors – analysed in considerable detail below – appear to play significant roles in shaping left parties' behaviour across all our case studies. As a result, many of the left parties considered here find themselves in key bargaining positions, especially in those countries where social democratic parties have fewer coalition options and/or historically better relationships with their cousins on the left. Consequently, as the authors in this volume have made clear, left parties are not substantially different from other parties in terms of the 'hard choices' that they are forced to make.

In this final chapter we seek to deepen our understanding of the nature and behaviour of left parties towards participating in government through an explicit comparison of three salient points raised in the introductory chapter. Drawing on the empirical evidence from our cases, we first consider factors tied to the party system that have framed, shaped and influenced left parties' strategic choices. The main question we analyse here is whether, in spite of specific sets of conditions that prevail at any one given time, there are any common influences that can explain the behaviour of left parties in terms of whether they enter government or more generally give greater priority to office-seeking goals. Secondly, we consider the potential impact of government participation on parties that do take the proverbial plunge. This question can be divided into two different parts: the effects of government participation/office-seeking behaviour on the electoral fortunes of these parties, and the effects of government participation/office-seeking behaviour on their internal dynamics and their strategic choices.

It should go without saying that in looking for answers to these questions we are acutely aware that national narratives and particularities always make generalisable propositions difficult. It has always been thus. Context – and agency – does matter, and in some cases it matters quite a lot. Having said this, however, we would be remiss if we did not attempt to gain a large-lens picture of left parties in government through intra- and inter-case comparisons. Thus, although we try to account for any 'deviations' from the general patterns we find, this chapter's chief purpose is to make explicit just those patterns while attempting to interpret and explain why they exist.

Understanding left parties' movement towards government: Party system effects

The first question we consider is whether there might be any common variables that can explain when, and under what conditions, left parties seek to enter government or to give greater priority to office-seeking goals. Although the range of possible influences is large, we believe that there are several in particular that merit closer scrutiny, all of which are connected to the party system. First, given the fact that social democratic parties are the only realistic coalition partner for left parties (either alone, or in combination with another 'bridge' party, such as the Greens), the narrowing of ideological/policy differences between left parties and their social democratic partners is crucial for any coalition between them to have a realistic chance of forming. We can throw some light on this by taking a policy-oriented approach based on data from the Comparative Manifesto Project (CMP). This data helps us illustrate the ideological distance between the parties (Budge et al., 1987, 2001). The CMP's left–right index combines parties' positions on 26 socio-economic, societal and foreign policy issues and enables us to place parties across the full breadth of the ideological spectrum (Budge and Klingemann, 2001: p. 21). The reliability of these data has, of course, often been disputed. According to the most exuberant of these criticisms, analyses of manifestos give us information about parties' willingness to ideologically move in the future rather than their real position at a given point of time (Janda et al., 1995: pp. 176–91; Pelizzo, 2003: pp. 83–6). These criticisms may well have some merit, but they do not stop the CMP approach from being methodologically consistent and therefore a reliable source of comparable data – and it is with such caveats in mind that we use the data here.

Furthermore, and specifically to help us avoid many of the conceptual problems associated with the original CMP data, we use the data in a modified form. On the one hand, we only refer to ideological distances, thus rendering the problem of the link between manifestos and parties' exact positions obsolete. On the other hand, we use the CMP data reanalysed by Simon Franzmann and André Kaiser (2006). They modified the original data in several respects: Franzmann and Kaiser differentiate not only left and right position issues, but also ideologically neutral valence issues. Additionally, they take into consideration that each issue can be both a valence and a position issue, as the character of an issue can vary, both over time and in different countries. Finally, Franzmann and Kaiser take into consideration the fact that manifestos represent signals rather than ideological positions. Accordingly, if a left party stresses the importance of the social-market economy as opposed to Marxism, this does not usually imply that this party is particularly 'right-wing'. Rather, it serves as a sign to potential voters that the party is not Marxist (any more). Franzmann and Kaiser take this into consideration by adapting a specific smoothing factor (2006: p. 173). Our expectation associated with this hypothesis is that distances between the two parties are narrower in government than in opposition. Table 11.1 below shows the results. The closer a score is to zero, the closer the parties are programmatically. The larger the score (the theoretical maximum being 10), the further apart parties are in programmatic terms. Bearing all aforementioned caveats in mind, the data reveal some interesting trends.

Table 11.1 Ideological distances between left parties and social democratic parties, 1990–2003

	DK*	FI*	FRA*	GER	ITA[a]	NL[b]	NOR	ESP	SWE*	All countries
1990/91	0.4	0.7	–	0.9	–	–	–	–	2.1	–
1992/93	–	–	0.8	–	0.4	–	0.2	2	–	–
1994/95	1	1	–	1.2	0.4	1.5	–	–	2.1	–
1996/97	–	–	1.2	–	1.5	–	0.4	2.1	–	–
1998/99	1.2	0.9	–	1.9	–	1.5	–	–	1.8	–
2000/01	0.8	–	–	–	n.a.	–	0.3	2	–	–
2002/03	–	1.3	1.5	2.5	–	1.4	–	–	1.3	–
Average	0.9	1	1.1	1.6	0.8	1.5	0.3	2	1.9	1.2
Average when in opposition	0.4	0.9	1	–	–	–	–	–	2	1.1
Average when a support party	1	–	–	–	–	–	–	–	1.3	1.2
Average when in government	–	1.1	1.5	–	–	–	–	–	–	1.3

* Average score of all parties defined as being left parties.
[a] Unless otherwise stated, figures for Italy are for the PCI/PDS and not the RC. The centre-left reference point for the 1992 and 1994 elections is the socialist PSI. The PSI left national government before the 1998 election and so cannot be included as a governing party in this election. In 2002 it is the Italian Renewal (RI).
[b] The Netherlands' score is the average of scores for SP and GL.
Source: Own calculations based on Franzmann and Kaiser (2006).

Table 11.1 tends to contradict our expectations; in those (admittedly limited) cases where a left party has entered into government as either a support party or a full coalition partner, the ideological distance between the left party and its social democratic partner does not appear to change significantly. This result may indicate that social democratic parties view left parties less as strategic partners in some future red–red 'project' and more as tactical partners to gain a parliamentary majority. As the cases of Norway, Sweden, Finland and Denmark demonstrate, coalitions or support arrangements between social democratic parties and left parties have been premised largely on reversing or ameliorating real or anticipated attacks on the traditional welfare state by parties of the right. This can hardly be said to constitute a 'project'.

Moreover, for social democratic parties, coalitions with left parties appear to us to indicate not so much some ideological evolution back towards the left (a kind of 'Blairism-in-reverse') as a search for new coalition options in a competitive party environment – an environment, it should be noted, that is no longer quite as conducive to social democratic parties' electoral success as it was in the (late) 1990s. For left parties, meanwhile, policy differences do not appear to represent an insurmountable barrier to government participation. Indeed, as we have seen in the case studies here, left parties enter government less because policy differences have narrowed and more because of the conviction that this represents the best way to weaken the power and influence of the centre-right. Participation also offers a way to prove left parties' importance in a rapidly changing electoral environment, a point brought home especially in the case studies in France, Italy and Finland. A move towards government represents the next – and, most probably, scarcely unavoidable – stage of their 'lifespan' if these parties wish to remain politically relevant.

This is not to say that the narrowing of policy differences is entirely unimportant, as several of our case studies have shown. Indeed, in Norway the perceived movement of the Labour Party back towards the left appears to have been one of the factors impacting the SV's evolution towards government. Even here, however, it is unclear whether the new priority given to office-seeking was really contingent upon this perception. This lack of an ideological barrier may also explain why, despite no significant lessening of policy divisions, coalitions with social democrats are still very much on the table for left parties in countries such as the Netherlands.

A second hypothesis we can examine is that the electoral strength of left parties and their coalition partners directly impacts these parties' decisions to enter coalitions. This hypothesis has two parts. First, it might be expected that, given competition on the left part of the political spectrum between Green parties and left parties, in those countries where Green parties are weak and/or nonexistent, the chances of left parties' participating in government rises. Second, it is reasonable to assume that these opportunities are reduced in those countries where their electoral strength vis-à-vis their possible social democratic partners is strong: where left parties are electorally strong, in other words, social democratic parties are loath to go into coalitions that lessen their

Table 11.2 The relative electoral strength of left parties and their coalition partners, 1990–2009

Status	Country	LP's share of the vote compared with the main SD party (%) (GOV/SUP)	LP's share of the vote compared with the main Green party (%) (GOV/SUP)	ENPP	Veto player index
Government	FI	42.9 *(43.9)*	137.8 *(138.7)*	5.1	4
	FRA[a]	24.9 *(14.5)*	126.8 *(145.5)*	3.1	7
	ITA[b]	23.7 *(9.3)*	271.4 *(–)*	5.1	7
	NOR	25.2 *(17.5)*	–	4.4	2
Support	DK	25.7 *(21.3)*	–	4.9	3
	ESP	17.2 *(8.6)*	–	2.5	6
	SWE	19 *(19.2)*	164.4 *(146.9)*	4.2	2
Opposition	GER	18	80.5	2.9	8
	NL[c]	26.3	–	5.3	7

[a] French scores are for PCF only.
[b] Italy's 2008 figures are for the Rainbow Left (Sinistra Arcobaleno, SA), all other elections RC.
[c] Netherlands score is average of scores for SP and GL.

Sources: Own calculations based on www.parties-and-elections.de; veto player index derived from Schmidt (2006: p. 352).

own power and influence. An indicator of what the reality might be can be seen in Table 11.2.

The evidence for the two parts of this hypothesis is somewhat ambiguous. Firstly, there seems to be no set proportion of the vote at which left parties and social democrats co-operate: although in nearly all the cases left parties' proportion of the social democratic vote is around 20–25 per cent, the range here runs from 42.9 per cent in Finland to 17.2 per cent in Spain. However, whenever left parties enter coalitions with social democratic ones, they lose significantly at the polls vis-à-vis their bigger partners, the best examples of this being Italy and Spain. The only (very moderate) exceptions to this trend are Finland and Sweden. The relative ability of the left parties to electorally stand their ground may have much to do with the general decline of social democratic parties in these countries, although – from this data alone – we cannot be sure of this. What we can be surer about, and as our case study on Germany makes clear, is that at the sub-state (i.e. *Land*, Provincial, etc., etc.) level social democrats have historically been wary of entering coalitions with *Die Linke* where the latter have been exceptionally strong electorally. Indeed, there seems to be some evidence that coalitions between social democratic parties and left parties are made considerably easier if the latter are not too strong vis-à-vis the former. Still, this part of the hypothesis cannot be confirmed in toto for left parties.

With regard to the second part of this hypothesis, the presence of a Green party is obviously no absolute barrier to government participation by left parties. Indeed, as we have seen, in Sweden, Finland, France and Italy left parties have participated as support parties or formal partners in coalitions that have included Green parties. On the other hand, the chances of left party participation in government appears to be greater where there is no electorally viable Green party (as in Norway and Denmark) to compete with it. Furthermore, left parties' chances of participation in government appear also to be greater in those countries (such as Finland, France and Italy) where left parties are more electorally successful than their Green brethren, making it harder for social democrats to cut deals with Green parties alone. Indeed, where Green parties do exist, the left parties' strategic environment undoubtedly becomes more complicated. Left parties and Greens often compete with the same themes for similar voter groups (despite voter demographics not being identical); they share (in part) the role of 'anti-establishment' or 'protest' parties, and relationships between the parties (as in Sweden, Germany and the Netherlands) are quite often strained. Moreover, this relationship is further complicated by the fact that both social democrats and Greens have considerably more coalition options: they can co-operate with each other (often to the exclusion of the left party) as well as with parties of the centre-right. We discuss this point further below.

Whether left parties enter coalitions, gain support party status or remain outside government seems to be related neither to the effective number of parliamentary parties (ENPP)[1] nor to the number of veto players (cf. Table 11.2). Values for both ENPP and veto players vary as much between countries as they do between the groups of countries in different categories (i.e. countries in which left parties enter government, gain support party status or remain outside government). However, if we analyse the coalitionability of parties represented in parliament (i.e. the segmentation of party systems[2]) in relation to the government prospects of left parties, the picture changes slightly. We hypothesise that both block dynamics and party system segmentation have an impact on the chances of left party government participation. It is reasonable to assume that in those cases where a block logic prevails – where, in other words, the party system is characterised by a block of parties on the right and a block of parties on the left, with no 'crossing' of blocks by the major parties in their coalition calculations – left parties stand a better chance of coming into government, as social democratic parties have need of them in putting together coalitions. We thought it also reasonable to assume that the greater the number of parties (making the putting together of larger coalitions a necessity), the greater the chances of left parties coming into government – this despite the complicated relationship (discussed above) that Greens and left parties enjoy. As Table 11.3 demonstrates, there is plenty of evidence to support this.

We begin Table 11.3 by including the average number of parties in the party system. This illustrates that, while some party systems have relatively few parties (e.g. Germany) and coalition negotiations are normally quite straightforward, others (e.g. Italy and Spain) can have many more, making – sometimes, although not always – coalition negotiations rather more complex. We also include (column three) the number of different coalition partners that the main centre-left party has actually had between 1990 and 2009, as well as the number of potential coalition partners to the right (as understood through CMP data) of the main social

Table 11.3 Segmentation and block dynamics, 1990–2009

Status	Country	Average number of parties in Parliament	Number of SD coalition partners	Number of coalition partners to SD's right	Electoral distance between biggest parties on left and right
Government	FI	8.8	6	3	–1
	FRA	7	2	–	13.4
	ITA	12	7[a]	–[a]	6
	NOR	7.6	2	–	–13.2
Support	DK	8.2	3	3	–6.4
	ESP	11	–	–	–0.3
	SWE	7	–	–	–17.3
Opposition	GER[b]	5	2	2	0.3
	NL	9.2	2	2	2.5

[a] These results refer to the period after the 1994 party system transformation.
[b] Although strictly speaking separate parties, the CDU and CSU are treated as one party here.

Sources: Own calculations based on www.parties-and-elections.de.

democratic party. Finally, and perhaps most interestingly, we include a column illustrating the distance between the single biggest party on the left of the party system (no matter what sort of left party it is) and the single biggest party on the right. A minus score indicates that the biggest left party (usually a social democrat one) has been stronger, while a positive number indicates that the right party has performed better at the polls. The larger the number, the greater the extent of this dominance (e.g. −17.3 in Sweden illustrates that the social democrats regularly outscored their single biggest competitor to the right, while 6 in Italy shows that the right has tended to do better there).

This data indicates that the greater the number of prospective coalition partners for social democrats in the 'left block', the greater the chance of left party participation in government. Similarly, the smaller the number of possible coalition partners on the right for social democratic parties, the greater also the chance that a left party will be in government. Furthermore, in the cases where this hypothesis concerning segmentation and block logic does not hold (in Denmark, for example), there is either a strong asymmetry (last column of Table 11.3) between the left and right – that is, the entire political spectrum is shifted towards the left, making participation by a left party more likely – or special circumstances governing coalition formation (as in Finland) take precedence. Conversely, when there is no strong block logic and/or where segmentation is low, left parties have less chance of coming into government (the Netherlands and Germany) because social democratic parties simply have more coalition options on the right of the political spectrum. Here, again, the importance of party system dynamics is fully illustrated; a left party's entrance into government depends upon the willingness of social democratic parties to countenance such coalitions (and the ability – read electoral strength – to do so, of course); and social democrats' calculations are in turn impacted by their relationship with the main party of the centre-right, other parties on the left, and parties in the centre that might bridge the gap between themselves and left parties.

The electoral impact of government participation on left parties

The next question we examine is the electoral impact of government participation on the parties themselves. As discussed in the introductory chapter, left parties face a serious dilemma in participating in government given both their historical legacies and their traditionally critical attitude towards governments in market economies. The effect, and indeed sometimes the trauma, of taking over the reins of power is sometimes not just politically chastening; it can also cause serious divisions and divides that have the power to develop into existential crises. Here we concentrate on the direct electoral impact of government participation on left parties. While parties that leave government will, almost by definition, have performed worse at the polls than they did before coming to power, it is still not unreasonable to assume – given what has been said above – that left parties will suffer more, and for longer, than most other parties in this position. Table 11.4 shows electoral results for left parties since 1990, dividing parties' results into those falling under 'parties in government' (or 'support') or 'in opposition'.

Not surprisingly, we can see that left parties' participation in government has led more or less across the board to election losses: where they have participated in government, left parties on average have lost about 25 per cent of their vote, declining from an average of 8.7 per cent before entering government to 6.8 per cent after participation in government.

Two things, of course, should be noted here. First, election losses range in each country from relatively small losses (and even a holding pattern, as in Denmark) to much more dramatic ones. Electoral loss appears to be especially pronounced in those countries where there are numerous 'outsider' parties (of the left or right) to which voters wishing to exercise a 'protest' vote can turn (France and Italy) and/or where the electoral system has traditionally discriminated against small parties (Spain). However, it is far from clear that participation in government is the only – or even the most important – reason for electoral decline, a point brought home in several of the case studies (for example in France, Italy, Finland and Sweden). Secondly, it remains to be seen whether these losses can be considered a permanent effect of participation – as these parties have disillusioned their core voters and been 'demystified' for voters – or whether these election losses are simply a 'normal' part of the electoral life cycle of any party. If the latter is true, then we can expect left parties to bounce back in the way that other parties might do.

Whether they do bounce back, however, depends on the 'lessons' they draw from their experience in government. As the case studies demonstrate, for some parties (e.g. the PCF in France) the lesson to be learned from participating in government is that such participation is simply too costly: it brings few benefits and a great deal of harm. For others, participation is still seen as a positive good, even if it has

Table 11.4 Election results of left parties, 1990–2009

	DK	FI	FRA[a]	GER	ITA[b]	NL[c]	NOR	ESP	SWE	Average
1990/91	8.3	10.1	–	2.4	–	–	–	–	4.5	–
1992/93	–	–	9.2	–	5.6	–	7.9	9.5	–	–
1994/95	7.3	11.2	–	4.4	6	2.4	–	–	6.2	–
1996/97	–	–	9.9	–	8.6	–	6	10.5	–	–
1998/99	7.5	10.9	–	5.1	–	5.4	–	–	12	–
2000/01	6.4	–	–	–	5	–	12.5	5.4	–	–
2002/03	–	9.9	4.8	4	–	6.6	–	–	8.4	–
2004/05	6	–	–	8.7	–	–	8.8	4.9	–	–
2006/07	13	8.8	4.3	–	5.8	10.6	–	–	5.9	–
2008/09	–	–	–	11.9	3.1	–	6.2	3.8	–	–
Average	8.1	10.2	7.1	6	5.7	6.3	8.3	6.8	7.4	7.3
Average in opposition[d]	9.1	10	7.8	–	6.2	–	8.8	7.6	7.6	8.2
Average as a support party	7.1	–	–	–	–	–	–	3.8	7.2	6
Average whilst in government	–	10.4	4.8	–	3.1	–	6.2	–	–	6.1
Average before governing/supporting	8.3	10.7	9.6	–	6.2	–	(8.8)[e]	(7.7)[e]	(7.6)[e]	8.7
Average after governing/supporting	8.5	8.8	4.3	–	5.4	–	–	–	–	6.8

[a] French scores are for PCF only.
[b] Italy's 2008 figures are for the Rainbow Left (*Sinistra Arcobaleno*, SA), all other elections RC.
[c] Netherlands score is average of scores for SP and GL.
[d] Averages in opposition have only been calculated for countries where left parties also entered government or gained support party status.
[e] Results for Norway, Spain and Sweden are not included in the average score because no data for periods after government participation / support status are available.

Source: www.parties-and-elections.de.

brought with it some inevitable disappointments or, at the very least, a sobering appraisal of what is possible as a formal coalition partner or support party (Denmark and Norway). For most of the parties, however, government participation remains a mixed bag. On the one hand, participation brings with it the benefits of experience and credibility, since a party that refuses on principle to assume power will either remain a pure protest party or simply fade into electoral irrelevance. Consequently, there simply seems to be no viable alternative to at least considering the prospect of entering coalition government. On the other hand, entering government comes with electoral costs, especially if a party (as happened in Finland, France and Italy) is viewed by its core voters as having not been able to draw firm lines in the sand regarding what policy objectives it is willing to compromise on with its coalition partners.

Consequently, as the case studies here suggest, left parties often come to believe that electoral loss can likely be ameliorated only through a reaffirmation of core policy positions. Not surprisingly, then, left parties that have gone back into the opposition will tend to 're-ideologise', stressing once more their opposition credentials and policy purity (as has been the case in Sweden, Italy and Finland). No matter whether government participation has been seen as largely negative or positive, the evidence from the case studies here suggests that left parties return after government participation to their more traditional role as (primarily) policy-seekers, something reflected in the fact that arguments and disputes (never far from the surface) over basic policy planks re-emerge after their time in government. As most left parties have, at the very least, factions within them that demand maximalist (rather than incremental) policy achievements, inner-party disputes over questions of policy remain stronger within left parties than in most other party families. In other words, because of their emphasis on policy-seeking, 'successful' participation in government – that is, the implementation of large parts of their policy agenda – becomes even more important for left parties than for other actors. The perception by many left parties that government participation has been 'unsuccessful' is therefore almost preprogrammed in light of both left parties' decidedly inferior power position as a minority party within coalitions and the invariable compromises that coalition government demands.

The discussion above illustrates that there is still plenty of scope for further analysing the role, impact and consequences for left parties when they (think about) enter(ing) national governments. To us, four things in particular seem to be particularly noteworthy. Firstly, most left parties were policy-orientated when they entered national government and remained so when they returned to opposition. Naturally the nature and extent of this policy-orientated political strategy differs across time and space, but it nonetheless remains at the heart of left party activity. Secondly, there does not appear to have been any noticeable de-mystification of left parties during their time in government. Left parties have indeed frequently found governing hard going, but they are by no means alone in this. Governing complex western democracies is indeed difficult, and pleasing both demanding electorates and partisan activists will never be easy. And yet left parties have generally not rendered themselves 'uncoalitionable' and they certainly have not fallen apart on account of internal contradictions. In short, they have dealt with governing in much the same ways as other parties have and do.

Thirdly, and linked in with the second point, left parties have consistently left government on the back of chastening sets of election results. This has generally prompted processes of consolidation, particularly in a policy sense, where parties instinctively look to retrench around core principles. But left parties have also – given time – been able to bounce back and again become candidates for office. In short, they do what all parties do when booted out of office; they reassess their strategy, analyse previous behaviour and try to learn from their mistakes, so, most importantly, that they can do a better job next time. Fourthly, and finally, we have seen that the key relationship in explaining the genesis of left–left coalitions is – not surprisingly – that between the left party and its main social democratic rival. This became evident in all of our case studies and gives further credence to the importance of agency in understanding political outcomes. If social democrats and left party politicians can find a working modus vivendi, then coalitions become both possible and practical.

Notes

1. The ENPP is defined as the reciprocal of the sum of all parties' squared seat numbers (Laakso and Taagepera, 1979). The less equally seats are distributed among parties, the bigger the difference between the effective and the actual number of parliamentary parties. If only one party is dominant, the ENPP's score approaches the value 1.
2. Segmentation refers to the number of coalition options parties in a party system have. In completely segmented party systems no coalition governments are possible, whereas in unsegmented party systems all parties are prepared to enter coalitions with each other (Niedermayer, 2003: p. 13).

Bibliography

Aardal, B. O. and H. Valen (1997), 'The Storting Elections of 1989 and 1993: Norwegian Politics in Perspective', in K. Strøm and L. Svåsand (eds.), *Challenges to Political Parties. The Case of Norway* (Ann Arbor: The University of Michigan Press), 61–76.

Abedi, A. and S. Schneider (2004), 'Adapt or Die! Organizational Change in Office-Seeking Anti-Political Establishment Parties', paper for presentation at the Annual General Meeting of the Canadian Political Science Association, Winnipeg, Manitoba, 3–5 June 2004.

Allern, E. H. and N. Aylott (2007), 'Overcoming the Fear of Commitment: Pre-Electoral Coalitions in Norway and Sweden', paper presented at the annual Political Studies Association conference, Bath, UK, 11–13 April.

Appleton, A. M. and D. S. Ward (1997), 'Party Response to Environmental Change. A Model of Organizational Innovation', *Party Politics*, 3 (3): 341–62.

Arter, D. (1999), *Scandinavian Politics Today* (Manchester, Manchester University Press).

Arter, D. (2001), *Scandinavian Politics Today* (Manchester: Manchester University Press).

Arter, D. (2002), '"Communists we are No Longer, Social Democrats we can Never be": The Evolution of the Leftist Parties in Finland and Sweden', *Journal of Communist Studies and Transition Politics*, 18 (3): 1–28.

Arter, D. (2003), 'Scandinavia: What's Left is the Social Democratic Welfare Consensus', *Parliamentary Affairs*, 56: 75–98.

Aylott, N. (2002), 'Let's Discuss this Later: Party Responses to Euro-Division in Scandinavia', *Party Politics*, 8 (4): 441–61.

Aylott, N. (2003), 'After the Divorce: Social Democrats and Trade Unions in Sweden', *Party Politics*, 9 (3): 369–90.

Aylott, N. (2008), 'Softer but Strong: Euroscepticism and Party Politics in Sweden', A. Szczerbiak and P. Taggart (eds.), *Opposing Europe? The Comparative Party Politics of Euroscepticism (Vol. 1)*, (Oxford: Oxford University Press), 181–200.

Aylott, N. (2009), *Danish PM, Swedish Opposition* (PSA Scandinavian Politics Specialist Group Newsletter), April 5.

Aylott, N. and N. Bolin (2007), 'Towards a Two-Party System? The Swedish Parliamentary Election of September 2006', *West European Politics*, 30 (3): 621–33.

Bale T. and T. Bergman (2006a), 'Captives No Longer, but Servants Still? Contract Parliamentarism and the New Minority Governance in Sweden and New Zealand', *Government and Opposition*, 41 (3): 422–49.

Bale, T. and T. Bergman (2006b), 'A Taste of Honey is Worse Than None at All? Coping with the Generic Challenges of Support Party Status in Sweden and New Zealand', *Party Politics*, 12 (2): 189–209.

Bale, T. and M. Blomgren (2008), 'Close but No Cigar? Newly Governing and Nearly Governing Parties in Sweden and New Zealand', in K. Deschouwer (ed.), *New Parties in Government: In Power for the First Time* (London: Routledge), 85–103.

Bale, T. and R. Dunphy (2006), 'In From the Cold: Left Parties, Policy, Office and Votes in Advanced Liberal Democracies Since 1989', paper given at the conference 'The Non Social Democratic Left and Government Participation', University of Sussex, 12 September.
Banholzer, V. M. (2001), *Im Schatten der Sozialdemokratie: Die Bedeutung der Kleinparteien in den politischen Systemen Norwegens und Schwedens* (Berlin: Berlin-Verlag Spitz).
Barker, P. (1998), 'From the SED to the PDS: Continuity or Renewal?' in P. Barker (ed.): *German Monitor – The Party of Democratic Socialism. Modern Post-Communism or Nostalgic Populism?* (Amsterdam: Rodopi B.V, 42), 1–17.
Bastian, J. (1995), 'The *Enfant Terrible* of German Politics: The PDS Between GDR Nostalgia and Democratic Socialism', *German Politics*, 4 (2): 95–110.
Beikler, S. (2003), 'Die heimliche Opposition', *Tagesspiegel*, p. 14.
Beikler, S. (2004), 'Profil schärfen, Streit vermeiden', *Tagesspiegel*, 28 September, p. 10.
Benedetto, G. and L. Quaglia (2007), 'The Comparative Politics of Communist Euroscepticism in France, Spain and Italy', *Party Politics*, 13 (4): 479–500.
Berg, N. J. (1982), *I kamp för socialismen. Kortfattad framställning av det svenska kommunistiska partiets historia 1917 – 1981* (Stockholm: Arbetarkultur).
Berglund, N. (2007a), 'State Puts Brakes on StatoilHydro,' *Aftenposten*, 19 October, at www.aftenposten.no (accessed on 1 June 2009).
Berglund, N. (2007b), 'Government Changes Loom after Election "Catastrophe"', *Aftenposten*, 11 September, at www.aftenposten.no (accessed on 1 June 2009).
Berglund, N. (2008a), 'Government Loses Popularity, New Split Looms over Wolves', *Aftenposten*, 23 June, at www.aftenposten.no (accessed on 1 June 2009).
Berglund, N. (2008b), 'Oil Industry Pesses for More Arctic Exploration Rights', *Aftenposten*, 27 May, at www.aftenposten.no (accessed on 1 June 2009).
Bergman, T. (2004), 'Sweden: Democratic Reforms and Partisan Decline in an Emerging Separation-of-Powers System', *Scandinavian Political Studies*, 27 (2): 203–25.
Bergounioux, A. and B. Manin (2005), *L'ambition et le remords* (Paris: Fayard).
Berliner Morgenpost (BM) (1999), 'Berliner PDS will einen rot-grünen Senat tolerieren', 28 February.
Berliner Zeitung (1996), 'Berliner PDS will Machtwechsel', 2 December 1996.
Berliner Zeitung (2001), 'Der lachende Vierte ist die PDS', *Berliner Zeitung*, 5 December.
Berstein, S. (2006), *Léon Blum* (Paris: Fayard).
Bertolino, S. (2004), *Rifondazione comunista: Storia e organizzazione* (Bologna: il Mulino).
Besancenot, O. (2003), *Révolution! 100 mots...* (Paris: Flammarion).
Betz, H-G. and S. Immerfall (1998), *The New Politics of the Right: Neo-Populist Parties and Movements in Established Democracies* (New York: St. Martin's Press).
Beyme, K. von (1985), *Political Parties in Western Democracies* (London: Gower).
Bille, L. (1989), 'Denmark: The Oscillating Party System', *West European Politics*, 12 (4): 42–58.
Bille, L. (1991), 'Politisk kronik 3. halvår 1999', *Økonomi og politik* (København: DJØF-Forlaget).

Bille, L. (1992), 'Denmark', in R. Katz and P. Mair (eds.), *Party Organizations: A Data Handbook* (London: Sage).
Bille, L. (2005), 'Denmark', *European Journal of Political Research*, 44: 994–1001.
Blomqvist, P. and C. Green-Pedersen (2004), 'Defeat at Home? Issue-Ownership and Social Democratic Support in Scandinavia', *Government and Opposition*, 39 (4): 587–613.
Boecker, A. (2004), 'Zeit der Pragmatiker', *Süddeutsche Zeitung*, 27 September, p. 5.
Boel, E. (1988), *Socialdemokratiets atomvåbenpolitik 1945–88* (Viborg, Akademisk Forlag).
Bourseiller, C. (1997), *Cet étrange monsieur Blondel* (Paris: De Bartillat).
Bortfeldt, H. (2003), 'Von Karl-Marx-Stadt nach Chemnitz. Programmparteitag der PDS in Chemnitz', *Deutschland Archiv*, 6: 936–944.
Bosco, A. (2001), 'Four Actors in Search of a Role: The Southern European Communist Parties', in P. Nikiforos Diamandouros and R. Gunther (eds.), *Parties, Politics, and Democracy in the New Southern Europe* (Baltimore: JHU Press), 329–387.
Botella, J. and L. Ramiro (eds.) (2003), *The Crisis of Communism and Party Change The Evolution of West European Communist and Post-Communist Parties* (Barcelona: ICPS).
Bozóki, A. and J. Ishiyama (eds.) (2002), *The Communist Successor Parties of Central and Eastern Europe* (Armonk, NY: M. E. Sharpe).
Brie, M. (1995), 'Das politische Projekt PDS – eine unmögliche Möglichkeit', in M. Brie, M. Herzig and T. Koch (eds.), *Die PDS – empirische Befunde und kontroverse Analysen* (Cologne: Papyrossa).
Brie, M. (2000), 'Strategiebildung im Spannungsfeld von gesellschaftlichen Konfliktlinien und politischer Identität', in M. Brie and R. Woderich (eds.), *Die PDS im Parteiensystem* (Berlin: Dietz), 15–49.
Brors, H. (2006), 'Lars Ohly traskar I Lars Werners spår', in *Dagens Nyheter*, 2 January, p. A29.
Brors, H. (2008), 'Dubbla budskap om skatterna', in *Dagens Nyheter*, 7 June, p. A10.
Brors, H. (2009a), 'Alliansen I knapp när väljarna flyr S', in *Dagens Nyheter*, 24 April, p. A07.
Brors, H. (2009b), 'MP och C slaktar heliga kor', in *Dagens Nyheter*, 16 May, p. A10.
Budge, I., H-D. Klingemann, A. Volkens, J. Bara and E. Tanenbaum (2001), *Mapping Policy Preferences. Estimates for Parties, Electors, and Governments 1945–1998* (Oxford: Oxford University Press).
Budge, I. and H-D. Klingemann (2001), 'Finally! Comparative Over-Time Mapping Party Policy Movement', in I. Budge et al., (eds.), *Mapping Policy Preferences. Estimates for Parties, Electors, and Governments 1945–1998* (Oxford: Oxford University Press), 19–50.
Budge, I., D. Robertson and D. Hearl (1987), *Ideology, Strategy and Party Change: Spatial Analyses of Post-War Election Programmes in 19 Democracies* (Cambridge: Cambridge University Press).
Buelens, J. and A. Hino. (2008), 'The Electoral Fate of New Parties in Government', in K. Deschouwer (ed.), *Newly Governing Parties*, (London: Routledge), 157–174.
Bull, M. and P. Heywood (eds.) (1994), *West European Communist Parties after the Revolutions of 1989* (London: Palgrave).
Burchell, J. (2001), '"Small Steps" or "Great Leaps": How the Swedish Greens are Learning the Lessons of Government Participation', *Scandinavian Political Studies*, 24 (3): 239–54.

Burchell, J. (2002), *The Evolution of Green Politics. Development and Change within European Green Parties* (San Francisco: Earthscan Publications Limited).
Buzzanca, S. (2008), 'Sinistra Arcobaleno, un voto su due al Pd', *la Repubblica*, 17 April, p.13.
Calculli, M. (2007), 'Scuola. Prc in piazza con i sindacati per il rinnovo dei contratti', http://home.rifondazione.it/dettaglio_01.php?id=1380.
Carlbom, M. (2002), 'V-förlust skylls på otydlighet', in *Dagens Nyheter*, 7 December, p. A11.
Carlbom, M. (2005), 'Brett samarbete kan bana väg för nytt vänsterparty', in *Dagens Nyheter*, 30 January, p. A08.
Carlbom, M. (2008a), 'V öppnar dörren för valsamarbete', in *Dagens Nyheter*, 7 June, p. A10.
Carlbom, M. (2008b), 'Grönt ljus för rödgrön regering', in *Dagens Nyheter*, 8 December, p. A06.
Carlbom, M. (2008c), 'V sager nej till valplatform', in *Dagens Nyheter*, 9 December, p. A10.
Centro de Investigaciones Sociológicas (2008), Study number 2750 (Madrid, January 2008).
Centro de Investigaciones Sociológicas (2008), Study number 2757 (Madrid, March 2008).
Chari, R. S. (2005), 'Why did the Spanish Communist Strategy Fail?', *Journal of Communist Studies and Transition Politics*, 21 (2): 296–301.
Christensen, D. A. (1996), 'The Left-Wing Opposition in Denmark, Norway, and Sweden: Cases of Euro-phobia?', *West European Politics*, 19 (3): 525–546.
Christensen, D. A. (1998), 'Foreign Policy Objectives: Left Socialist Opposition in Denmark, Norway and Sweden', *Scandinavian Political Studies*, 21 (1): 51–70.
Christensen, D. A. (2001), 'The Norwegian Agrarian-Center Party: Class, Rural, or Catchall Party?', in D. Arter (ed.), *From Farmyard to City Square? The Electoral Adaptation of the Nordic Agrarian Parties* (Aldershot: Ashgate).
Cleven, T. (1996), 'PDS möchte Konservative in Schwerin ablösen', *OZ*, 12 August.
Cleven, T. (1997), 'PDS-Chef kam mit blauem Auge davon', *Ostsee Zeitung (OZ)*, 17 February 1997.
Closa, C. (2001), 'Las raíces domésticas de la política europea de España y la Presidencia de 2002', *Etudes et Recherches*, 16: 320–338.
Colomer, J. M. (1999), ''The Spanish 'State of the Autonomies': Non-institutional Federalism, in P. Heywood (ed.), *Politics and Policy in Democratic Spain: No Longer Different?* (London: Frank Cass).
Communistische Partij van Nederland (1986), *Verkiezingsprogram van de CPN voor 1986–1990* (Amsterdam: CPN).
Communistische Partij van Nederland (1984), *Partij Program van de CPN: Machts Vorming voor een Socialistisch Nederland* (Amsterdam: CPN).
Corbetta, P., P. Marcotti and V. Vanelli (2008), 'Elezioni 2008 – Flussi elettorali in 15 città', Istituto Cattano, http://www.cattaneo.org/pubblicazioni/analisi/pdf/Analisi %20 Cattaneo%20%20Flussi%20elettorali%202008%20in%20 15%20citt%C3%A0%20(25%20giugno%202008).pdf.
Courtois, S. and M. Lazar(1995), *Histoire du Parti communiste français* (Paris: PUF).
Coustal, F. (2009), *L'incroyable histoire du nouveau parti anti-capitaliste* (Paris: Demopolis).

Cullberg, J. (2008), 'Nedtonad mp-kritik ny strategi av v', in *Dagens Nyheter*, 17 February, p. A08.
Dagens Nyheter (2008), 'Rekordstort gap mellan blocken', 18 February, p. A11.
Dagens Nyheter (2008), 'Kamrat demokrat', 5 June, p. A02.
Dagens Nyheter (2008a), 'Vänstervridningen', 18 December, p. A02.
Dagens Nyheter (2008b), 'Ohly alliansens baste valarbetare', 18 December, p. A06.
D'Alimonte, R. and S. Bartolini (1997), ' "Electoral Transition" and Party System Change in Italy', in M. Bull and M. Rhodes (eds.), *Crisis and Transition in Italian Politics* (London: Frank Cass), 110–134.
Damgaard, E. (1992), *Parliamentary Change in the Nordic Countries* (Oslo: Scandinavian University Press).
Damgaard, E. and P. Svensson (1989), 'Who Governs? Parties and Policies in Denmark', *European Journal of Political Research*, 17: 731–45.
Derfler, L. (1977), *Millerand: The Socialist Years* (Hague: Mouton).
Deschower, K. (2004), 'New Parties in Government: A Framework for Analysis', paper presented to the workshop on 'New Parties in Government, ECPR Joint Sessions of Workshops, University of Uppsala, 13–18 April.
Deschouwer, K. (2008), 'Comparing Newly Governing Parties', in K. Deschouwer (ed.), *Newly Governing Parties* (London: Routledge), 1–16.
Dolez, B. (1997), 'Les "petits" partis au regard de la réglementation du financement de la vie politique', in L. A. Villalba and B. Villalba (eds.) *Les petits partis* (Paris: L'Harmattan).
Dumont, P. and H. Bäck (2006), 'Why so Few, and so Late? Green Parties and the Question of Government Participation,' *European Journal of Political Research*, 45 (1): 35–67.
Dunphy, R. (2004), *Contesting Capitalism? Left Parties and European Integration*, (Manchester: Manchester University Press).
Dunphy, R. (2007), 'In Search of an Identity: Finland's Left Alliance and the Experience of Coalition Government', *Contemporary Politics*, 13: 1: 37–55.
Dunphy, R. and T. Bale (2007), 'Red Flag Still Flying? Explaining AKEL – Cyprus's Communist Aanomaly', *Party Politics*, 13 (3): 287–304.
Einhorn, E. S. and J. Logue (1988), 'Continuity and Change in the Scandinavian Party Systems', in S. B. Wollinetz (ed.), *Parties and Party Systems in Liberal Democracies* (London: Routledge).
Elseveir (2006), *Ook Halsema wil niet met Bos regeren* (Amsterdam), 13 December.
Elvik, Å. (2007), Interview with author, Tuesday, 12 June, Oslo.
Eriksson, G. (2002), 'Regeringsfrågan: V backar om utrikespolitik', in *Dagens Nyheter*, 30 September, p. A05.
Eriksson, G. (2004), 'S och mp planer fördjupat samarbete', in *Dagens Nyheter*, 7 July, p. A08.
European Commission (2005), *The European Constitution: Post-referendum Survey in Spain*. (Brussels: Flash Eurobarometer 168).
Fabbrini, S. (2009), 'The Transformation of Italian Democracy', *Bulletin of Italian Politics*, 1 (1): 29–47.
Fehst, G. (2003), 'Helmut Holter will Lösungen für die Leute im Land', *PDS Mitgliederzeitschrift Disput*, available on http://archiv2007.sozialisten.de/politik/publikationen/disput/view_html?zid =2788&bs=1&n=2 (viewed on 4 September 2009).

Felfe, E. (2006), 'Warum? Für wen? Wohin? 7 Jahre PDS Mecklenburg-Vorpommern in der Regierung', in Cornelia Hildebrandt and Michael Brie (eds.), *Die Linke in Regierungsverantwortung: Analysen, Erfahrungen, Kontroversen* (Berlin: Rosa Luxemburg Stiftung), 52–58.

Felfe, E., E. Kischel and P. Kroh (eds.) (2005), *Warum? Für wen? Wohin? 7 Jahre PDS Mecklenburg-Vorpommern in der Regierung* (Schkeuditz: GNN Verlag).

Field, B. (2006), 'Transition Modes and Post-transition Inter-party Politics: Evidence from Spain (1977–82) and Argentina (1983–89)', *Democratization* 13 (2): 205–226.

Folkesocialisten (1980), party membership papers (Copenhagen: SF, number 3 and number 5).

Folkesocialisten (1986), party membership paper (Copenhagen: SF, number 10).

Frankland, E. G. and D. Schoonmaker (1992), *Between Protest and Power: The Green Party in Germany* (Boulder: Westview Press).

Franzmann, S. and A. Kaiser (2006), 'Locating Political Parties in Policy: A Reanalysis of Manifesto Data', *Party Politics*, 12 (2): 163–188.

Fronteers (2009), *The Sacred Rules of Dutch Politics:* Available at: http://www.quirksmode.org/politics/rules.html. (Viewed 01 July 2009).

García Escribano, J. J. (2002), 'El pacto PSOE-IU: un acuerdo de conveniencia', in I. Crespo (ed.), *Las campañas electorales y sus efectos en la decisión del voto: las elecciones generales de 2000 en España* (Madrid: Volume 2), 149–180.

Gay, P. (1962), *The Dilemma of Democratic Socialism* (New York: Collier).

Gerth, M. (2003), *Die PDS und die ostdeutsche Gesellschaft im Transformationsprozess* (Hamburg: Dr. Kovac).

Gildea, R. (1992), *The Past in French History* (Yale: Yale University Press).

Ginsborg, P. (1990), *A History of Contemporary Italy: Society and Politics 1943–1988* (London: Penguin).

Goll, S. (2008), 'No JSF veto from Socialist Left Party', *Aftenposten*, 31 October, at www.aftenposten.no (accessed on 1 June 2009).

Goul Andersen, J. and J. Bendix Jensen (2001), 'The Danish Venstre: Liberal, Agrarian or Centrist?', in D. Arter (ed.), *From Farmyard to City Square? The Electoral Adaptation of the Nordic Agrarian Parties* (London: Ashgate), 96–131.

Green-Pedersen, C. (2001), 'Minority Governments and Party Politics: The Political and Institutional Background to the "Danish Miracle"', *Journal of Public Policy*, 21 (1): 53–70.

Green-Pedersen, C. and K. van Kersbergen (2002), 'The Politics of the Third Way. The Transformation of Social Democracy in Denmark and the Netherlands,' *Party Politics*, 8 (5): 507–524.

GroenLinks (1989), *Programma Groen Links Tweede-Kamerverkiezingen 1989* (Amsterdam: GroenLinks).

GroenLinks (1992), *Uitgangspunten van Groen Linkse Politiek 1992* (Amsterdam: GroenLinks).

GroenLinks (1994), *GroenLinks verkiezingsprogramma 1994–1998: voor de Tweede Kamer en Europees Parlement* (Utrecht: GroenLinks).

GroenLinks (1997), *Statuten* (Utrecht: GroenLinks).

GroenLinks (2002), *Overvloed en onbehagen Verkiezingsprogramma* 2002–06 (Utrecht: GroenLinks).

GroenLinks (2006), *Groei Mee: Programma van GroenLinks Tweede-Kamerverkiezingen 22 November 2006* (Utrecht: GroenLinks).

Bibliography

GroenLinks (2007), *Groei Mee: Het huishoudboekje van GroenLinks verkiezingsprogramma 2007-2011* (Utrecht: GroenLinks).
GroenLinks (2008), *Programma van Uitgangspunten zoals gewijzigd op het Toekomstcongres, 22 November 2008 Versie 1 December 2008* (Utrecht: GroenLinks).
Grzymała-Busse, A. M. (2002), *Redeeming the Communist Past: The Regeneration of Communist Parties in East Central Europe* (Cambridge: CUP).
Haahr, J-H. (1993), *Looking to Europe: The EC Policies of the British Labour Party and the Danish Social Democrats* (Aarhus: Aarhus University Press).
Hamrud, A. (2009), 'Ohly rejält missnöjd med resultatet', in *Dagens Nyheter*, 8 June, p. A06.
Harmel, R. and K. Janda (1993), *Performance, Leadership, Factions, and Party Change: An Empirical Analysis*, Manuscript presented at the 1993 APSA meeting.
Harmel, R. and K. Janda (1994), 'An Integrated Theory of Party Goals and Party Change', *Journal of Theoretical Politics*, 6 (3): 259–287.
Harmel, R., U. Heo, A. Tan and K. Janda (1995), 'Performance, Leadership, Factions and Party Change: An Empirical Analysis', *West European Politics*, 18, 1: 1–33.
Harmel, R. and A. Tan (2003), 'Party Actors and Party Change: Does Factional Dominance Matter?', *European Journal of Political Research*, 42: 409–24.
Harmsen, R. (2005), 'The Dutch Referendum on the Ratification of the European Constitutional Treaty 1 June 2005' *European Parties Elections and Referendums Network: Referendum Briefing Paper No.13* (University of Sussex, Brighton: EPERN Briefing).
Harmsen, R. (2002), 'Europe and the Dutch Parliamentary Election of May 2002' *European Parties Elections and Referendums Network: Referendum Election Briefing No.3* (University of Sussex, Brighton: EPERN Briefing).
Heidar, K. (2005), 'Norwegian Parties and the Party System: Steadfast and Changing,' *West European Politics*, 28 (4): 807–833.
Heinisch, R. (2003), 'Success in Opposition – Failure in Government: Explaining the Performance of Right-Wing Populist Parties in Public Office', *West European Politics*, 26: 91–130.
Hippe, J., R. Koroeze, P. Lucardie., N. van de Walle and G. Voerman (2007), 'Kroniek 2005. Overzicht van de partijpolitieke gebeurtenissen van het jaar 2005', in *Jaarboek 2005 Documentatiecentrum Nederlandse Politieke Partijen* (Groningen: DNPP). *Kroniek 2005: Overzicht van de partijpolitieke gebeurtenissen van het jaar 2005* (Groningen DNPP).
Hippe, J., R. Kroeze, P. Lucardie and G. Voerman (2006), 'Kroniek 2004. Overzicht van de partijpolitieke gebeurtenissen van het jaar 2004', in *Jaarboek 2004 Documentatiecentrum Nederlandse Politieke Partijen* (Groningen: DNPP). *Kroniek 2004: Overzicht van de partijpolitieke gebeurtenissen van het jaar 2004* (Groningen DNPP).
Hippe, J., P. Lucardie and G. Voerman (2005), 'Kroniek 2003. Overzicht van de partijpolitieke gebeurtenissen van het jaar 2003', in *Jaarboek 2003 Documentatiecentrum Nederlandse Politieke Partijen* (Groningen: DNPP). *Kroniek 2003: Overzicht van de partijpolitieke gebeurtenissen van het jaar 2003* (Groningen: DNPP).
Hippe, J. ,P. Lucardie and G. Voerman (2004), 'Kroniek 2002. Overzicht van de partijpolitieke gebeurtenissen van het jaar 2002', in *Jaarboek 2002 Documentatiecentrum Nederlandse Politieke Partijen* (Groningen: DNPP). *Kroniek 2002: Overzicht van de partijpolitieke gebeurtenissen van het jaar 2002* (Groningen: DNPP).

Holmås, H. (2007), Interview with author, Thursday, 14 June, Oslo.
Holter, H. (2000), 'Mehrheiten gewinnen durch eine Politik für Mehrheiten. Rede auf dem Landesparteitag der PDS Mecklenburg-Vorpommern am 25 November 2000 in Greifswald', *PDS Pressedienst*, 48 (PDS: Berlin).
Hough, D. (2000) ''Made in Eastern Germany': The PDS and the Articulation of Eastern German Interests', *German Politics*, 9 (2): 125–148.
Hough, D. and J. Olsen (2004), 'The PDS and Participation in Eastern German Land Governments', *GFL*, 3: 117–142.
Hough, D. and M. Koß (2009), 'Populism Personified or Reinvigorated Reformers? The German Left Party in 2009 and Beyond', *German Politics and Society*, 27 (2): 76–91.
Hough, D., M. Koß and J. Olsen (2007), *The Left Party in Contemporary German Politics* (London: Palgrave).
Hough, D., W. Paterson and J. Sloam (eds.) (2006), *Learning from the West? Policy Transfer and Programmatic Change in the Communist Successor Parties of Eastern and Central Europe* (Oxford: Routledge).
Hough, Dan and T. Verge (2009), 'A Sheep in Wolf's Clothing or a Gift from Heaven? Left-Left Coalitions in Comparative Perspective', *Regional and Federal Studies*, 19 (1): 37–55.
Hudson, K. (2002), *European Communism since 1989* (London: Palgrave).
Ishiyama, J. (ed.) (1999), *Communist Successor Parties in Post-Communist Politics* (Hauppauge, NY: Nova Science).
Italian National Election Study (2001), available on http://www.itanes.org/index.asp (viewed on 26 November 2009).
Izquierda Unida (2003), *Informe Político* (Madrid: IU party conference resolutions, VII Federal Assembly).
Izquierda Unida (2004), *Informe Político* (Madrid, IU party conference resolutions, VIII Federal Assembly).
Izquierda Unida (2008a), *Más Izquierda* (Madrid: IU).
Izquierda Unida (2008b), *The Lisbon Treaty* (Brussels: IU's Parliamentary Party in the European Parliament).
Izquierda Unida (2009), *Plan de trabajo de la secretaría federal de refundación y de relaciones políticas y sociales*, (IU: Madrid). Viewed 20 April 2009 at <http://www1.izquierda-unida.es/doc/PLAN_ REFUNDACION_ PRESIDENCIA_090404.pdf>.
Jacobsen, B. (2007), Interview with author, 12 June, Oslo.
Janda, K., R. Harmel, C. Edens and P. Goff (1995), 'Changes in Party Identity: Evidence from Party Manifestos', *Party Politics*, 1 (2): 171–96.
Jensen, L. (2007), Interview with author, 13 June, Oslo.
Jesse, E. and J. P. Lang (2008), *Die Linke – der smarte Extremismus einer deutschen Partei* (Munich: Olzog).
Johnsson, G. and L-O. Pettersson (2009), 'Sahlins samarbete stort hot mot partiet', in *Dagens Nyheter*, 14 April, p. A06.
Jungar, A-C (2002), 'A Case of a Surplus Majority Government: The Finnish Rainbow Coalition', *Scandinavian Political Studies*, 25(1): 57–83.
Karlsson, L-I. (2007), 'Nu laddar de för koalitionen', in *Dagens Nyheter*, 16 April, p. C10.
Karlsson, L.-I and O. Wijnbladh (2006), 'Röd-grön samarbete skjuts på framtiden', in *Dagens Nyheter*, 19 September, p. A14.

Keith, D. (2010), *Organisational and Programmatic Change in Western European (Post-) Communist Parties* (Brighton: University of Sussex DPhil Thesis, forthcoming).
Kirchheimer, O. (1966), 'The Transformation of the Western European Party System', in J. LaPalombara and M. Weiner (eds.), *Political Parties and Political Development* (Princeton: University Press), 177–200.
Kite, C. (1996), *Scandinavia Faces EU, debates and decisions on membership 1961–1994* (Umeå: University: Department of Political Science).
Kitschelt, H. (1990), 'New Social Movements and the Decline of Party Organization', in R. J. Dalton and M. Kuechler (eds.), *Challenging the Political Order. New Social and Political Movements in Western Democracies* (Cambridge: Polity Press).
Kjöller, H. (2007), 'Mentalt majoritetsparti', in *Dagens Nyheter*, 25 April, p. A02.
Koeneman, L., I. Noomen and G. Voerman (1989), *Kroniek: Overzicht van de partijpolitieke gebeurtenissen van het jaar 1988* (Groningen: DNPP).
Konstitutionsutskottet (2003), *Regeringens förhållande till riksdagen* (KU 2002/03: 30).
Knutsen, O. (1998), 'Expert Judgments of the Left-Right Location of Political Parties: A Comparative Longitudinal Study', *West European Politics*, 21 (2): 63–94.
Laakso, M. and R. Taagepera (1979), 'Effective Number of Parties: A Measure with Application to Western Europe', *Comparative Political Studies* 12 (1): 3–27.
Lacouture, J. (1974), *Léon Blum* (Paris: Seuil).
Lago, I. (2009), 'Distorted Mirrors: Strategic Voting and Contamination Effects'. Barcelona: Universitat Pompeu Fabra. Viewed 9 August 2009, <http://www.upf.edu/dcpis/_pdf/paper_forum_lago.pdf>.
Laguiller, A. (2002), *Mon communisme* (Paris: Plon).
Land, R. and R. Possekel (1995), 'On the Internal Dynamics of the PDS', *Constellations*, 2: 51–59.
Langeland, H. (2007), Interview with author, Thursday 14 June, Oslo.
Larsen, H. (1994), 'Efter P. Much. De Radikale og dansk udenrigspolitik 1945–1992', *Vandkunsten*, 9/10: 285–314.
Lazar, M. (1997), 'L'idéologie communiste n'est pas morte', *Esprit*, March–April: 83–91.
Lazar, M. (1999), 'La gauche communiste plurielle', *Revue française de science politique*, 49, no.4–5, August–October: 605–705.
Lazar, M. (2003), 'Le discours de la gauche extrême', *Le débat*, 127, November–December: 176–91.
Lees, C. (2000), *The Red-Green Coalition in Germany. Politics, Personalities and Power* (Manchester: Manchester University Press).
Lenin, V. I. (1997), *Left-wing Communism: An Infantile Disorder* (London: Bookmarks).
Lijphart, A. (1999), *Patterns of Democracy* (London and New Haven, Yale University Press).
Lindahl, R. and D. Naurin (2005), 'Sweden: The Twin Faces of a Euro-Outsider', *Journal of European Integration*, 27 (1): 65–88.
Lindén, J. (2005), 'Radical Left in Government – Finnish Experiences', unpublished paper delivered to a Norwegian Socialist Left (SV) seminar in Kristiansand on 1 April 2005.
Linke, Die (2007), *Heiligendamm – erfolgreicher Protest und ein Gipfel hinter Stacheldraht* (Berlin: Die Linke). Also available on http://die-linke.de/partei/

organe/parteitage/gruendungsparteitag/ beschluesse/heiligendamm_ erfolgreicher_protest_und_ein_gipfel_hinter_stacheldraht/.
Linke, Die (2009a), *Solidarität, Demokratie, Frieden – Gemeinsam für den Wechsel in Europa! Europawahlprogramm 2009 der Partei DIE LINKE* (Berlin: Die Linke). Also available on http://die-linke.de/fileadmin/tpl/gfx/wahlen/pdf/europawahlprogramm2009_neu.pdf.
Linke, Die (2009b), *Konsequent sozial. Für Demokratie und Frieden. Bundestagswahlprogramm 2009* (Berlin: Die Linke). Also available on http://die-linke.de/fileadmin/download/wahlen /pdf/485516_LinkePV_LWP_BTW09.pdf.
Lipset, S. M. and S. Rokkan (1967), *Party Systems and Voter Alignments* (New York: Free Press).
Lopapa, C. (2007), '"Rispetto I soldati, ma li vorrei a casa" Vicenza: Errore madornale il sì agli Usa. Adesso serve il referendum per ribaltare la decisione', *la Repubblica*, 28 January.
Lopapa, C. (2008), 'E nelle urne i partiti trovano un tesoro', *la Repubblica*, 17 April, p.4.
Lucardie, P. (1994), 'General Elections in the Netherlands, May 1994: The Triumph of Grey Liberalism', *Environmental Politics*, 4 (1): 119–123.
Lucardie, P. (1999), 'Dutch Politics in the Late 1990s: "Purple" government and "green" opposition', *Environmental Politics*, 8 (3): 153–158.
Lucardie, P. (2007), 'The Netherlands' in *European Journal of Political Research*, 46 (1): 1041–1048.
Lucardie, P and C. P. Ghillebaert (2008), 'The Short Road to Power and the Long Way Back: Newly Governing Parties in the Netherlands', in K. Deschouwer (ed.) *New Parties in Government: In Power for the First Time* (Oxon: Routledge).
Lucardie, P. and G. Voerman (2003), 'The Organisational and Ideological Development of GreenLeft', in J. Botella L. Ramiro (eds.), *The Crisis of Communism and Party Change The Evolution of West European Communist and Post-Communist Parties* (Barcelona: ICPS).
Lucardie, P. and G. Voerman (2005), 'The Netherlands', *European Journal of Political Research*, 44 (1): 1124–1133.
Lucardie, P. and G. Voerman (2006), 'The Netherlands: Results of the National Referendum' in *European Journal of Political Research*, 45, (7–8): 1201–1206.
Lucardie, P. and G. Voerman (2008), 'Amateurs and Professional Activists: De Groenen and GroenLinks in the Netherlands' in E. Frankland et al., (eds.) Green *Parties in Transition: The End of Grass-roots Democracy?* (Oxon: Ashgate).
Lucardie, P. and W. van Schuur (2009), 'More Moderate than Militant: The Members of the Dutch GroenLinks', (Groningen: DNPP).
Lucardie, P., I. Noomen and G. Voerman, G. (2001), *Kroniek 2001: Overzicht van de partijpolitieke gebeurtenissen van het jaar 2001*, (Groningen DNPP).
Lucardie, P., J. van der Knoop, W. van Schuur and G. Voerman (1995), 'Greening the Reds or Reddening the Greens? The Case of the GreenLeft in the Netherlands', *Green Politics Three*: 90–111.
Lucardie, P., M. Breewold, G. Voerman and N. van de Wall (2006), *Kroniek 2006: Overzicht van de partijpolitieke gebeurtenissen van het jaar 2006*, (Groningen: DNPP).
Luther, K. R. (2003), 'The Self-Destruction of a Right-Wing Populist Party? The Austrian Parliamentary Election of 2002', *West European Politics*, 26 (2): 136–152.

Lysbakken, A. (2007), Interview with author, Tuesday 12 June, Oslo.
Madeley, J. S. (1998), 'The Politics of Embarrassment: Norway's 1997 Election,' *West European Politics*, 21 (2): 187–194.
Madeley, J. S. (1999), 'The 1998 Riksdag Election: Hobson's Choice and Sweden's voice,' *West European Politics*, 22 (1): 187–94.
Madeley, J. S. (2002), 'Outside the Whale: Norway's Storting Election of 10 September 2001', *West European Politics*, 25 (2): 212–222.
Madeley, J. S. (2003), '"The Swedish Model is Dead! Long Live the Swedish Model!" The 2002 Riksdag Election', *West European Politics*, 26 (2): 165–73.
Mair, P. (2008), 'Electoral Volatility and the Dutch Party System: A Comparative Perspective', *Acta Politica*, 43 (2–3): 235–253.
Mannheimer, R. (2008), 'Vince il bipolarismo Carroccio e Di Pietro nuove «ali radicali»', *Corriere della Sera*, 15 April, p.3.
March, L. (2008), *Contemporary Far Left Parties in Europe* (Bonn: Friedrich Ebert Stiftung).
March L. and C. Mudde (2005), 'What's Left of the Radical Left? The European Radical Left after 1989: Decline and Mutation', *Comparative European Politics*, 3 (1): 23–49.
Markovits, A. and P. S. Gorski (1993), *The German Left: Red, Green and Beyond* (Cambridge: Polity Press).
Marx. K. (1852), *Eighteenth Brumaire of Louis Bonaparte* (London: Wishart).
Mauro, A. (2007a), 'Leggere la Finanziaria 2007', http://home.rifondazione.it/dettaglio_01.php?id=544.
Mauro, A. (2007b), 'Le nuove sfide del Prc', http://home.rifondazione.it/dettaglio_01.php?id=1286.
Meuche-Mäker, M. (2005), *Die PDS im Westen 1990–2005: Schlussfolgerungen für eine neue Linke* (Berlin: Dietz, 2005).
Miller, Tobias (1997), 'Wir wollen Magdeburger Verhältnisse', *Berliner Zeitung*, 24 November.
Minkenberg, M. (2001), 'The Radical Right in Public Office: Agenda-setting and Policy Effects', *West European Politics*, 24: 1–21.
Mjøset, L., Å. Cappelen, J. Fagerberg and B. S. Tranøy (1994), 'Norway: Changing the Model,' in P. Anderson and P. Camiller (eds.), *Mapping the West European Left* (London/New York: Verso).
Möller, T. (1999), 'The Swedish Election 1998: A Protest Vote and the Birth of a New Political Landscape?', *Scandinavian Political Studies*, 22 (3): 261–73.
Möller, T. (2007), 'Sweden: Still a Stable Party System?', in K. Lawson and P. Merkl (eds.), *When Parties Prosper. The Uses of Electoral Success*, Boulder (CO: Lynne Rienners), 27–42.
Montero, J. R. (1999), 'Stabilising the Democratic Order: Electoral Behaviour in Spain', in P. Heywood (ed.), *Politics and Policy in Democratic Spain: No Longer Different?* (London: Frank Cass).
Morata, F. (1997), 'Modernization through Integration', in K. Hanf and B. Soetendorp (eds.), *Adapting to European Integration* (London: Longman), 100–115.
Moreau, J. (1998), *Les socialistes français et le mythe révolutionnaire* (Paris: Hachette).
Morlino, L. (2009), 'Transition from Democracy to Democracy: Is it Possible in Italy?', *Bulletin of Italian Politics*, 1 (1): 7–27.
Mudde, C. (2007), *Populist Radical Right Parties in Europe* (Cambridge: CUP).

Müller, W. C. (1997), 'Inside the Black Box: A Confrontation of Party Executive Behavior and Theories of Party Organizational Change', *Party Politics*, 3 (3): 289–313.
Müller, W. C. and K. Strøm (eds.) (1999), *Policy, Office, or Votes? How Political Parties in Western Europe Make Hard Decisions* (Cambridge: Cambridge University Press).
Narud, H. M. (1995), 'Coalition Termination in Norway: Models and Cases', *Scandinavian Political Studies*, 18 (1): 1–24.
Narud, H. M. (1996), *Voters, Parties and Governments. Electoral Competition, Policy Distances and Government Formation in Multi-Party Systems* (Oslo: Institute for Social Research).
Narud, H. M. and H. Valen (2007), 'The Storting Election in Norway, September 2005', *Electoral Studies*, 26: 219–223.
Neubegauer, G. and R. Stöss (1999), 'Nach der Bundestagswahl 1998: Die PDS in stabiler Seitenlage?,' in Oskar Niedermayer (ed.) *Die Parteien nach Der Bundestagswahl 1998* (Opladen: Leske & Budrich), 119–140.
Newell, J. L. (2000), 'Party Finance and Corruption: Italy', in R. Williams (ed.), *Party Finance and Political Corruption* (Basingstoke and London: Macmillan), 61–87.
Newell, J. L. (2009a), 'The Man Who Never was?', *Journal of Modern Italian Studies*, 14 (4), 395–412.
Newell, J. L. (2009b), 'Centro-sinistra, sinistra radicale, antipolitica e centro: Quattro opposizioni in cerca di rivincita', in G. Baldini and A. Cento Bull (eds.), *Politica in Italia: I fatti dell'anno e le interpretazioni* (Bologna: il Mulino), 97–117.
Niedermayer, O. (2003), 'Die Entwicklung des deutschen Parteiensystems bis nach der Bundestagswahl 2002', in O. Niedermayer (ed.), *Die Parteien nach der Bundestagswahl 2002* (Opladen: Leske & Budrich), 9–42.
Norris, P. (2005), *Radical Right: Voters and Parties in the Regulated Market* (Cambridge: CUP).
NRC Handelsblad (2006a), *'GroenLinks wil niet in coalitie als SP wegvalt'* (Amsterdam: NRC, 29 November).
NRC (2006b), *'Met ChristenUnie erbij gaat inhoud meespelen'* (Amsterdam: NRC, 16 November).
NRC (2006c), *'Afhaken bij formatie is historische fout van GroenLinks'* (NRC Amsterdam, 28 December).
Nurmi. H. and L. Nurmi (2007), 'The Parliamentary Election in Finland, March 2007', *Electoral Studies*, 26: 797–803.
Office of the Prime Minister of Norway (2005), 'The Soria Moria Declaration on International Policy', at www.regjeringen.no/en/dep/smk/documents/ Reports-and-action-plans/Rapporter/ 2005/The-Soria-Moria-Declaration-on-Internati.html?id=438515, accessed on 10 June 2008.
Ohly, L. (2004), 'Perssons usla ledarskap ökar högervridningen', in *Dagens Nyheter*, 4 December, p. A06.
Olsen, J. (2002), 'The PDS in Western Germany: An Empirical Study of Local PDS Politicians', *German Politics*, 11 (1): 147–172.
Oswald, F. (2002), *The Party that came out of the Cold War: The Party of Democratic Socialism in United Germany* (London: Praeger).
Olsen, J. (2001), 'The Merger of the PDS and WASG: From Eastern German Regional Party to National Radical Left Party?', *German Politics*, 16 (2): 205-221.
Pacifistisch Socialistische Partij (1981), *Socialisme en Ontwapening* (Amsterdam: PSP).

Pacifistisch Socialistische Partij (1986), *Programma PSP Tweede-Kamerverkiezingen 1986* (Amsterdam: PSP).
Pallarés, F. and M. Keating (2003), 'Multi-level Electoral Competition: Regional Elections and Party Systems in Spain', *European Urban and Regional Studies*, 10 (3): 239–55.
Paniagua, J.L. and L. Ramiro-Fernández (2003), *Voz, Conflicto y Salida. Un Estudio sobre Faccionalismo: Nueva Izquierda, 1992–2001* (Madrid: Editorial Complutense).
Paolucci, C. and J. L. Newell (2008), 'The Prodi Government of 2006 and 2007', *Modern Italy*, 13 (3): 283–291.
Passarini, P. (2007), 'Maggioranze variabili i dubbi del Quirinale', la Stampa, 6 March, p.5.
Patton, D. (2006), 'Germany's Left Party.PDS and the "Vacuum Thesis": From Regional Milieu Party to Left Alternative?', *Journal of Communist Studies and Transition Politics*, 22 (2): 206–227.
PCE (2005), *Reconstrucción del PCE*. Draft resolutions prepared for the XVII PCE's Conference, May 2005.
PCE (2006), Report to the PCE's Federal Committee, 18 June 2006.
PDS Parteivorstand (1998), *Das Rostocker Manifest. Für einen zukunftsfähigen Osten in einer gerechten Republik* (Berlin: Parteivorstand der Partei des Demokratischen Sozialismus).
Pedersen, M. (1982), 'Towards a New Typology of Party Lifespans and Minor Parties', *Scandinavian Political Studies*, 5 (1): 1–16.
Peil (2009). 'Nieuw Haags Peil van 5 september 2009' Available at https://n6.noties.nl/peil.nl/ (viewed 1 September 09).
Pelizzo, R. (2003), 'Party Positions or Party Direction? An Analysis of Party Manifesto Data', *West European Politics* 26 (2): 67–89.
Pergande, F. (2004), 'Massenverelendung', *Frankfurter Allgemeine Zeitung*, 28 June 2004, p. 3.
Pergande, F. (2005), 'Schweriner Koalition streitet über EU-Verfassung', *FAZ*, 27 May, p. 2.
Perrineau, P. (2003), *le Désenchantment démocratique* (Paris: FNSP).
Perrineau, P. and C. Ysmal (2003), (eds.), *Le vote de tous les refus* (Paris: Presses de Sciences Po).
Persson, G., G. Schyman, B. Schlaug, M. Samuelsson (1998), 'Vi samarbetar hela mandatsperioden', in *Dagens Nyheter*, 18 December.
Petersen, N. (1994), 'Vejen til den europæiske Union 1980–93', in T. Swienty (ed.), *Danmark i Europa 1945–93* (København: Munksgaard), 195–271.
Petersen, N. (1995), 'Denmark and the European Community 1985–93', in C. Due-Nilsen and N. Petersen (eds.), *Adaption and Activism. The Foreign Policy of Denmark 1967–1993* (Købehavn: DJØF-Forlaget), 189–224.
Pingaud, D. (2000), *La gauche de la gauche* (Paris: Seuil).
Platone, F. and J. Ranger (2000), 'Les adhérents du Parti communiste français en 1997' *Cahiers du cevipof*, 27 March.
Poguntke, T. (1993), *Alternative Politics: The German Green Party* (Edinburgh: Edinburgh University Press).
Poguntke, T. (2002), 'Green Parties in National Governments: From Protest to Acquiescence?' in F. Müller-Rommel and T. Poguntke (eds.), *Green Parties in National Governments* (London: Routledge), 133–145.

Politieke Partij Radicalen (1977), *Programma PPR Tweede-Kamerverkiezingen 1977* (Amsterdam: PPR).
Politieke Partij Radicalen (1986), *Programma PPR Tweede-Kamerverkiezingen 1986* (Amsterdam: PPR).
'Programmatische Eckpunkte. (2007), Programmatisches Gründungsdokument der Partei DIE LINKE. Beschluss der Parteitage der WASG und der Linkspartei. PDS', see http://die-linke.de/partei/dokumente/programm_der_partei_die_linke_programmatische_eckpunkte/iv_fuer_einen_richtungswechsel/, section 4, accessed on 15 November 2008.
Rada, U. (2001), 'PDS spart am besten', *taz*, 25 June, p. 19.
Ramiro-Fernández, L. (2004), 'Electoral Competition, Organizational Constraints and Party Change: The Communist Party of Spain (PCE) and United Left (IU), 1986–2000', *Journal of Communist and Transition Politics*, 20 (2): 1–29.
Ramiro-Fernández, L. (2005), 'The Crisis of the Spanish Radical Left: The PCE and IU. A rejoinder', *Journal of Communist and Transition Politics*, 21 (2): 303–305.
Raunio, T. and M. Wiberg (2008), 'The Eduskunta and the Parliamentarisation of Finnish Politics: Formerly Stronger, Politically Still Weaker?', *West European Politics*, 31: 3: 581–599.
Reißig, R. (2005), *Mitregieren in Berlin. Die PDS auf dem Prüfstand* (Berlin: Rosa-Luxemburg-Stiftung, Texte 22).
Richter, C. (2003a), 'Die Hauptstadt-PDS will auch mal die Faust ballen', *Berliner Zeitung*, 19 December, p. 20.
Richter, C. (2003b), 'PDS: Das Studium darf nichts kosten', *Berliner Zeitung*, 8 December, p. 20.
Ricolfi, L. (2008), 'Perché le sinistre hanno perso', in R. Mannheimer and P. Natale (eds.), *Senza più sinistra* (Milan: il Sole 24 Ore), 49–59.
Robrieux P. (1980), *Histoire intérieure du parti communiste 1920–1982* (Paris: Fayard).
Rommetvedt, H. (2003), *The Rise of the Norwegian Parliament.* (London: Frank Cass).
Salvadori, M. L. (1994), *Storia d'Italia e crisi di regime* (Bologna: il Mulino).
Sannerstedt, A. and M. Sjölin (1992), 'Sweden: Changing Party Relations in a More Active Parliament', in E. Damgaard (ed.), *Parliamentary Change in the Nordic Countries* (Oslo: Scandinavian University Press), 100–51.
Sartori, G. (1976), *Parties and Party Systems: A Framework for Analysis* (Cambridge: Cambridge University Press).
Sassoon, D. (1996), *One Hundred Years of Socialism. The West European Left and the Twentieth Century* (London: I.B.Tauris Publishers).
Sastre García, C. (1997), 'La transición política en España: una sociedad desmovilizada', *Revista Española de Investigaciones Sociológicas*, 80: 33–68.
Schattschneider, E. E. (1960/75), *The Semisovereign People. A Realist's view of Democracy in America* (Hinsdale: The Dryden Press).
Schmidt, M. G. (2006), *Demokratietheorien: Eine Einführung* (Wiesbaden: VS Verlag für Sozialwissenschaften).
Schou, T. L. and D. J. Hearl (1992), 'Party and Coalition Policy in Denmark', in M. J. Laver and I. Budge (eds.), *Party, Policy and Government Coalitions* (Basingstoke: St. Martin's Press).
Schyman, G. (2000), 'Krav på regeringssamarbete står kvar', in *Dagens Nyheter*, 13 April, p. A04.

Seierstad, D. (2006), 'Die jüngsten Entwicklungen der norwegischen Linken: Herausforderungen und Perspektiven', in M. Brie and C. Hildebrandt(eds.), *Die Linke im Aufbruch* (Berlin: Dietz).
Seierstad, D. (2007), Interview with author, Thursday 14 June, Oslo.
SF-Status (1984), *SF's Officielle Dokumenter og Vedtagelser* (SP Forlag).
SF-Status (1986), *SF's Officielle Dokumenter og Vedtagelser* (SP Forlag).
SF-Status (1993), *SF's Officielle Dokumenter og Vedtagelser* (SP Forlag).
Shull, T. (1999), *Red and Green. Ideology and Strategy in European Political Ecology* (Albany: State University of New York Press).
Sitter, N. (2006), 'Norway's Storting Election of September 2005: Back to the Left?', *West European Politics*, 29 (3): 573–580.
Siune, K., P. Svensson and O. Tonsgaard (1994), *Fra et nej til et ja* (Aarhus: Politica).
Sjöblom, G. (1968), *Party Strategies in a Multiparty System* (Lund: Studentlitteratur).
Sjöstedt, J. (2006), 'Vänsterpartiet måste inse att valet var en katastrof', in *Dagens Nyheter*, 27 September, p. A06.
Skidmore-Hess, D. (2003), 'The Danish Party System and the Rise of the Right in the 2001 Parliamentary Election', *International Social Science Review*, 78 (3/4): 89–101.
Snels, B. (2005), 'We moeten gezamenlijke plannen maken: Links aan de macht' in *Spanning*, 7 (12) (Rotterdam).
Socialistiese Partij (1974), *Beginselen van de Socialistiese Partij: Vastgesteld door het Tweede Partijkongres 2 en 3 Februari 1974 in Nijmegen* (Rotterdam: SP).
Socialistiese Partij (1987), *Beginselen van de Socialistiese Partij: Algemmeen Geschienis en Klassenstrijd* (Rotterdam: SP).
Socialistiese Partij (1991), *Handvest 2000* (Rotterdam: SP).
Socialistische Partij (1999), *Heel de mens* (Rotterdam: SP).
Socialistische Partij (2002), *SocialistischePartij: Eerste Wed Links* (Rotterdam: SP).
Socialistische Partij (2004), *Wie zwijgt stemt toe! voor de Europese verkiezingen van 2004* (Rotterdam: SP).
Socialistische Partij (2005), *Spanning*, 7 (12) (Rotterdam).
Socialistische Partij (2006a), *Een beter Nederland, voor hetzelfde geld: Verkiezingsprogramma van de SP, 2006–2010* (Rotterdam: SP).
Socialistische Partij (2006b), *Een neter Europa begint in Neerland* (Rotterdam: SP).
Socialist Left Party (2005), *Different People. Equal Opportunities. Election Manifesto of the Socialist Left Party of Norway (SV), 2005–2009*, at www.sv.no (accessed on 5 June 2009).
Spanning SP (2005a), 'Linkse samenwerking?', *Spanning* (Rotterdam: SP).
Spanning SP (2005b), 'Linkse samenwerking?', *Spanning* (Rotterdam: SP).
Spiegel (2003), 'Oskar, der Rettungsanker', 29 September 2003.
Spiegel (2005), 'Ein Himmelfahrtskommando', 30 May 2005, p. 57.
Spiegel (2008), 'Mosaik des Chaos', 16 January 2008.
Spiegel (2008), 'Linken-Abgeordnete hat Sehnsucht nach der Stasi', 14 February 2008.
Spiegel (2008), 'Umstrittener Pit Metz will in Landesvorstand', 23 August 2008.
Spier, T., F. Butzlaff, M. Micus and F. Walter (eds.) (2001), *Die Linkspartei. Zeitgemäße Idee oder Bündnis ohne Zukunft?* (Wiesbaden: VS Verlag für Sozialwissenschaften).
Spier, T. and C. Wirries (2007), 'Ausnahmeerscheinung oder Normalität? Linksparteien in Westeuropa', in T. Spier et al., (eds.), *Die Linkspartei – Zeitgemäße*

Idee oder Bündnis ohne Zukunft? (Wiesbaden: VS Verlag für Sozialwissenschaften), 71–116.

Ştefuriuc, I. and T. Verge (2008), 'Small and Divided Parties in Multi-Level Settings: Opportunities for Government Participation, the Case of Izquierda Unida in Spain', *South European Society and Politics*, 13 (2): 155–173.

Strøm, K. (1990a), 'A Behavioral Theory of Competitive Political Parties', *American Journal of Political Science*, 34(2), 566–568.

Strøm, K. (1990b). *Minority Government and Majority Rule* (Cambridge: Cambridge University Press).

Strøm, K. and L. Svåsand. (1997), 'Political Parties in Norway: Facing the Challenges of a New Society,' in K. Strøm and L. Svåsand (eds.), *Challenges to Political Parties. The Case of Norway* (Ann Arbor: The University of Michigan Press).

Strøm, K., H. M. Narud and H. Valen (2005), 'A More Fragile Chain of Governance in Norway,' *West European Politics*, 28 (4): 781–806.

Strøm, K., I. Budge and M. J. Laver (1994), 'Constraints on Cabinet Formation in Parliamentary Democracies', *American Journal of Political Science*, 38 (2): 303–335.

Süssner, H. (2006), 'Good-bye Lenin? Die schwedische Linkspartei 1998–2005', in M. Brie and C. Hildebrandt (eds.), *Parteien und Bewegungen. Die Linke im Aufbruch* (Berlin: Dietz), 191–205.

Süssner, H. (2008), 'Schweden – Langer Marsch in die Koalition', in B. Daiber and C. Hildebrandt (eds.), *Die Linke in Europa: Analysen linker Parteien und Parteiallianzen* (Berlin: Rosa-Luxemburg-Stiftung), 66–70.

Svåsand, L. and U. Lindström (1996), 'Scandinavian Political Parties and the European Union', in J. Gaffney (ed.), *Political Parties and the European Union* (London: Routledge).

Svensson, P. (1993), 'The Danish Yes to Maastricht and Edinburgh. The EC Referendum of May 1993', *Scandinavian Political Studies*, 17 (1): 69–82.

Tarschys, D. (1977), 'The Changing Basis of Radical Socialism in Scandinavia', in K. H. Cerny (ed.), *Parliaments and Majority rule in Western Europe* (Frankfurt: Campus Verlag).

Tiefenbach, P. (1998), *Die Grünen: Verstaatlichung einer Partei* (Cologne: PapyRossa).

Tisdall, J. (2007), 'Voter trouble for alliance partners,' *Aftenposten*, 21 March, at www.aftenposten.no (accessed on 1 June 2009).

Torreblanca, J. I. (2005), *The Three Points of Dissensus on the European Constitution* (Madrid: Real Instituto Elcano, ARI 22/2005). Viewed 14 April 2009, http://www.realinstitutoelcano. org/analisis/689.asp.

van der Steen, P. (1994), *De doorbraak van de 'gewone mensen'-partij De SP en de Tweede-Kamerverkiezingen van 1994* (Groningen: DNPP).

van Holsteyn, J. (2006), 'The Dutch Parliamentary Elections of 2006', *West European Politics*, 30 (5): 1139–1147.

van Raak, R. (2005) 'Geen huwelijk, maar ook geen slippertje: Linkse zaken doen', *Spanning*, 7 (12): XXX.

Vänsterpartiet (2008), *Partiprogram* (Stockholm: Vänsterpartiet).

VAS (2007), *The Left Road to a Just World: the Left Alliance Party Programme* (Helsinki: VAS).

Verge, T. (2007), *Partidos y representación política: Las dimensiones del cambio en los partidos políticos españoles, 1976–2006* (Madrid: CIS).

Verge, T. (2010), 'The Spanish Left and the European Constitution', in K. Roder and M. Holmes (eds.), *The Left and the European Constitution: from Laeken to Lisbon* (Manchester: Manchester University Press).
Voerman, G. (1995), 'The Netherlands: Losing Colours, Turning Green' in D. Richardson and C. Rootes (eds.) *The Green Challenge: the Development of Green Parties in Europe* (London: Routledge).
Voerman, G. (1997), 'Fusie rood en groen ligt niet in het verschiet', *de Volkskrant* 18 June.
Voerman, G. (1998), 'Snelle groei SP heeft risico's', *de Volkskrant*, 16 February 1998.
Voerman, G. (2002), 'De ideologische overeenkomsten en verschillen tussen PvdA en SP', *Tijdschrift voor cultuur, religie en politiek*, 7 (2): 8–12.
Voerman, G (2007), 'Ten strijde tegen de eigen geest', *Socialisme & Democratie*, 64 (7–8): 43–51.
Voerman, G (2007b), *Hoe Mao moeiteloos werd ingeruild voor Jezus Voerman* (Groningen DNPP).
Voerman, G. (2008), 'The Disappearance of Communism in the Netherlands' in U. Backes and P. Moreau (eds.), *Communist and Post-Communist Parties in Europe* (Göttingen: Vandenoek and Ruprecht).
Voerman, G. and P. Lucardie (2007), 'De sociaal-democratisering van de SP' in R. Cuperus and F. Becker, (eds.), *Lost Battle. De PvdA en de verkiezingen van november 2006* (Amsterdam: Mets & Schilt), 139–164.
de Volkskhrant (2006), 'Balkenende gaat Bos het hof maken' (Amsterdam), 8 December.
Waller, M. (1995), 'Adaptation of the Former Communist Parties of East Central Europe', *Party Politics*, 1 (4): 473–490.
Walter, K. (2003), 'PDS-Landesspitze wehrt sich gegen Kritik der Basis', *OZ*, 15 September, p. 4.
Ward, S. and G. Voerman (1999), *New Media and New Politics: Green Parties, Intra-Party Democracy and the Potential of the Internet (an Anglo-Dutch Comparison)* (Groningen: DNPP).
Weis, F. (2005), 'Die PDS in den westlichen Bundesländern: Anmerkungen zu keiner Erfolgsgeschichte', *Utopie kreativ*, 173: 257–265.
Welt, Die (2009), 'Jetzt ist Ramelow bereit, der SPD alles zu geben', *Welt*, 3 September.
Wenz, D. (1998), 'Wir fühlten uns an DDR-Zeiten erinnert', *FAZ*, 18 August.
Worre, T. (1992), 'Folkeafstemningen om Maastricht-Traktaten 2 juni 1992', *Dansk Udenrigspolitisk Årbog* (København, 112–132).
Zeitschrift für Sozialistische Politik und Wirtschaft – ZSPW (1997), *Erfurter Erklärung*, 1 (97), accessible on http://www.spw.de/9701/erfurt.html.
Ziblatt, D. F. (1998), 'The Adaptation of Ex-Communist Parties to Post-Communist East Central Europe: A Comparative Study of the Hungarian and East German Ex-Communist Parties', *Communist and Post-Communist Studies*, 31 (2): 119–137.

Index

Afghanistan 28, 36, 63, 146, 162
Almunia, Joaquín 89, 104 (notes)
Alternative Space (Espacio alternativo) 101
Amato, Giuliano 63
Anderson, Claes 72, 74, 77
Anguita, Julio 89, 104 (notes)
'Another Netherlands' 166
Anti-Capitalism 14, 42, 50, 56, 80, 97, 102, 140, 145, 146, 147, 152, 163
Anti-Capitalist Left Party (Spain), see Alternative Space
Anti-fascism 42
Antikapitalistische Linke (Anti-Capitalist Left) 145, 147
Anti-militarism 16, 62, 106, 122, 123
Anti-nuclearism 16, 76, 79, 81, 107, 115, 119, 124, 129
Antori, Christine 131
Arhinmäki, Paavo 78, 79, 82, 84, 85, 86 (notes)
ATTAC 45, 146

Bartolini, Stefano 57
Berlin 139, 142, 145, 150, 151, 153
Berlin Wall 2, 54, 146
Berlusconi, Silvio 58, 59, 60, 64
Bernstein, Eduard 33
Bertinotti, Fausto 37, 60, 61, 63
Besancenot, Olivier 42, 45
Bisky, Lothar 143
Björklund, Jan 119
Blackmail potential 12, 56, 57
Bloc dynamics within party systems 109, 181, 182
Blum, Léon 35
Bos, Wouter 166
Bovè, José 45
Brandenburg 139, 142
Brekk, Lars Peder 28

Brie, Andre 152
Brouwer, Ina 159
Buchholz, Christine 145
Buffet, Marie-George 37, 38, 39

Captive Parties 94, 106, 111, 113, 114
Central Organisation of Finnish Trade Unions (SAK) 71, 72, 85 (notes)
Centre Democrats 121, 125
Centre Party (Finland) 70, 71, 72, 82, 83, 84
Centre Party (Italy) 66
Centre Party (Norway) 17–23, 24, 25, 27, 28
Centre Party (Sweden) 107, 109–110, 114
Charter 2000 159
Chemnitzer Program 148
Christian Democratic Appeal (Netherlands) 155, 156, 157, 161, 162, 166–172
Christian Democratic Union (Germany) 140, 148, 149
Christian Democrats (Finland) 104
Christian Democrats (Italy) 52, 53, 54, 66, 67 (notes)
Christian Democrats (Sweden) 109
Christian People's Party (Denmark) 125, 127, 128, 132
Christian People's Party (Norway) 17, 19, 21, 23
Christian Social Union (Germany) 140
Christian Union Party (Netherlands) 155
Coalition potential of parties 12, 30, 56, 57, 58, 93, 110, 179
Coalition theory 7
Cold War 5, 36, 52, 70, 74
Comisiones Obreras (Joint Commissions) 101

Common Foreign and Security
  Policy (CFSP) 152
Communist Party of Denmark
  (DKP) 122, 123, 125
Communist Party of Finland
  (SKP) 65, 70, 85 (notes)
Communist Party of Germany
  (DKP) 145
Communist Party of Italy (PCI) 5,
  52–57, 60, 66, 67 (notes)
Communist Party of Spain
  (PCE) 87–88, 91, 92, 93, 95, 97,
  98, 99–102, 104 (notes)
Communist Party of the Netherlands
  (CPN) 156, 157, 158, 159, 163
Communist Party of the Soviet
  Union (CPSU) 36
Communisti Unitari (United
  Communists) 58
Communist Party of Sweden
  (SKP) 106, 117
Comparative Manifesto Project 175
Confédération Général du Travail
  (CGT) 49
Confédération Paysanne 45
Conservative Party (Finland) 72,
  73, 82
Conservative Party (Norway) 17, 19,
  22, 23
Conservative Party (Spain) 94, 99
Conservatives/Conservative
  People's Party (Denmark) 122,
  127, 128, 132
Contract Parliamentarism 105–106,
  109, 116, 118
Corrienta Roja (Red Current) 101
Cossuta, Armando 55
Cossuttiani 55
Courant, Pierre Lambert 44
'Crisis Agreement' in Norway 22

D66/Liberals (Netherlands) 155, 157,
  160, 170
D'Alimonte, Roberto 57
De Lorenzo, Giovanni 66
Democratic Left (SD) 4, 64
Democratic Party (PD) 64
Democratic Party of the Left
  (PDS) 54, 57, 58

'Demystification' of Left Parties
  182–184
De-pillarisation 155
DNA (see Labour Party, Norway)
Dolez, Marc 40

Eastern Europe 2, 106, 107, 123, 124,
  130, 135, 136
EC (see EU)
Effective Number of Political Parties
  (ENPP) 178, 180, 185 (in notes)
EFTA 110
Election losses after
  Incumbency 181–185
Elections, European Parliament 47,
  63, 65, 84, 86 (notes), 90, 96,
  98, 125, 133–135
Electoral Alliance for Labour and
  Social Justice 139, 141,
  142–144, 145, 146
Erfurt Declaration 150
Ernst, Klaus 143
EU Constitutional Treaty 96–97,
  132, 137, 152, 165
Eurocommunism 70, 95, 106
European Economic Area (EEA) 22,
  25, 27
European Integration 15
European Left Party (ELP) 81
European Union (EU) 7, 18, 22, 23,
  27, 30, 31, 42, 44, 70, 74, 77, 78,
  79, 80, 81, 84, 96, 97, 110, 111,
  113, 115, 116, 118, 119, 120
European United Left/Nordic Green
  Left (GUE/NGL) 46
External shocks 10, 173

'Federation of the North' 40
Féderation syndicale unitaire (FSU) 49
Ferrero, Paulo 65, 68 (note)
Forum Demokratischer Sozialismus
  (Forum of Democratic
  Socialism) 147
Free Democratic Party (FDP) 148
Frutos, Francisco 91, 104 (notes)

Gade, Steen 131
Gayssot, Jean-Claude 37
Gehrcke, Wolfgang 145

German Democratic Republic 138, 140, 145, 149
German unification 138, 140, 141, 142
Girodano, Franco 63
Gleiss, Thies 146
Gluckstein, Daniel 44
Gonzalez, Felipe 89, 104 (notes)
Green Party (Finland) 71, 72, 73, 75, 76, 82–84, 85
Green Party (Germany) 139, 140, 148, 149, 150, 153, 154
Green Party (Italy) 64
Green Party (Spain) 98, 100, 104 (notes)
Green Party (Sweden) 105, 107, 109, 111, 112, 113, 114–115, 116, 117, 118, 119
Green Party/*Les Verts* (France) 37, 46
Gremetz, Maxime 37
Gustavson, Fin 24
Gysi, Gregor 143, 150

Halema, Femke 162, 166, 167, 168, 169
Halvorsen, Kristin 25, 27, 30
Hamburg 141
Hartz Reforms 142
Havana an de Waal' 171
Hollande, François 50
Höppner, Reinhard 149
Hue, Robert 37–38
Huttu-Juntunen, Terttu 72
Hynönen, Pekka 72

Initiative of Catalonian Greens (ICV), see Green Party (Spain)
International Monetary Fund (IMF) 27, 165
Iraq War 45, 68 (notes), 94, 113, 172
Italian Renewal Party (RI) 176

Jagland, Thorbjørn 21
Jospin, Lionel 37

Kauffman, Sylvia-Yvonne 152
Keldorf, Søren 134
Keynesian Economics 19, 146

Khrushchev, Nikita 36
Kok, Wim 170
Kommunistische Platform (Communist Platform) 140, 145, 147
Korhonen, Martti 75, 77, 78, 84
Kosovo 25, 162, 169
Kox, Tiny 158, 159, 166
Kritisch GroenLinks 168
Kyllönen, Merja 79, 84, 86 (notes)

Laakso, Jaakko 77, 79
Labour Party (Norway) 16–22, 23, 24, 25, 26, 27, 28, 29, 30, 31 (notes)
Lafontaine, Oskar 41, 139, 143, 148, 153
Laguiller, Arlette 42, 46
Lara, Cayo 101–102
Le Pen, Jean-Marie 42, 47
Left Liberals (Norway) 17
Left Socialist Party (Denmark) 122, 123, 128
Left-libertarianism 6, 160, 163, 168
Les Verts, see Green Party, France
Liberals (Denmark) 127, 128, 129, 132
Ligue communiste révolutionnaire (LCR) 42, 43, 45, 46, 47, 49
Lipponen, Paavo 71–73, 75, 76
Lisbon Treaty 38, 45, 46, 81, 96, 151, 152
List Pim Fortuyn 155, 170
Llamazares, Gaspar 91, 92–93, 100–101
Lower Saxony 146
Lutte Ouvrière (LO) 42, 43, 44
Lysbakken, Audun 30

Maastricht Treaty 95, 97, 110, 123, 130, 136, 137
Marijnissen, Jan 158, 159, 166, 170, 172
Marx, Karl 34, 37
Marxistische Forum (Marxist Forum) 140, 145
Mecklenburg-Western Pomerania 139, 142, 145, 150
Mélanchon, Jean-Luc 40

Moderates (Sweden) 109
Modern Socialists (within *Die Linke*) 140, 144, 151, 153
Monje, Daan 158
Mussolini, Benito 53

National Coalition Party (Finland) 71, 72–73, 74, 76, 83
'National Compromise' 130–132, 136–137
NATO 16, 18, 25, 27, 28, 76, 77, 78, 79, 81, 82, 86, 96, 97, 98, 111, 112, 113, 121, 123, 124, 125, 132, 145, 152, 153, 157, 158, 162, 165, 169
Negative Parliamentarism 106, 108, 173
Neo-Liberalism 7, 42, 47, 80, 109, 110, 143, 147, 159, 163, 164
New Left 16, 40, 55, 78, 85, 86 (notes), 90, 98, 106, 122, 157, 163
New Left Democratic Party (Spain) 99
Nielsen, Holger K. 131
Norwegian Communist Party (NKP) 16
Nouveau Parti anti-capitaliste (NPA), see LCR

Ochetto, Achille 55
OECD 75
Ohly, Lars 113, 116–117, 118, 119

Pacifist Socialist Party (Netherlands) 156–157, 158, 163
Parti de Gauche 40, 41
Parti de Travailleurs; see Parti Ouvrière Indépendant
Parti Ouvrière Indépendant (POI) 44
Party of Radicals (Netherlands) 155–157, 158, 163
Party of Socialist Action (Spain) 99
People's Democratic League of Finland (SKDL) 69–70, 72
People's Movement Against the EC 133, 135
People's Party (Sweden) 109

Persson, Gorän 112, 113
Picquet, Christian 47
'Policy influence differential' 24
Popular Party (PP), see Conservative Party, Spain
Pragmatists (within *Die Linke*) 144, 149, 153
Prodi, Romano 54, 63–64
Progress Party (Denmark) 125, 127, 130
Progress Party (Norway) 17, 26
Proletarian Democracy (Italy) 55
Publicly funded employment programmes 141
Purple Government 160, 164, 170

Radical Left Parties vs. Extreme Left Parties 7-May
Radical Liberals (Denmark) 127, 128, 129, 132, 137
Radicals (France) 34, 36, 37
Rainbow Left 63, 178, 183
Ramelow, Bodo 148
Red Alliance (Norway) 17
Red Bloc 126, 129
Red Cabinet 123
Red-Centre Alliance' 127
Red-Green cooperation 22, 69, 88, 114, 119, 121
Red-Green Unity List 123–124
Red-Red cooperation 148, 150, 176
Republicans (France) 34, 53
Republican Left of Catalonia 101
Rosenmöller, Paul 159, 150, 161, 166, 169, 170
Rossi, Fernando 63
Rostock Manifesto 141

Saarland 139, 143, 148
Sahlin, Mona 115
Sansonetti, Piero 65
Sarkozy, Nicolas 48, 50
Saxony 139, 142
Saxony-Anhalt 139, 142, 149
Schivardi, Gerárd 44
Schröder, Gerhard 142–143
Schyman, Gudrun 107, 110, 112, 113–114, 115–117
Segmentation 179–181, 186 (notes)

Segni, Antonio 66
Seppänen, Esko 74, 77, 83
SFIO 35–36
Siimes, Suvi-Anne 72, 73, 74, 75, 76, 77–79, 80, 83, 86 (notes)
Single European Act 129, 133, 134–135
Sjöstedt, Jonas 117
Snels, Bart 166
Social Democratic Party (Denmark) 122, 123, 124, 125, 126, 127, 128, 129, 130, 131, 132, 135, 136, 137
Social Democratic Party (Finland) 70, 72, 73, 74, 75, 76, 78, 79, 80, 81, 83, 84, 85
Social Democratic Party (Germany) 140, 142, 143, 145, 146, 148, 149, 150, 151, 152, 153, 154
Social Democratic Party (Spain) 87–95, 98–101, 103, 104 (notes)
Social Democratic Party/Labour Party (Netherlands) 155, 156, 161, 162, 164, 166–168, 170, 171–172
Social Democratic Workers Party (Sweden) 106–109, 110, 111, 112, 114–115, 116, 117, 118, 119
Socialist Party (France) 38, 39, 40, 42, 43, 44, 46, 47, 48, 50, 51
Socialist Party of Italy (PSI) 53, 55, 66
Sociality Unity Party (SED) 138
Soria Moria Declaration 27
SOS-Racisme 45
Soviet Union (see USSR)
Søvndal, Villy 126
Sozialistische Linke (Socialist Left) 147
Statoilhydro 28
Stoltenberg, Jens 20–22, 27, 28
Support parties 13, 15, 16, 24, 87, 93, 94, 103, 108, 111, 112, 113, 114, 115–118, 195, 120 (notes), 121, 123, 139, 149, 176, 179, 184
Swedish People's Party (Finland) 71, 72, 73, 83, 84

Tennilä, Esko Juhani 77
Thuringia 139, 142, 148, 153
Tobin tax 97, 165
Trasformismo 53
Trotskyism 34, 38, 40–45, 46–50, 51, 56, 62, 169
True Finnish Party (PS) 71, 77, 84
Turigliatto, Franco 63

Ulivo (Olive Tree Coalition) 58, 59
Union National des Syndicats Autonomes (UNSA) 49
Union syndicale Groupe des Dix-Solidaires (SUD) 49
Unity List (UL), see 'Red-Green Unity List'
USSR 36, 42, 46, 55, 69, 70, 79, 95, 106, 117, 123, 124

Vacuum thesis 20
van der Spek, Fred 157
van Raak, Ronald 166
Veltroni, Walter 64
Vendola, Nichi 65
Vestager, Margrethe 129
Veto Players 179
VVD/Liberal Party (Netherlands) 155, 160

Wagenknecht, Sarah 145
WASG, see Electoral Alliance for Labour and Social Justice
Werner, Harald 145
Werner, Lars 107
Western European Union (WED) 130
Wissler, Janine 145
Workers Party/PdT (France) 43, 44, 45, 49
World Trade Organisation (WTO) 27

Zapatero, José Luis Rodríguez 102